THE **STORY** OF
WOODSTOCK

BACK

to the

GARDEN

**PETE
FORNATALE**

A Touchstone Book
PUBLISHED BY SIMON & SCHUSTER

NEW YORK   LONDON   TORONTO   SYDNEY

Touchstone
A Division of Simon & Schuster, Inc.
1230 Avenue of the Americas
New York, NY 10020

First Touchstone hardcover edition July 2009

For information about special discounts for bulk purchases,
please contact Simon & Schuster Special Sales at 1-866-506-1949 or
business@simonandschuster.com.

The Simon & Schuster Speakers Bureau can bring authors to your live event.
For more information or to book an event contact the Simon & Schuster Speakers Bureau
at 1-866-248-3049 or visit our website at www.simonspeakers.com.

Designed by Ruth Lee-Mui

Manufactured in the United States of America

1 3 5 7 9 10 8 6 4 2

Library of Congress Cataloging-in-Publication Data
Fornatale, Pete.
Back to the garden: the story of Woodstock /
Pete Fornatale.—1st Touchstone hardcover ed.
        p.   cm.
Includes index.
1. Woodstock Festival (1969: Bethel, N.Y.)
2. Rock music—History and criticism. I. Title.
ML38.B43W64 2009
781.66079'74735—dc22
2008051386

ISBN 978-1-4165-9119-1
ISBN 978-4165-9677-6 (ebook)

This one is for all the people who have ever listened to me
on the radio and liked what they heard.

CONTENTS

Sunday

BRING BACK THE SIXTIES, MAN

Joe McDonald

Woodstock is in your mind
Not the present or the past
It can happen anywhere, anytime
Bring back the sixties, man

Woodstock is not a dream
Not an image on a movie screen
And we can make it happen if we try
Bring back the sixties, man

Oh, this might be mountain moving time
Close your eyes can you see
Pictures in your mind?
Pictures in your mind?

People are laughing you know
They're clapping their hands
Digging the music and
The rock 'n' roll bands
Don't you know it could be such a
Beautiful trip
Screamin' and shoutin' you know it's
Fantastic!

Woodstock is our dream
It's not an image on a movie screen
And we can make it happen if we try
Anywhere and anytime
We can make it happen if we try
Let's bring back the sixties, man!
Let's bring back the sixties, man!

Words and music by Joe McDonald

© 1978 Alkatraz Corner Music BMI

I wanted to be a part of, not to feel apart from. And what a miracle it was that I became a part of Woodstock! What a dream come true. And to be such an important part. A highlight, some say. But not by myself. It took everyone there to make it happen. Like a good potluck dinner. We all brought something. We brought our special sauce. Our secret recipes. And our best behavior.

Why go to all the trouble? one might ask. The obvious reason for those who were a part of it was that they were out to get us. We had only ourselves. Those of us who knew, knew. The film crew, the stage crew, the sound crew, the roadies, the musicians, the audience—we all knew: They wanted to kill us! They hated us! They wanted to send us to war or put us in jail. They never would have allowed it to happen if they knew before what it would become. And, by the grace of a higher power, we slipped between the cracks and it happened. After Woodstock, much of it would become against the law for real. But for that one time we did it. We collectively made it happen. And, boy, did it happen!

People always ask me what was it like, and I always say like a family picnic. They always say that they are sorry that they were not there, and I always say don't be. I have played hundreds of Woodstocks before and after. In places all over the world. Small ones and big ones. All it is, in my opinion, is good vibes, nice music, outdoors, and some snacks. It don't get better than that.

It was too long. It was too big. It was too muddy. It was too cold. It was too hot. . . . It was too much. But in my family we have a saying that we always want too much. One of my kids when young and you asked "How much do you want?" always said, "Too much." And that is my own personal character defect: I want too much. And at Woodstock in 1969 we all got too much.

I love music. I love the outdoors. I love the unpredictable. I love good vibes. And I got my dream come true for those three days. I was there for the beginning and I was there for the end. What a treat.

And I also shared the collective dream of peace and love with most of my generation. And for three days we had peace and love. In the midst of a country full of hate and violence, confusion and despair, over half a million of us had three full days of peace and love.

The haters blamed us for all the bad things that happened after Woodstock. Even forty years later the haters are busy spinning their disinformation. We are responsible for AIDS, drug addiction, unwanted pregnancies, lack of patriotism, hippies—for Christ's sake, lack of ambition. The list has no end. They take no responsibility and put it all on the sixties generation. But the world knows the truth, and young people all over the world still keep the dream of Woodstock alive.

I always wondered what went on in the White House during the Woodstock Festival. How did the president and his pals talk about us? Did they see the writing on the wall? It was the beginning of the end for them and a start for us.

We were not stupid and lazy. We took the weekend off and had some fun, then many of us went back to work. Some of us building a new world. Some of us defending the old world. But all of us knowing that the world would never be the same because of what happened at Yasgur's farm.

INTRODUCTION

Just after midnight on July 27, 1969, twenty minutes into my debut program at WNEW-FM in New York, I did my first live commercial. As instructed during orientation, I looked at the program log, opened up the alphabetized copybook in front of me, and rifled through it until I came to the Ws. When the vinyl record on the turntable to my right ended, I turned on the mic switch and did a quick back-sell of the music I had just played ("Sing This Altogether" by the Rolling Stones, "All Together Now" by the Beatles, and "You Can All Join In" by Traffic). I then proceeded to read these exact words from that copybook:

"The Woodstock Music and Art Fair is a three-day Aquarian exposition at White Lake in the town of Bethel, Sullivan County, New York. Friday, August 15, you'll hear and see Joan Baez, Arlo Guthrie, Tim Hardin, Richie Havens, the Incredible String Band, Ravi Shankar, and Sweetwater.

"Then on Saturday, August 16, it's Canned Heat, Creedence Clearwater, the Grateful Dead, Keef Hartley, Janis Joplin, the Jefferson Airplane, Mountain, Santana, and the Who—the hottest group on the scene right now.

"Sunday, August 17, the Band; Jeff Beck; Blood, Sweat and Tears; Iron Butterfly; Joe Cocker; Crosby, Stills and Nash; Jimi Hendrix; the Moody Blues; Johnny Winter; and that's not all. Tickets are available by mail or at your local ticket agency for any one day at $7.00, two days at $14.00, and for all three days, just $18.00. A special two-day ticket is available by mail for only $13.00.

"For tickets and information, you can write the Woodstock Music and Art Fair, Box 996, Radio City Station, New York, one-zero-zero-one-nine, or phone Murray Hill 7-0700. M-U-seven-zero-seven-zero-zero. Remember, the Woodstock Music and Art Fair is being held at White Lake in the town of Bethel, Sullivan County, New York.

"They've had their hassles, but it looks like everything's gonna be okay."

That last line was an ad-lib—a fairly pithy one at that—but no one had any idea at the time just how important that three-day festival would turn out to be, not only to music fans but also to commentators, journalists, politicians, pundits, sociologists, writers, and members of the youth movement. These were my first few minutes on the air at the most important of the new breed of FM-rock radio stations in the country, and I was talking about an event that would soon redefine the culture, the country, and the core values of an entire generation.

Woodstock was, without question, the high-water mark of the '60s youth revolution—musically, politically, and socially. A gathering of close to half a million people in one place at one time is bound to get attention, no matter what the reason. But half a million *young* people gathered in one place at one time to flex their cultural muscle and celebrate their life-altering music sent shock waves from upstate New York to the rest of the country. Even in the technologically primitive stages of our global village, this legendary tribal gathering put Woodstock front and center in the consciousness of citizens around the world.

Without initially intending to, Woodstock made a statement. It became a symbol for all the changes that bubbled up during the first half of the American '60s and boiled over during the second half. Just eight years earlier, John F. Kennedy had galvanized the nation during his inaugural address with his declaration that "the torch has been passed to a new generation." He was talking about the torch handed off by the pre–World War II generation to the men and women who actually fought it. Woodstock was about the passing of the torch to the next generation—from the World War II veterans to their children, the already labeled "baby boomers," who grew up very differently than their forebears, with affluence, education, television, and, of course, with rock 'n' roll.

So now it is forty years later. In some respects, Woodstock is just as much of a mess today as Max Yasgur's farm was on that Monday morning when Jimi Hendrix played his final note. At least figuring it out is. There are still so many stories to tell, even after all of these years. And many of those stories contradict one another. To borrow a phrase from Kris Kristofferson, that baptismal blast in Bethel was ". . . a walking contradiction, partly truth and partly fiction." Woodstock is an elephant. Perhaps even a big pink one, depending on what you were ingesting back then. (Big Pink was even the name of "the trips tent" set up by the Hog Farm at the site to deal with drug-related casualties.) And we are all blind men and women trying to describe this behemoth based on the part of its body that we touch.

In the end, they are all partly correct, but all mostly wrong. So it is with Woodstock. You simply can't make any definitive judgments or observations about the whole of it until you have learned something about the totality of its parts. Jainists call it the Theory of Manifold Predictions.

We have attempted in these pages to avoid the pitfalls of selective dissection by providing as many first-person accounts as we can from every strand of the Woodstock freak flag, every tile of the Woodstock mosaic, and every thread of the Woodstock tapestry—even when they are totally at odds with one another. But *caveat emptor!* Even this approach will not solve or resolve a more bewildering, confounding dilemma about the festival—namely, all of the diametrically opposed viewpoints and anecdotes about the *very same* "truths" that you will encounter. And I'm not talking about mere mild differences of opinion. I'm talking about wildly divergent, red-in-the-face rants and polemics about everything that happened during those very same sixty-five hours on Yasgur's farm in Bethel, New York, in August of 1969.

Thankfully, there is a name for this dichotomy as well. It's called the Rashomon effect. It's based on the late Japanese director Akira Kurosawa's landmark 1950 film, *Rashomon,* in which four individuals witness the same exact crime, yet describe it subjectively, in four radically contradictory ways. The idea is that despite our different experiences of the same events, each account can still be plausible. Each person has a unique set of life experiences that influence the way he or she experiences the world.

We hope that providing you with the widest possible assortment of first-person accounts dating back to the historic weekend itself, as well as those sifted through the mists of time during those four rapidly passing decades, will give you *very* reliable eyewitness testimony upon which to base *your* opinions about Woodstock. But here too, we offer you this warning. Take the four hundred thousand versions of the truth from the estimated number of persons who attended the actual event, then add to that the accounts of those who *swear* they were there but weren't. Finally, calculate into the equation the hundreds of millions who experienced Woodstock vicariously through the movie, recordings, documentaries, books, articles, and word-of-mouth recollections that have been bouncing all around the globe for forty years now. Massage the quantitative facts about the event together with the myths and legends, and you end up with some idea of how chameleonlike anything Woodstock-related is. One might even say, "It all depends on what your definition of *is,* is!"

So let's return once more to Max Yasgur's farm in Bethel, New York, that weekend in August of 1969 when the shit hit the fan (or, in some cases, when the fans hit the shit) and see what sense we can make of it all on this auspicious fortieth anniversary.

> **Graham Nash:** The legend, the myth of Woodstock has grown. It was undeniably a tremendous social event. A lot of great music. A lot of good times had by a lot of people. I think as we get into the future, the legend, the myth of Woodstock becomes greater than the actual reality.

I think Graham has it exactly right. With each passing day, week, month, or year, it becomes much less important how many nails were used to build the stage at Woodstock, and far more important what people have embroidered in their DNA about the very word *Woodstock*. The myth making began as early as the week after the festival itself:

> The baffling history of mankind is full of obvious turning points and significant events: battles won, treaties signed, rulers elected or disposed, and now seemingly, planets conquered. Equally important are the great groundswells of popular movements that affect the minds and values of a generation or more, not all of which can be neatly tied to a time or place. Looking back upon the America of the '60s, future historians may well search for the meaning of one such movement. It drew the public's notice on the days and nights of Aug. 15 through 17, 1969, on the 600-acre farm of Max Yasgur in Bethel, NY.
>
> —<u>Time</u> magazine, August 29, 1969

Next witness?

Say what you will about Abbie Hoffman's role as a hippie, Yippie, fighter, inciter, ad man, madman, he was early into the Woodstock myth-making business. He even gave it a name. It's all on the record, either in his book *Woodstock Nation* or in his public testimony at the notorious Chicago Eight trial, from April 1969 to February 1970, where he and his codefendants were tried for crimes related to the riots at the 1968 Democratic National Convention. The following is taken from the transcript of those hearings in the courtroom of Judge Julius Hoffman:

Mr. Weinglass:	Will you please identify yourself for the record?
The Witness:	My name is Abbie. I am an orphan of America.
Mr. Schultz:	Your Honor, may the record show it is the defendant Hoffman who has taken the stand?
The Court:	Oh, yes. It may so indicate . . .
Mr. Weinglass:	Where do you reside?
The Witness:	I live in Woodstock Nation.
Mr. Weinglass:	Will you tell the Court and jury where it is?
The Witness:	Yes. It is a nation of alienated young people. We carry it around with us as a state of mind in the same way as the Sioux Indians carried the Sioux nation around with them. It is a nation dedicated to cooperation versus competition, to the idea that people should have better means of exchange than property or money, that there should be some other basis for human interaction. It is a nation dedicated to—
The Court:	Just where it is, that is all.
The Witness:	It is in my mind and in the minds of my brothers and sisters. It does not consist of property or material but, rather, of ideas and certain values. We believe in a society—
The Court:	No, we want the place of residence, if he has one, place of doing business, if you have a business. Nothing about philosophy or India, sir. Just where you live, if you have a place to live. Now you said Woodstock. In what state is Woodstock?
The Witness:	It is in the state of mind, in the mind of myself and my brothers and sisters. It is a conspiracy. Presently,

the nation is held captive, in the penitentiaries of the institutions of a decaying system.

We will address Abbie's specific involvement with Woodstock later on, but let it suffice for now to say that he was a controversial, polarizing character about whom widely divergent opinions were held. (In the interest of full disclosure, I will tell you that when I met Abbie at a Washington Square concert in the '80s, he called me "golden throat," which edged me closer to the pro-Abbie contingent after years of dismissing him as the clown prince of 1968 politics.)

Let's continue our sampling of Woodstock witnesses with the then-most trusted man in America. Here is Walter Cronkite's summation of Woodstock on his decade-ending radio documentary called *I Can Hear It Now/The Sixties:*

Twenty-seven days after "Tranquility Base," on an untranquil sea of mud, there was a walk in space that four hundred thousand long-haired pilgrims in and out of sweatshirts called "the greatest weekend since the creation." It came to be known as the "Woodstock Nation." In search of rock, acid rock, acid, pot, peace, and just being together, four hundred thousand Americans between fifteen and twenty-five flocked to Max Yasgur's dairy farm in Bethel, New York, for a weekend with Sly and the Family Stone; Country Joe and the Fish; Janis Joplin; the Jefferson Airplane; Santana; Crosby, Stills and Nash; the Who; Joan Baez; and Arlo Guthrie, among others.

The festival was declared a disaster area, and if there had been a riot, the commission that would have investigated it would have probably blamed negligent planning by the promoters; lack of water, food, medical and sanitary facilities; and stormy weather. It would have cited also the abundance of marijuana, some hard drugs, communal living, the exploitation of thousands of turned-away ticket holders who never got their eighteen dollars back. Yet there was no violence, relatively little illness for a population of this size. Three people died, two were born, and in a rare happening, even the police got rave notices. There was some paranoia. The establishment was blamed by some for having seeded the clouds causing the downpour. Some critics of the festival called it an orgy organized by the communists. And the promoters ended up suing each other.

Another early indication of Woodstock's potential as a sociological phenomenon can be found in the attention paid to it by renowned anthropologist Margaret Mead. Her widely respected theories, including studies about the healthy attitudes toward sex held by residents of the South Pacific, made her a perfect candidate to offer insights into the social, sexual, and psychological aspects of Woodstock. She plumbed the event for meaning and significance in the January 1970 issue of *Redbook* magazine:

> I do not think the Woodstock festival was a "miracle"—something that can happen only once. Nor do I think that those who took part in it established a tradition overnight—a way of doing things that sets the pattern of future events. It was confirmation that this generation has, and realizes that it has, its own identity.
>
> No one can say what the outcome will be; it is too new. Responding to their gentleness, I think of the words "Consider the lilies of the field . . ." and hope that we—and they themselves—can continue to trust the community of feeling that made so many say of those three days, "It was beautiful."

"It was beautiful!"

That was certainly one side of the Woodstock coin. The other side wasn't nearly as amiable and benign. That one came from the poison pen of the Russian-born American philosopher, novelist, and playwright Ayn Rand. She originated the belief system called Objectivism, which espouses that all humans must base their actions and values solely upon the tools of reason. Her books *The Fountainhead* (1943) and *Atlas Shrugged* (1957) were wildly successful in this country and all over the world. She vented her disdain for rock 'n' roll music, the hippies who liked it, and the so-called counterculture in her book *The New Left: The Anti-Industrial Revolution*.

Seizing on the coincidence of the successful Apollo 11 flight and Woodstock taking place exactly one month apart, she praised to the skies the former and lashed out unmercifully at the latter. Drawing on Friedrich Nietzsche's *The Birth of Tragedy* from the Spirit of Music, Rand cleverly used the dichotomy of the Greek gods Apollo and Dionysus to frame her attack on Woodstock by contrasting it with the moon landing. Rational, civilized thought is Apollonian; drunkenness and madness are Dionysian. The delicious coincidence of the mission being called Apollo must have made it irresistible for Rand to mount her blistering attack on the hedonism of Woodstock by bashing it with the rational triumph of NASA's accomplishment. On the one hand:

> In my article "Apollo 11," I discussed the meaning and the greatness of the moon landing . . . "No one could doubt that we had seen an achievement of man in his capacity as a rational being—an achievement of reason, of logic, of mathematics, of total dedication to the absolutism of reality."

On the other hand:

> The hippies are the living demonstration of what it means to give up reason and to rely on one's primeval "instincts," "urges," "intuitions"—and whims. With such tools, they are unable to grasp even what is needed to satisfy their wishes—for example, the wish to have a festival. Where would they be without the charity of the local "squares" who fed them? Where would they be without the fifty doctors, rushed from New York to save their lives—without the automobiles that brought them to the festival—without the soda pop and beer they substituted for water—without the helicopter that brought the entertainers—without all the achievements of the technological civilization they denounce? Left to their own devices, they literally didn't know enough to come in out of the rain.

Then-President Richard M. Nixon or even Vice President Spiro T. Agnew could not have put it any more condescendingly.

There's a word for this too: dualism. In general, dualism refers to something consisting of two parts. For example, in theology, the concept that the world is divided into opposing forces of good and evil. Dualism about Woodstock began to unfold almost at the exact moment that the event itself got under way. An early testament to the potential hurricane strength of the festival is the roaring battle that was waged very privately behind the scenes and very publicly on the front page and editorial pages of the esteemed *New York Times*. Woodstock was and had been a magnet for the music journals and alternative papers that had grown up with the rock 'n' roll of the mid-'60s. The establishment press didn't jump on board full-tilt until the event became a legitimate news event because of the sheer size of the festival and the huge number of attendees that it attracted.

The *Times* had a reporter on the scene filing stories as early as Friday, August 15. The first headline was:

"200,000 THRONGING TO ROCK FESTIVAL JAM ROADS UPSTATE."

On the next day:

"300,000 AT FOLK-ROCK FAIR CAMP OUT IN A SEA OF MUD."

Times rock critic Mike Jahn filed his first review on August 18:

"ROCK AUDIENCE MOVES TO DUSK-TO-DAWN RHYTHMS."

Barnard Law Collier's next bylined story read:

"TIRED ROCK FANS BEGIN EXODUS."

But the real fun began on Monday, August 18, when the *Times* printed an editorial with the headline "Nightmare in the Catskills," which read in part:

The dreams of marijuana and rock music that drew 300,000 fans and hippies to the Catskills had little more sanity than the impulses that drive the lemmings to march to their deaths in the sea. They ended in a nightmare of mud and stagnation that paralyzed Sullivan County for a whole weekend.

What kind of culture is it that can produce so colossal a mess?

The reporters who were on the front lines filing stories were *furious* with the executives back at the paper sitting in comfort in the *Times* building passing judgments that were completely at odds with what the troops in the trenches had experienced and tried to communicate in their reporting.

John Morris: I had the <u>New York Times</u> staff in my office. And the ones who went back to New York and went into Arthur Sulzberger's office and said, "We quit!" He said, "What are you talking about?" "The editorial in <u>The New York Times</u> today trashing Woodstock, taking it apart, calling it filthy, mud-soaked is so inaccurate and is so different from all the reports that we've been sending down, and all the things that we've told everybody, that we don't want to work for the paper anymore." And he went, "Ooops!" And they changed the editorial the next day. <u>The New York Times</u> doesn't recant editorials. But they did.

The new version on August 19 was headlined "Morning After at Bethel" and read in part:

> Now that Bethel has shrunk back to the dimensions of a Catskill village and most of the 300,000 young people who made it a "scene" have returned to their homes, the rock festival begins to take on the quality of a social phenomenon, comparable to the Tulipmania or the Children's Crusade. And in spite of the prevalence of drugs—sales were made openly, and "you could get stoned just sitting there breathing," a student gleefully reported—it was essentially a phenomenon of innocence.
>
> The music itself was surely a prime attraction. Where else could aficionados of rock expect to hear in one place Sly and the Family Stone, Creedence Clearwater Revival, Jefferson Airplane, and all those other lineal descendants of the primeval Beatles?
>
> Yet it is hardly credible that they should have turned out in such vast numbers and endured, patiently and in good humor, the discomforts of mud, rain, hunger, and thirst solely to hear bands they could hear on recordings in the comfort of home. They came, it seems, to enjoy their own society, free to exult in a life style that is its own declaration of independence. To such a purpose a little hardship could only be an added attraction.

Now *that's* duality!

Here's reporter Barnard Law Collier's take on the dustup:

> Every major <u>Times</u> editor up to and including executive editor James Reston insisted that the tenor of the story must be a social catastrophe in the making. It was difficult to persuade them that the relative lack of serious mischief and the fascinating cooperation, caring, and politeness among so many people was the significant point. I had to resort to refusing to write the story unless it reflected to a great extent my on-

the-scene conviction that "peace" and "love" was the actual emphasis, not the preconceived opinions of Manhattan-bound editors. After many acrimonious telephone exchanges, the editors agreed to publish the story as I saw it, and although the nuts-and-bolts matters of gridlock and minor lawbreaking were put close to the lead of the stories, the real flavor of the gathering was permitted to get across. After the first day's _Times_ story appeared on page 1, the event was widely recognized for the amazing and beautiful accident it was.

As blindly as the straight press pounced on Woodstock's inadequacies, _Rolling Stone_, the most successful "serious" rock magazine, trumpeted its glories:

> Chicago was only the labor pains. With a joyous three-day shriek, the inheritors of the earth came to life in an alfalfa field outside the village of Bethel, New York. Slapping the spark of life into the newborn was American rock and roll music provided by the Woodstock Music and Art Fair.
>
> And Dylan's Mr. Jones, who has, indeed, been aware of what is happening, but has preferred to denounce the immorality of fucking around with his values, is now forced to acknowlege [sic] both the birth and its legitimacy . . .
>
> Out of the mud and hunger and thirst, despite the rain and the end-of-the-world traffic jams, beyond the bad dope trips and the garish confusion, a new nation had emerged into the glare provided by the open-mouthed media.

So far, we've heard from some journalists, an anthropologist, a philosopher, a social scientist, a network news anchorman, and a Yippie. Now let's put Woodstock on the couch. The late, renowned psychotherapist Rollo May mused about the festival in the November 1969 issue of _Mademoiselle_ magazine:

> We're living in a transitional age, and the young people are developing the new myths and symbols by which people can communicate. Bethel is a way of forming the symbols of community. It's not the answer to everything, nor a blueprint for the new society, but it is a valuable signpost. I hope it's the forerunner to a new age. But what this age will be—beyond something that comes out of the absolute needs for humanness, something that puts more emphasis on love and community

and less emphasis on money and machines and trips to the moon—I just don't know . . .

Of all the "in the moment" instant analyses of the "meaning" of Woodstock, Dr. May's might just be the most honest, accurate, and disarming of all. Why? Because the true test of Woodstock, the real proof in the pudding about it, could not and would not really be known until the march of time did its tricky business. It would not be until decades passed that one could look back at actual societal changes, not projected or imagined ones, and come to some completely objective and accurate conclusions about how the festival did or did not affect the unfolding of American history.

Many of those changes will flash before your eyes as you read the testimony gathered here. Interwoven throughout the text are opinions, indictments, and glorifications of all things pre- and post-Woodstock. Our primary focus will be on the music and musicians, but none of their stories can be told without a clear-eyed view of all the societal, technological, and generational changes that have taken place between August 15, 1969 and August 15, 2009.

In the end, the single unifying thread that continues to make Woodstock a subject of intense fascination for the ages, and that made this project such an exciting and affirming one to undertake, is this observation from the late Joseph Campbell, author of *The Power of Myth:*

> People say that what we're all seeking is a meaning for life. I don't think that's what we're really seeking. I think what we're seeking is an experience of being alive, so that our life experiences on the purely physical plane will have resonances within our own innermost being and reality, so that we actually feel the rapture of being alive.

Apart from everything else you can say about it, Woodstock made us feel the rapture of being alive. It's time to get back to the garden.

PLAYERS

Billy Altman is a rock critic.

Miller Anderson was the guitarist for the Keef Hartley Band.

Joan Auperlee was an audience member who was backstage at Woodstock.

Joan Baez is a singer-songwriter, political activist, and the ultimate folk Madonna.

Marty Balin was the co–lead singer and founder of Jefferson Airplane.

Dale Bell was the associate producer on the film *Woodstock*.

Bill Belmont was the artist coordinator at Woodstock. During the show, he was a key part of keeping the musicians calm and happy.

Mike Bloomfield was a virtuoso guitarist with the Butterfield Blues Band and the Electric Flag.

Joe Boyd is the producer and author who represented the Incredible String Band at the time of Woodstock.

Marty Brooks is a publishing, media, and software development executive who has always been thrilled that he attended Woodstock, even though he now lies and tells people he was only three years old at the time.

Michael Brown was the Left Banke's principal writer and keyboardist.

Paul Butterfield, virtuoso harmonica player and founder of the Butterfield Blues Band.

Jack Casady was the bass guitarist for Jefferson Airplane.

Felix Cavaliere is a founding member of the Rascals and a follower of Swami Satchidananda.

Dick Cavett is the comedian and talk show host who showcased Woodstock-era musicians on his late-night show.

Joe Cocker is the British singer-songwriter famous for his eccentric performing style.

Bobby Colomby was the original drummer and founding member of Blood, Sweat and Tears.

Stu Cook played bass guitar for Creedence Clearwater Revival.

Roger Daltrey, lead singer and founding member of the Who.

Clive Davis was the president of Columbia Records at the time of Woodstock.

Henry Diltz was a rock photographer stationed on stage during the festival.

Alan Douglas, Jimi Hendrix's producer.

Spencer Dryden was the drummer for Jefferson Airplane.

Mike Eisgrau was the WNEW newsman who covered Woodstock.

Greg Errico was a member of Sly and the Family Stone.

Ahmet Ertegun was the president of Atlantic Records.

Christopher Farley is the culture editor at the *Wall Street Journal*.

John Fogerty was the lead singer for Creedence Clearwater Revival.

Myra Friedman, journalist, Janis Joplin's friend and biographer, worked for Albert Grossman at the time of Woodstock.

Stan Goldstein coordinated a variety of components of the festival such as the campgrounds and the Hog Farm.

Bill Graham was an entrepreneur, manager, and promoter who opened and ran the famous Fillmores West and East.

Larry Graham, member of Sly and the Family Stone at Woodstock and founder of the funk group Graham Central Station.

Nick Gravenites, rock 'n' roll songwriter and musician.

Henry Gross performed with Sha Na Na and was the youngest person to take the stage at Woodstock.

Arlo Guthrie, the singer-songwriter made famous by his eighteen-minute song "Alice's Restaurant."

Bill Hanley was the sound designer for the Fillmore East and the Woodstock Festival.

George Harrison was a member of the Beatles and a student of Ravi Shankar.

Mickey Hart was the drummer and percussionist for the Grateful Dead.

Richie Havens is the seminal figure of folk music who opened the festival.

Jimi Hendrix, virtuoso rock 'n' roll guitarist.

Dave Herman was a Philadelphia, then New York area, DJ originally hired to be an emcee at Woodstock.

Bob Hite, aka "Bear," was the lead singer for Canned Heat.

Abbie Hoffman was a political activist and author known for his involvement at the Democratic National Convention in Chicago in 1968.

Mike Jahn, former *New York Times* critic and author.

Larry Johnson headed up the sound department for the Woodstock film and now is Neil Young's film producer.

Al Kooper is a rock 'n' roll legend and a founding member of the Blues Project and Blood, Sweat and Tears.

Artie Kornfeld was a record company executive who worked closely with Michael Lang in creating Woodstock.

Paul Krassner is a humorist, author, and a political activist.

Roy Landis was an audience member at Woodstock.

Michael Lang was the executive producer for the Woodstock Festival. The man with the plan.

Chris Langhart was the technical director at the Woodstock Festival.

Lisa Law was a member of the Hog Farm and wife of Tom Law.

Tom Law was a dedicated member of the Hog Farm famous for teaching yoga at the festival.

Mel Lawrence was the director of operations at the festival.

Alvin Lee headed up Ten Years After.

Phil Lesh was a founding member and bass guitarist for the Grateful Dead.

Arthur Levy, a rock historian who has written extensively about Joan Baez.

Michael Lydon, critic and author who wrote the book *Rock Folk*.

Tom Malone, a teenage concert attendee at Woodstock.

Greil Marcus is a well-known rock critic and author.

Jim Marion is a self-described "Fillmore rat" who attended Woodstock.

Dave Marsh is a music critic and author.

Peter Max is an artist known for his iconic posters who was a follower of Swami Satchidananda.

Joe McDonald, aka Country Joe, is the political folk singer-songwriter who performed both as a solo act and as the frontman for Country Joe and the Fish.

Melanie (Safka) is a folksinger who performed on Friday.

Barry Melton was a member of Country Joe and the Fish. He is now a lawyer and judge in Marin County.

Chip Monck worked at the Fillmore East before designing the lighting for Woodstock. He is also famous for his distinct announcements at the festival.

John Morris was the production manager of the Woodstock Festival. He had worked closely with Bill Graham at the Fillmore East.

John Morthland is a rock critic and author.

Graham Nash was a founding member of Crosby, Stills, Nash and Young as well as a solo artist.

Nancy Nevins, lead singer of Sweetwater.

Felix Pappalardi was the producer of Cream and a founding member of Mountain.

Chip Rachlin has been an agent, manager, promoter, and entrepreneur for more than forty years.

Kenny Rankin, multitalented singer, songwriter, interpreter.

John Roberts is the Woodstock founder who financially backed the festival, along with Joel Rosenman.

Robbie Robertson, singer, songwriter, producer, and founding member of the Band.

Joel Rosenman was one of the "young men with unlimited capital" who made Woodstock possible, along with John Roberts.

Lillian Roxon was a rock critic and author.

Ellen Sander is a rock critic famous for her work in the '60s and '70s.

Carlos Santana is the founder and frontman for the band Santana.

Bob Santelli, renowned author, critic, and museum curator.

Swami Satchidananda was a yogic guru who spoke at the festival.

Stan Schnier worked at the Fillmore. After Woodstock, he went on the road with Country Joe and the Fish and later became the bassist for the Incredible String Band, then a personal manager and music publisher. He's been a professional photographer and amateur lap steel guitarist for the last 20 years.

Harriet Schwartz was a young Warner Bros. employee in 1969 and a Woodstock audience member.

John Sebastian was a central figure in the post–British Invasion revival of American rock 'n' roll and a member of the Rock and Roll Hall of Fame with his group the Lovin' Spoonful.

Bob See worked at the Fillmore East under Bill Graham and later started the legendary music production company See Factor.

Ravi Shankar is an Indian musician famous for popularizing the sitar.

Michael Shrieve was the drummer for Santana.

Jeffrey Shurtleff was a West Coast singer-songwriter-musician who performed with Joan Baez.

John Simon was a music producer of the '60s and '70s famous for his work with Simon and Garfunkel; Blood, Sweat and Tears; Janis Joplin; and the Band.

Rose Simpson was a member of the Incredible String Band.

Grace Slick was one of Jefferson Airplane's lead singers.

P. J. Soles is a cult actress who dated Joshua White at the time of Woodstock.

Bert Sommer, singer-songwriter who performed at Woodstock.

Robert Spitz is the author of *Barefoot in Babylon,* a book about Woodstock.

Patrick Stansfield is a famous production manager and friend of Chip Monck.

Stephen Stills is a guitarist, singer-songwriter, and founding member of Crosby, Stills, Nash and Young.

Sly Stone was the founder and frontman for Sly and the Family Stone.

Bill Thompson acted as a temporary manager for Jefferson Airplane.

Elliot Tiber is a writer who provided the festival permit for Woodstock in Bethel, New York.

Pete Townshend, founding member of the Who who wrote the rock opera *Tommy.*

Michael Wadleigh is a filmmaker, photographer, and writer most famous for his Academy Award–winning documentary about Woodstock.

Wavy Gravy, aka Hugh Romney, is the political comedian who headed up the Hog Farm.

Bob Weir is a singer-songwriter, guitarist, and founding member of the Grateful Dead.

Jann Wenner is the founder of *Rolling Stone* magazine.

Leslie West, founding member of the Vagrants and Mountain.

Joshua White created the psychedelic Joshua Light Show made famous at the Fillmore East.

Ellen Willis was a rock 'n' roll journalist.

Johnny Winter is a blues singer, guitarist, and producer.

Max Yasgur owned the farm in Bethel that became the Woodstock site.

Miriam Yasgur was Max Yasgur's wife.

Sam Yasgur is the son of Max and Miriam Yasgur.

Neil Young, occasional member of Crosby, Stills, Nash and Young, solo artist, and so-called Godfather of Grunge.

Friday

RICHIE HAVENS

Jt is 5:07 p.m. on Friday, August 15, 1969. You are standing on the stage in the far end of the cow pasture's natural amphitheater. The stage is set, and you can smell the fresh lumber used for its recent construction. As you look out in front of you, a sea of bobbing heads stretches for miles. It is a wave of humanity unlike any in the annals of recorded history. Certainly, the crowd is unusual for its size and more so for the ostensible reason all these people are here—for a unique type of American music barely fourteen years old called rock 'n' roll. If you accept the crowd estimate of five hundred thousand, that makes it the second-largest city in New York.

It is also notable because until the actual first day of the festival, absolutely no one involved in the event in any capacity had accurately surmised how huge it was going to be. Just ask one of the first men who stood onstage and looked out at that crowd.

John Morris: The night before the festival opened, we suddenly realized that it was going to be a lot bigger than we thought.

Bill Hanley: I went to the site and I custom-built the speakers for the upper levels in the back. If you look at the thing from overhead, you'll see the big green planes on either side that were meant to force the audience to be in front of the loudspeakers. They were expecting a big crowd, not anywhere near as big as what happened.

John Morris: We were figuring we'd have seventy-five thousand people. My mother had always told me to never use profanity in public—she's dead now, so I can say this—the first two words said over the sound system the night before we opened were "holy shit." I'd taken my crew out to dinner, we came back—it took us two hours to do something that had usually taken five to six minutes. And we were sort of going, "OOOOOOHHH!" and I walked up onstage and [Bill] Hanley was testing the sound. And so those were the first two intelligible words that were said into a live mic, which was right there but I didn't know was on. There were a good three or four hundred thousand, later six or seven hundred thousand people in that field! And the sun was coming up, so I could see them. What went through my head very quickly was, Well, forget the fences. They're gone. There were so many more than we guessed. The Beatles had drawn fifty thousand people to Shea Stadium. Monterey, which was a year or two before, was thirty-five thousand people over three days. The idea of putting one hundred thousand in the same place is normal to us now, but the idea of putting something like that together then and having that many people was just beyond the pale. I had a bet with Michael Lang—which he never, never collected, or ever asked to collect. I bet him a hundred dollars for every thousand people over fifty thousand!

Bill Belmont: I don't think anybody expected half a million people. How many people were you going to expect? This was before the big stadium shows. The difficulty was that you had a bunch of bands that were capable of drawing three thousand to ten thousand people on their own.

Some of the performers didn't have an idea how large the crowd was going to be until it came time to head over from the hotel to the stage.

Melanie: I get in the helicopter and now we are flying—I had never been in a helicopter before—we're flying over this stuff, and I say, "What is that, down there?" And the helicopter guy says, "It's people." "No, that's not possible, how could that be possible—where's the stage?—that's a stage?—and I have to?—oh, no!" I was terrified from the minute this whole thing started, and then they dropped me down on the field.

John Sebastian: I get in the helicopter and, we take off over this incredible sea of people. It was absolutely astonishing. Going over it in a helicopter really told the story. When I landed, I knew more than the people who were on the ground because I could see the scale of the thing already and the tent city that was out behind it and the dilapidated cars that were gonna be hopeless at the end of that weekend with all the mud and everything. I could see it all.

By midday on Friday, the route to the festival had more clogged arteries than Elvis Presley. Here is a recorded conversation that took place near the site between WNEW radio newsman Mike Eisgrau and a couple of local town police officers directing traffic on Saturday afternoon:

Mike Eisgrau: Did you ever expect to have this many people in the town of Bethel?

Policeman #1: Not right offhand, I didn't.

Policeman #2: The traffic is terrible. It is backed up four deep and has been four deep from White Lake right back through on the quick way right past Monticello— backed up from White Lake through Swan Lake and Liberty under the quick way—and a—there's no place to park. Everything is full.

Mike Eisgrau: What's the estimate as to how many people have come up?

Policeman #2: Well, we don't estimate it, but Woodstock Ventures estimated it at a hundred and seventy thousand.

Mike Eisgrau: So far?

Policeman #2: So far.

Mike Eisgrau: How do you handle this type of thing?

Policeman #2: Well, we've got every available policeman on corners directing traffic.

Mike Eisgrau: But there's no place to park the cars.

Policeman #2: Not at this point.

Mike Eisgrau: You've got a full weekend ahead of you.

Policeman #2: Oh boy, have I!

Later, Eisgrau described the scene from above.

Mike Eisgrau: This sight is hard to believe. We're over White Lake in the midst of this music festival encampment—we're up over the trees now—we're coming in over the top of the main stage of this music festival, and for easily a half a mile all we can see on this hilltop are people—fifty, a hundred, possibly two hundred thousand people sitting there—the music going on day and night and despite the rain, despite the mud, despite the water, despite the hardship, these people, apparently, are going to stick it out.

Despite the horrific road conditions, people made the best of it.

Arthur Levy: A lot of people just chickened out when they saw the traffic and the mess of the whole thing. But the people who had schlepped and decided to stay wanted to be part of it. Every year somebody else makes a different photographic scientific analysis about how many people were at Woodstock.

Joan Auperlee: The drive to the festival was a short one for us. Getting onto the main road should have been a breeze, but even though we set out early, the line of traffic was incredible. We merged in, radio cranking, and slowly made our way to the festival site creeping along. I had a '67 Camaro with five people inside. Many people were walking faster than the car could travel, so people were sitting all over the cars, on the hoods and on the top of the car. Wine and marijuana was freely and happily shared by all. Nobody was in a rush and everyone was so polite. It was a delightful trip.

Ellen Sander: On the way in, the ground was already muddy and there were a lot of people. The wheels of the car got stuck in the muddy shoulder. Some of the people walking pushed us out. We didn't even have to ask, didn't even have to get out of the car. People just helped other people. That was great.

Dave Herman: My wife Jayne and I left Philly about nine a.m. and when we left the Thruway to take the local highway to Yasgur's farm, it was about noon and the road was already jammed. As we literally inched our way down the road I knew I would be very late. It so happens that my sister, Judy, and her husband owned and operated a sleepaway camp called Camp Ranger on White Lake only about half a mile from the Woodstock site, so knowing the back roads from previous visits, I was able to wend my way to her camp where I left my car and walked with Jayne the half mile to the farm. We were dumbstruck as we got closer by the awesome throngs of concertgoers already streaming in through the knocked-down fences.

Jim Marion: I don't recall very much traffic on the way up until we got to Monticello to get onto route 17B into White Lake. It would take us more than ten hours to go the last eight miles. At first, cars were abandoned one or two deep on both sides of the road, then three or four deep; and it became evident that we were basically stuck in a one-way tunnel of traffic with no way to get out. Most of the time, the car went nowhere, so we put down the tailgate, turned up the radio, and partied on the back of the car, oblivious to the fact that there was intermittent rain. It was a real party atmosphere and we'd come prepared with beer and food, which we shared with the people around us. At one point, I noticed that the car stuck in back of us had California license plates, and we all thought it was pretty incredible that somebody would drive from California to come to this festival. Everyone on the road was curious about what was happening and we'd ask anyone who was headed away from the festival what was going on. "Hendrix is playing." "The whole thing's been canceled." "Sly was playing." "I don't know, it's a bunch of folkies with guitars." In retrospect, the people leaving knew as much as we did, which was nothing, but I recall one guy who did seem to have a grasp of the situation. "It's a fucking mess," he told us.

One incident on the road that I recall vividly occurred when my friend Mike and I wandered off the road a bit in the pitch-dark to relieve ourselves of some of the beer we'd consumed. The road must have been elevated, because we found ourselves rolling down a hill and smack into a yard that was filled with a get-together of Hasidic Jews. It appeared to be a vacation cabin, and there were probably thirty people, all well dressed in their white shirts, black hats, and their curls; and every single one of them staring, with jaws dropped, at the two scruffy, long-haired intruders who had fallen into their domain as if we were from a different planet, which, in a sense, I guess we were. We muttered an apology and started to head back up toward the road, which was no more than twenty yards away, when one of the young men asked, "What's going on?" We told him there was a rock festival in White Lake and we were headed there, which caused a few laughs, shrugged shoulders, and a number of "what, are you crazy?" looks from the group. The young man who had asked the question smiled and said, "Whatever that is, have a good time."

Mike Jahn: I heard about Woodstock from the <u>New York Times</u>. I was never big on industry gossip: I was focused on the music. So I didn't really have any idea that the Woodstock festival was coming up. And when I heard about it, I thought, I don't want to go to this. I told the <u>Times</u> that I'd rather go to Newport and they said, "We want you to go to Woodstock."

I got about halfway there in my rented car and it was trafficky. You just couldn't get anywhere. So I had to leave my car by the side of the road and walk to a sleazy motel and checked in. I called the <u>Times</u> and told them what was going on. I said, "Look, you better send a hard news team here. I cannot do this myself. This is a major story." They sent a helicopter for me and that's how I got in.

There was supposed to be a plan to help deal with all the traffic, but it was never implemented.

Stan Goldstein: We had hired three hundred New York City cops. On Wednesday, the police commissioner of the City of New York withdrew those cops and told them if they participated, they would be fired. At the same time, people started arriving in large quantities days in advance of the event. We asked the highway patrols to put into effect our traffic plan. The highway patrols did not. We lost control of the roads. We had no authority to turn roads one way or close others. By losing the cops, who were supposed to be directing traffic into the parking lots we had rented, no one parked in the lots. Thousands of acres we had rented for parking sat empty. People parked willy-nilly on the side of the roads. The traffic would and should have been mitigated by all the plans we had made.

The crowd was patient and well behaved but starting to get restless. The nominal reason that they came to this gathering was to hear live music and, so far, with the exception of an occasional soundcheck, there wasn't even a struck chord emanating from the sound system that Bill Hanley had built to reach the maximum number of listeners with the maximum amount of power. All of that would change in an instant, of course, but not without an equally maximum amount of tension, aggravation, frustration, and negotiation as to who would actually be the first artist to step out on that stage and attempt to command the undivided attention of the masses.

Picking the pecking order of the performers should have been the least of the organizers' problems. Just choose the lineup, notify the managers, cue the soundman, alert the roadies, roll the cameras, announce the star that would do the opening honors, then take your seat, sit back, relax, and enjoy the show, right? Not so much.

Backstage in the performers' tent and one of the organizers' trailers, some drops of nervous perspiration appeared. Why? The designated opening act, Sweetwater, an LA band with a well-received debut album on Warner Bros. Records, was hopelessly trapped in the long, unending, unmoving traffic jam on Route 17B. It was clear that they had no chance of arriving in time for the announced 4:00 p.m. kickoff. What to do?

One of the solutions was a matter of sheer practical deduction. It would be easier to put a solo artist onstage, or a group with a few acoustic instruments, than it would be to put a full-tilt rock 'n' roll band up there. The promoters had a little breathing room on that score because opening day had already been designed to feature the softer, more acoustic acts that were scheduled to appear that weekend: Joan Baez, Arlo Guthrie, et al. Sweetwater would have been perfect, but fate determined otherwise, and various alternative options had to be looked at in a hurry.

Bill Belmont: Well, the original plan called for a number of local bands to open the show on Friday. By Friday, it was clear that being able to do an actual programmed timely show was sort of out the window. It was really difficult to try and figure out who was around. It was a very sunny day. It was very warm. There were tons of people in the audience. I don't think the crowd was at its peak, but there were tons and tons of people in the audience. It was a huge stage. It was perhaps sixty or seventy feet by forty feet. It might have been bigger than that. I don't remember. But the stage itself, it was really basically just a lot of people hanging around.

Richie Havens was originally scheduled to perform later in the day, but that was about to change.

Richie Havens: We were back at the hotel. I was supposed to go on fifth and there was no way to get anyone there. There wasn't gonna be a Woodstock, to tell you the truth. It was gonna be the world's largest riot, because seven miles away were all the musicians in two hotels, and they couldn't get to the site at all—no road to get there. And no one could carry tons of amps and equipment down to the stage from seven miles away.

Michael Lang: It was a question of who we could get on the quickest, who was ready, and who needed the least preparation and the least gear. Tim Hardin was an idea. He wasn't ready. Tim, I think, was a little blitzed, a little too blitzed. He was a friend, and I was hoping that playing at Woodstock would bring him back, because he had been blitzed for a while. And I thought it would be a good opportunity for him to get his shit together, and straighten up long enough at least to get some public recognition. But he wasn't ready.

Richie Havens: Tim Hardin was there, but he decidedly refused to go on first. He was not coming out from under the stage.

Chip Monck: Tim was absolutely unable to fathom or to deal with the fact of opening the show. He couldn't be presented without some help. So he politely declined.

Richie Havens: All of a sudden, they said, "Richie! We've got a guy with a helicopter who's gonna come over. You've got the least number of instruments, so you'll go over first."

I said, "Okay, fine."

Then he came back and said, "No, he's not coming," then "Yes! He _is_ coming!"

Now the concert is three hours late already and in the Holiday Inn driveway comes this little helicopter right outside my window and I hear this noise, so we run out with our two conga drums, two guitars, and the three of us, and we hunch into this bubble helicopter and they took us over.

Michael Lang: Well, Richie was scared, frankly, as I recall. But I think that was a kind of natural reaction to looking at a crowd of that size. But he didn't make it a problem.

Richie Havens: I actually was afraid to go on first. I knew the concert was late and that maybe it would be a little nuts. I didn't want to be trampled by a billion people. So I said, "Don't do this to me, Michael. I'm only one guy. My bass player isn't even here."

His bass player, Eric Oxendine, got caught in the traffic jam leading to the site, and decided to walk the fifteen or twenty miles from where the traffic was stopped dead to the stage. He would have made it in time for Richie's set if the order hadn't changed, but that was not meant to be. Lang continued to beg, plead, and cajole. Richie relented and walked out onstage.

Chip Monck: And suddenly, it was showtime. I said, "Sit down, stand up, do whatever you wish to do, but we're ready to start now and I bet you're pleased with that. And, ladies and gentlemen—please—Mr. Richie Havens."

Joshua White: He was the first guy they could get on and he's a great-looking guy and he did his job. And so, the festival was launched!

He was twenty-eight years old, dressed magnificently in white trousers and a long, flowing orange caftan. Richie Havens was born on January 21, 1941, in Brooklyn, New York. He was a product of that borough's rough and tough Bedford-Stuyvesant neighborhood who somehow escaped the dead-end fate of many of his peers and schoolmates, in part because of his devotion to music and the arts. He moved to Greenwich Village at the dawn of the '60s and made his living as a portrait artist and poet. For a while, he lived down the hall from Noel Paul Stookey who was performing as a solo musician-comedian at clubs in the Village before joining forces with Peter Yarrow and Mary Travers and rewriting American music history as the folk trio Peter, Paul and Mary. Stookey befriended Richie and encouraged him to flex his musical muscles. They've remained lifelong friends.

Richie took the advice and began transforming his poems into songs, which he performed to great acclaim and growing audiences throughout the rest of the decade. One major factor that helped Richie gain an audience was the change happening on FM radio. When FM radio came into being, every AM station simply used FM to simulcast its programming. But in 1966, the FCC mandated that the FM signal must broadcast something different. This led to more creative, progressive stations playing the hipper music of the day and gearing their free-form programming to a decidedly younger crowd. One of the early favorites on these so-called Freak-quency Modulation stations was Richie Havens. His invitation to perform at Woodstock was a no-brainer.

Joshua White: Richie Havens was quite popular at that time. He was a folksinger in the tradition of Leadbelly and Josh White—the other Josh White. He was a favorite on free-form radio stations. He was a very good and impassioned singer, and he was one of the earliest black folksingers who developed credibility with this white audience. The audience loved him.

Mike Jahn: One of the reasons I decided to go to Woodstock was that Richie Havens was going to be there. Richie and I were friends, and I figured if he was going to be there, I could be there. I knew him back in 1966. Somebody gave me a copy of Mixed Bag and I loved it. I got in touch with him and met him in his apartment in the East Village. He took me to Slug's, a legendary jazz club, and I was probably the only white man in the place. There was some animosity with the guy at the door. He didn't want to let me in, but Richie said, "He's cool," so he let me in. So we went in together to see Sun Ra. Richie was such a sweetheart.

Stan Schnier: When Richie was doing shows at the Fillmore, he didn't have a road crew. There was a guy named Dino who played backup guitar, and Dino used to come over to our apartment all the time and jam with us. It was a very small world then. Funny enough, most of the time when he and Richie were onstage, you couldn't even hear Dino, because Richie sang and played so full and loud and Dino was kind of in the back, twiddling. It wasn't a defined rhythm-lead relationship. It was just something that they had between them that kept Richie locked in. I never saw anybody like Richie before, and I haven't seen anybody since. He was totally unique.

Tom Law: I met him through Albert Grossman. I'd see him when I was working for Peter, Paul and Mary. I think he's one of the most soulful people on the planet; I put him at the top of the list.

Billy Altman: I saw Richie Havens open for Cream in the fall of 1967. He was somebody I was familiar with. A great performer. His energy was impressive. He used a tuning where his guitar was tuned to a chord and it allowed him to do all these great rhythmic things. And that made him the perfect act for that point at Woodstock. He was able to get people into the music physically, because of how rhythmic it was, and that's not something a lot of people could have done.

Mike Jahn: As a performer, Richie was magnetic and charismatic. He had an amazing rich sound, and he used that open E tuning on his guitar and it just sounded amazing. He had huge hands. Piano player hands. You can't bring your thumb around over the bass strings and bar the strings unless you have immense hands. His voice is very expressive. Here's a comparison that most rockers will hate, but hearing Richie play "San Francisco Bay Blues" was on the level of hearing Streisand's rendering of "Happy Days Are Here Again." Taking an old jolly-time tune and making it into something entirely different. It blew me away. He is a wonderful talent.

Stan Schnier: He uses these great open tunings. Joni Mitchell uses them, too. I think a lot of guitar players are always kind of mystified by them. "How did she do that? How did he do that?"

You can't talk about Richie Havens without discussing his ability to perform covers—to interpret other artists' material. At a time when most of his contemporaries were dismantling the notion of being handed other people's songs to record and perform by the A&R (artists and repertoire) man at the record company, Richie clearly had it going both ways.

Billy Altman: He was a great singer and a great interpreter also. There aren't many people who can do Bob Dylan as good as Bob Dylan, or even half as good as Bob Dylan, and he's one of the few people who's always been able to do a great job with Dylan's material. And I say that with the utmost respect. The same is true with the Beatles. Even with songs that you wouldn't necessarily think would be open to that kind of interpretation like "Here Comes the Sun." He is able to find things in songs and make them his own. That's what Richie Havens does.

He wasn't the opening act; he was the opening "act-cident." The good luck charm. The omen that in some way everyone at the festival backstage, onstage, and in front of the stage hoped could make you believe that everything was going to be all right. He did his job and he did it magnificently. He was the perfect candidate to spark the flame to light the fire that would burn brightly and tangibly for almost four straight days. His peace-love demeanor and childlike jargon definitely set the tone for the entire weekend of hippie chic:

Richie Havens from the stage, August 15, 1969: A hundred million songs are gonna be sung tonight. All of them are gonna be singing about the same thing, which I hope everybody who came, came to hear, really. And it's all about you—actually—and me and everybody around the stage and everybody that hasn't gotten here, and the people who are gonna read about you tomorrow. Yes! And how really groovy you were—all over the world, if you can dig where that's at—that's really where it's really at!

The lightness of his spoken message was in direct contrast to the unrelenting power of his music and his message. He did "High Flying Bird," the lead-off track from his stunning Verve-Forecast debut album *Mixed Bag*. He did Gordon Lightfoot's "I Can't Make It Anymore." He performed a trilogy of classic Beatles songs, "With a Little Help from My Friends," "Strawberry Fields Forever," and "Hey Jude."

Richie was well past the twenty minutes he was expecting to play, but even after double that amount of time, then triple that amount of time, there was still no sign that anyone wanted him to come off the stage. Nobody frantically giving him the "cut" sign, so he surmised, correctly, that his follow-up wasn't ready yet. He soldiered on. Literally. His searing performance of the antiwar song "Handsome Johnny," cowritten with the then-folksinger, now Academy Award–winning actor Lou Gossett Jr., once again brought the crowd to its feet. Having accrued enough show business savvy to leave them clamoring for more, Richie attempted, once and for all, to leave the stage. It was not to be. Pushed back out once again to face the roaring crowd, Richie looked squarely into the eyes of a moment of truth that few performers in any of the arts ever face. And then it just came to him—an instance of otherworldly creativity that simply defies expectation, but not imagination.

Richie Havens: Two and a half hours—two hours and forty-five minutes later, as I walked off the eighth time, they said, "No, no one's here yet, go back." [Laughs.] For the seventh time. I decided I didn't know what else to sing, you know, it's like everything I could think of, you know? So, I really had an inspiration. I looked out over the audience, which I could not see the end of because what most people don't see in the movie is, as far as you could see people in the picture that they show, when I'm onstage, there was the other side of that hill that was equally as large. And the people on that side of the hill never even saw the stage; they just lied down in the field and listened, and that was probably the best sound. It could be heard fifteen miles away actually. Best sound I ever played outdoors, in that sense. But the thing was that I was onstage and I didn't know what to sing, so I—I looked out and I said, you know, "Freedom isn't what they've made us even think it is. We already have it. All we have to do is exercise it. And that's what we're doing right here." So I just started playing, you know, notes—trying to decide what am I gonna sing and the word came out, "Freedom," you know. I started singing "Freedom." And then, of course, "Motherless Child," which I hadn't sung in probably seven years—six or seven years, came out. And then there was another part of a hymn that I used to sing back when I was about fifteen that came out in the middle of it. "There's a telephone in my bosom and I can call him from my heart." And—that's how it came together.

Arthur Levy: He used to perform with his eyes closed. I didn't know if he did that because the amount of sweat he generated stung his eyes or if he just had to block out the audience. It was certainly the largest crowd he'd ever played to. It could have been very daunting and intimidating to perform to that number of people. "Freedom" is one of the great transcendental moments in rock history.

Bob Santelli: Havens saved the day. The manner in which Richie plays, hard strums, open tunings that would allow him to play the guitar as if it were some kind of weapon, as if the notes and the chords that would come flowing out of his guitar were meant to disable any doubters. This is the kind of acoustic music that was ideal for an outdoor setting, especially to kick off the festival. He rose to the occasion. Look at the intensity in Richie Havens's face and match that with the intensity of his guitar playing and then the rhythms of his conga player. This was a powerful and driving rock band, and he was creating it with a guitar that seemed to have vengeance in mind in some way, shape, or form. It was a powerful performance and it was very lucky that it occurred because there wasn't a whole lot else that was as compelling or as intense on Friday as Richie Havens.

It couldn't have started off any better. There are many characters from all facets of the festival who have laid claim to or been given the title "Father of Woodstock." Some are certainly worthy of the sobriquet. But, more than most, Richie Havens can wear that mantle with pride and dignity and humility. At this writing, he is still the greatest living embodiment of the Woodstock ethos.

On the occasion of this fortieth-anniversary milestone, Richie is still recording, still touring, still painting, still acting, and still making his voice heard on a variety of issues as he completes his seventh decade on the planet. I'd like to illustrate his generosity and commitment with a personal observation. In the 1980s, after the death of singer-songwriter Harry Chapin, I cohosted an annual twenty-four-hour fund raiser at the United Nations for World Hunger Year, the charitable organization cofounded by Harry and my friend Bill Ayres. On the afternoon of the broadcast, Richie came by to perform and lend a hand before a scheduled concert that evening on Long Island. He sang, he talked, he played, then he left for his gig. That was it. I put it out of my head and moved on to the next guest. At about three o'clock in the morning, the really dead hours of a twenty-four-hour Hungerthon, there was an unexpected knock on the door at the UN. It was Richie! He had taken a collection for World Hunger Year at the concert and brought the proceeds back with him to the city after the show! *That* is the ethos of Woodstock!

Richie's performance crystallized and clarified the real underlying reason these half a million people had gathered together here in the single-word clarion call repeated over and over and over again, and screamed right back at him by the throng, "Freedom! Freedom! Freedom! Freedom! Freedom . . . !"

Richie's power as a performer is still evident today. He puts his whole mind, heart, soul, and body into each mesmerizing performance. He seems transfixed, transformed, transported. Is it real? Is it an act? I've seen it up close and personal for over forty years now and I'm here to tell you that it's no act. It's just Richie being Richie—taking himself and his audience (whether one other person in a radio studio or five hundred thousand on a dairy farm) to somewhere between gravitational reality and supernatural transcendence.

For forty years now, Richie Havens has taken upon himself the Olympian task of carrying the Woodstock torch, and keeping it burning for his own and all subsequent generations.

Stan Schnier: He's still the same person today as he was then. He's totally unpretentious. If you saw him on the street, he's wearing a caftan, he treats everybody like a brother.

Richie Havens's name will always be inextricably intertwined with Woodstock, and he appreciates the connection. He relishes his role, both at the festival and in explaining what happened there to others.

Richie Havens: I have been straightening out the record on Woodstock from an infrastructure perspective. Why did all those people come there? It wasn't just the music. It was not just sex, drugs, and rock 'n' roll, as the media has constantly portrayed it. I get to tell people what really happened at Woodstock, which is that a lot of people came together because of like-minded problems we were all having, issues that we all had to deal with in the '60s coming out of the '50s, and that spanned a great span from women's rights through Vietnam, through civil rights—through all of that. Consequently, what happened is what I call a "cosmic accident." No one knew eight hundred and fifty thousand people were gonna show up. And, as far as the music goes, more than half the people onstage, no one had ever seen before. And that was the magic of it.

THE SWAMI

The Woodstock Festival was a destination of biblical proportions. In the tumultuous time of the late '60s, millions of kids were forging a new way of life, and these Three Days of Peace and Music provided the perfect microcosm to put their cultural, political, and social ideals into action.

The spiritual quest of half a million kids brought them to the Woodstock Festival. Sensing the spiritual significance of the festival before it even happened, *Woodstock* director Michael Wadleigh set out to assemble what he describes as a modern retelling of the *Canterbury Tales*. One of the film's most famous documentary segments features a young man and woman, two hitchhikers on their way to the festival. To Wadleigh, and to the international audience that the film reached, those kids perfectly represented the Woodstock pilgrim.

My father was asking whether I was in a communist training camp or something in the house that I lived in. And I could understand where he's coming from. Because he's an immigrant, and so he came over here to better himself economically and so forth and all that other rot to make it better for me, and he can't understand why I didn't play. He said, "Why aren't you playing the game? Here's all this opportunity, here are all these things which have so much value." But they only have value to him, and he can't understand why they don't have value to me. But then again he does have wisdom to allow me to be who I am. I will, by doing what I'm doing, learn for myself how to live. And that's what he wants me to do.

Mike Wadleigh: The things that kid says about America, about his father, about finding himself, the counterculture movement. He was so far beyond his years. What he said was an articulation of a generation. His father was an immigrant from an impoverished background, came to America for what the kid calls "the old American Dream" which was to make a lot of money, make a good life financially. He says I grew up with that, and now I have enough money, and I want to find myself. He didn't of course just mean spiritually, he meant intellectually as well. It was Socrates, it was Plato. It was exploration. Going back to "Back to the Garden" . . . "I don't know who I am, but life is for learning." That kid was really saying it, and saying how he had to strike out and find the values for himself. He gave us an analysis. People don't know, even people coming to the festival, they're looking to find themselves, they don't know what life is about, and they're thinking that maybe someone else has something to tell them, maybe the musicians or other people they'll meet. I think that is the true value of the Woodstock Festival. That people were able to find out what was going on from other people who were there in a natural environment.

So those children looked up at that "simple, unpainted stage . . . the cathedral" looking for answers. For a generation that was routinely seeking alternatives to nearly every aspect of life handed down from family, church, state, and school, exploring new forms of worship and spirituality was certainly to be expected. And given the power of pop stars to focus attention on their interests and whims du jour, it was no surprise when legitimate holy men (or self-proclaimed shamans) hopped on their magic carpets (or a commercial airliner) and brought their meditation methods (or snake oil) to all those young American seekers.

Among these voices was the Indian spiritual figure Swami Satchidananda. The child of two wealthy Hindu landowners in India, Swami was already a guru in India, where he headed an ashram in Sri Lanka. He moved to New York in 1966 after visiting a guru there. In the time that elapsed between his move to the States and Woodstock, he developed quite a following loyal to his teachings of yoga and enlightenment.

In regards to the guidance-seeking flower children prevalent at Woodstock, Swami remarked: "They are all searching for the necklace that's around their necks. Eventually they'll look in the mirror and see it."

While benedictions and convocations are commonplace at all manner of American gatherings—communion breakfasts, political conventions, sports award dinners, et cetera—no one connected with Woodstock had given a moment's thought to have someone deliver an opening prayer. And yet it happened.

The mad scramble to reorganize the opening night schedule continued full-tilt even as Richie Havens was sitting onstage performing. In the middle of the blur of John Sebastian, Tim Hardin, Country Joe negotiations, a member of Swami Satchidananda's inner circle made his way right up to John Morris, catching his attention in the chaos.

John Morris: Somebody out of his entourage came over and said that the Swami would like to speak to the crowd. And I said "Why not?!?" And so we set it up for him to do.

Ellen Sander: Swami Satchidananda was a culture hero at the time. He worked with a lot of major celebrities.

The pop artist Peter Max tells a story about meeting the Swami in Paris and encouraging him to come to America.

Peter Max: I knew that in America, everybody was experimenting and trying to find another way of expanding the mind. The yogic type of thinking, about love and peace, was in the air, it was part of the fashion. But for it to really become part of your lifestyle, not just an idea, was very, very big. And I said to him, "Swami, America needs you." And he laughed and slapped his knee and said, "Well, if America needs me, maybe I'll come."

Swami Satchidananda: The first group of people who were around me, they were just lying down on the floor, putting their feet up in my face, blowing their cigarettes, and saying, "Swami, can you tell us something about yoga." [Laughs.] Oh boy. Certainly, there was a little cultural difference.

Felix Cavaliere: Being in a rock band at that time was to be exposed to every kind of vice known to man. I had been given a book by a friend of mine called Autobiography of a Yogi and toward the end of the book it said, "If you want a teacher, ask, and he shall come." Within two weeks, we were asked to do a television program, and I walked in, and there he was.

No less than the ways in which Richie Havens or Sly Stone or Alvin Lee rose to the occasion and caught lightning in a bottle, Swami Satchidananda said the right words, at the right time, in the right place, for the right people:

My beloved brothers and sisters, I am overwhelmed with joy to see the entire youth of America gathered here in the name of the fine art of music. In fact, through the music, we can work wonders. Music is a celestial sound, and it is the sound that controls the whole universe, not atomic vibrations. Sound energy, sound power, is much, much greater than any other power in this world. And, one thing I would very much wish you all to remember is that with sound, we can make—and at the same time, break. Even in the war field, to make the tender heart an animal, sound is used. Without that war band, that terrific sound, man will not become animal to kill his own brethren. So, that proves that you can break with sound, and if we care, we can make also.

So I am very happy to see that we are all here gathered to create some sounds—to find that peace and joy through the celestial music. And I am really very much honored for having been given this opportunity of opening this great, great music festival. I should have come a little earlier to do that job, but as you all know, thousands of brothers and sisters are on the way, and it's not that easy to reach here.

Swami went on to praise the American youth as emerging international leaders, embracing a more holistic look at life, beyond the material.

And the future of the whole world is in your hands. You can make or break. But, you are really here to make the world and not to break it. I am seeing it. There is a dynamic manpower here. The hearts are meeting. Just yesterday I was in a monastery, where about two hundred or three hundred Catholic monks and nuns met and they asked me to talk to them under the heading of "East and West—One Heart." Here, I really wonder whether I am in the East or West. If these pictures or the films are going to be shown in India, they would certainly never believe that this is taken in America. For here, the East has come into the West. And with all my heart, I wish a great, great success in this music festival to pave the way for many more festivals in many other parts of this country . . .

The entire world is going to watch this. The entire world is going to know that what the American youth can do to the humanity. So, every one of you should be responsible for the success of this festival.

John Morris: He came out, and he was wonderful! He talked about peace, and loving each other.

I will not pretend to you that everyone at the festival embraced the Swami's message. Many were skeptical, and even a little creeped out, by the droves of über flower children whom he attracted.

Joshua White: I was watching it from the back. I was standing directly behind him, fifty feet back and twelve feet in the air, looking down as I set up my equipment and looking down, not so much at the Swami but at his people. And I said I have no desire to go down and hug these people.

The whole kind of blissed-out spiritualism was beginning to take hold and it did among many of the Fillmore people. There was nothing that preceded it. It began with people deciding they were vegetarians, which meant that they ate nothing but rice.

A swami is a swami and he just sits there . . . but watching the ritu-alistic people preparing everything and that blissed-out look on their faces . . . it was pod-people time . . . it just scared me. I just didn't like that. But that's just me. I have other friends who deeply embraced it and grew because of it.

Regardless of personal preferences, the influence of Swami and the Eastern invasion cannot be diminished.

Joshua White: Because of Woodstock and for many years afterward, you couldn't present something that didn't have an overriding peace theme, love theme, universality. People are only just beginning to understand that now.

FRIDAY

22

FREE CONCERT

There is no such thing as a free lunch, and there is certainly no such thing as a "free festival." John Morris knew this even as he uttered one of the most famous Woodstock quotes:

It's a free concert from now on. That doesn't mean that anything goes. What that means is we're going to put the music up here for free. What it means is that the people who're backing this thing, who put up the money for it, are going to take a bit of a bath. A big bath. That's no hype, that's true, they're going to get hurt. What it means is that these people have it in their heads that your welfare is a hell of a lot more important, and that the music is, than the dollar . . . Now, the one major thing that you have to remember tonight, when you go back up to the woods to go to sleep or if you stay here, is that the man next to you is your brother. And you damn well better treat each other that way because if you don't, then we blow the whole thing, but we've got it, right there.

Though these words were beautiful and perfect for the occasion, it would be naïve to think that the festival had been envisioned as an act of charity to the Woodstock generation. The festival was envisioned and executed as a capitalist enterprise.

Stan Goldstein: Often lost in what you hear about Woodstock is the understanding that this was an enterprise with commercial intent. We hadn't intended it to be a free festival, we sold tickets and had concessions and intended to exploit the festival in whatever ways we could to make a profit.

Tom Malone: We made it through the traffic, parked the car in a freshly plowed down field full of corn, and marched off to the hill with the tents on top and the towers of scaffolding off in the distance. We arrived on the hill Friday morning before noon.

As we approached the bottom of the hill, we were behind the stage. A small army of really strong-looking guys were still building the stage and putting stuff on the biggest speaker towers I have ever seen. I being the good Catholic schoolboy, was looking for an entrance gate and someone to give my ticket to. I looked to the left and the right of the stage, there were no fences, no gate, just all these kids walking up the hill coming and going from all directions. Approaching us was the most colorful clown-looking hippie freak playing a kazoo. For some reason he looked like he would be part of the festival. I asked him, "Who do we give our tickets to?" He replied, "Tickets, tickets. I'll take your ticket." I handed him my three-day ticket, he tore the Friday stub portion off the ticket, and handed me back the Saturday Sunday part, which I still have. It was years later that I figured out that the colorful character who took my Friday ticket stub was Wavy Gravy.

Wavy Gravy: I, as chief of police, was surveying the bowl when this guy came up to us and said, "Well, they just about got the tents up and they're ready to start taking tickets, you wanna clear the infield?" And I looked out there were about thirty thousand people there already, and I said, "Look, do you wanna have a good movie or a bad movie?"

John Morris: There's a scene in the movie where there's a whole group of us standing there. It's probably Michael and Artie and Stan Goldstein and maybe Langhart and myself, and I walk away from the thing and throw my hands in the air. And what the conversation was Artie Kornfeld saying, "We're gonna lose everything and we're not gonna make any money on this. It's terrible. Can't we do like they do in the Catholic church and get girls in diaphanous gowns"—and I was a Catholic, I didn't know about girls in diaphanous gowns—"to go out in the crowd with collection baskets and ask if they'd give us money?" And that's why I walked away and threw my hands in the air, and walked straight to my trailer. We were the first people to use Winnebagos, that's what we lived in. I walked into the office, picked up the phone, and called Joel and John.

Joel Roberts and John Rosenman—the money guys behind Michael Lang and Artie Kornfeld's vision—never got to the Woodstock site because they were stuck in the office trying to come up with money to pay the acts.

John Roberts: We had a backstage operation that was being handled by Michael Lang—and about a mile from the site, we had what we called our "staging area" or our so-called executive offices, where we were coordinating the security, traffic, medical, press—and that's where Joel and I were stationed. The last time I got to the actual site was Friday, around the time Richie Havens was going on. And from then until Monday morning, about two in the morning, I was in that other building and working—and I never got back to the site.

John Morris: I said to them, "Look. There's two ways we can play this right now. I told them Artie's idea, and I was still laughing at that point. The other thing is I could go up onstage and say that this is a free concert, which is stating the patently obvious. It is a free concert. We can't make them go out of the gates and pay us the money when they come in. Or we could keep going. And if we don't keep going—I'd already been on the phone with [Governor] Nelson Rockefeller's chief of staff earlier in the morning, who wanted to send in the National Guard to clear the place out. We almost had an Attica. They said, "Alright, give us a couple of minutes," and they called us in a couple of minutes and said, "Go with it." Now, they were digging themselves a gigantic financial hole, but they said, "This is what it is. This is what we have to do."

John Morris is one of the unsung heroes of Woodstock. His actions bring to mind Kipling's line, "If you can keep your head while all about you are losing theirs . . . you'll be a Man, my son." Morris was a little different in appearance and lifestyle than most of the young counterculture types who made Woodstock happen.

John Morris: Yeah, I was straight. I was East Coast prep school. East Coast college. One thing I've always done is that I've always worn jackets. It's a prep school habit. Then all of a sudden, it was like everything was totally different—tie-dye and long hair and no bras.

Surrounded by the mostly "kid army" that assembled at Woodstock, Morris was the grown-up who saw to it that even under the most adverse circumstances, there was an adult around who could kiss the boo-boo and make it feel better.

John Morris: I've joked for years now that my one disappointment in my time in the music business was that nobody ever got me a baseball jacket that said "Éminence Grise" on the back of it because that's what I was. I was the older guy who'd lived a different kind of life whose job it was to be in control of what was going on. Anarchy was my enemy.

Though only thirty years old at the time, Morris was not a stranger to being the grown-up in the room. He had already established relationships with the top agents of the day through his various booking gigs, and most specifically through his position at the Fillmore East.

John Morris: And some of the people who had offices upstairs in the Fillmore thought I was the enemy. I was very old world as far as they were concerned. I didn't do drugs; they were not part of my life. It took me an awful long time to convince them that while I came from the straight world, I was really someone who was interested in what was going on, but I just felt that somebody had to manage it.

And Morris, with his inimitable charm, eventually won over his detractors.

Joshua White: John Morris was particularly interesting because he was not a dope smoker and he was not from the hip scene, but he was a very cool guy and he would stand there in espadrilles and no socks—because that was his style—and he would tell them about some resort that he thought was a great place to visit in Mystic, and they would listen with rapt attention.

Stan Schnier: Oh yeah, he was clean as a whistle. He and I were and are like brothers, in constant communication. John was the exact right man for the job.

Morris straddled the line between the hip and straight worlds perfectly.

Bob See: John always came off as being the proper, the upper crust, Upper East Side kind of kid. You would not consider him a hippie. He was very much dressed and had the attitude of a straight guy. He could deal with the straight world, and they'd accept him as being part of that. They'd listen to him.

Morris's dynamism made him the perfect person to run the Fillmore East. They were pioneering a new way of presenting music.

John Morris: This was a whole new direction for a whole new audience who really wanted something different. There were kids out there in the East Village and around the country—ten years younger than I was, at least—who were really interested in having somebody bring the music to them. I was the one with some experience, not in the music business but in theatrical production. And if you brought the music to them and you did it with great production values, it blew their mind.

The Fillmore East knew how to put on the best show with the best sound, the best lights, the best everything. And John Morris was one of the few people who could be trusted by both the money people and the talent. The reputation Morris gained at the Fillmore helped land him an interesting opportunity.

John Morris: It was April of 1969. I had been running Fillmore East. And then I left Fillmore East to take the Doors and the Airplane to Europe. When I came back from Europe, I found that I was unemployed. Then I started hearing about this festival and was approached and fairly quickly met Michael Lang. And we talked about my coming and helping and working on the festival.

Stan Goldstein: Chip Monck arranged that we would meet at Morris's apartment. Neither Michael Lang nor I knew John until that time. At that meeting, we learned about John's involvement at the Fillmore as its general manager. John indicated that he was interested and could be of value to us. By virtue of his experience at the Fillmore, he was in touch with a lot of people that we weren't in touch with, and he had experience with a lot of people we didn't have experience with.

FREE CONCERT

Mike Wadleigh: John Morris really ran the stage. The promoters really weren't that experienced, and John was. He had a really good mellow manner of keeping control.

Morris ensured that the Woodstock train made it along with as few catastrophes and casualties as possible. As the crowd grew, a monumentally wise decision was made about who should introduce the acts and fill time. The original plan called for a rotating crop of progressive rock DJs such as Rosko from New York and Dave Herman from Philadelphia to do the honors. As the scope of this responsibility dawned on the organizers, the plan was jettisoned. While my personal prejudice tells me that my colleagues could have risen to the occasion, I also realize that the burden of this pressure was very real. Obviously, announcements were needed that rose above the level of "How you doin', Woodstock?" or "Hey, Bethel, are you ready to rock?" Plan A was scratched. Plan B was put into effect.

Dave Herman: A meeting had just been held where it was decided that "crowd control" would have to be handled from the stage, and they were reluctant to give that awesome responsibility to the three DJs.

Thus, Chip Monck and John Morris were knighted the de facto hosts of the affair. Between the two of them, they knew and understood the inner workings of the festival. They were the best equipped to make impromptu decisions based on whatever wild cards got tossed their way. Plus, they were both charming in totally different ways.

Joshua White: [Morris] was a hipper version of Dick Clark. He was very comfortable being onstage, and you thought he was giving you great content, but really he was just filling the time. The attitude was, as long as you kept talking to the crowd, you could get away with an hour before the next band came on.

While Morris embodied the cool, gentle parental figure, technical director and lighting designer Chip Monck carried a different appeal.

Michael Wadleigh: A quiet guy. A tall, blond, good-looking guy who generally walked around pretty much naked. He had the real spirit of the counterculture.

Because of his role in the *Woodstock* movie, Chip Monck quickly and unwittingly became the "voice of a generation."

Patrick Stansfield: One night, Chip had rented us a flashy used convertible from Hollywood Rent-a-Wreck to make a very late night mad dash drive to San Diego. And so there we were, blazing down Interstate 5 toward the border wild-eyed and bushy-tailed. We stopped off at a Union 76 gas station in San Juan Capistrano on the way. We had been up it seemed for the entire obligatory three-day run of a really big rock show in LA. Chip was as always at the wheel, long blond hair flowing behind him in the wind. Stroking his bushy cavalier's mustache, Chip swerved off the freeway into the gas station and announced to the uniformed pump jockey in his booming "Voice of Woodstock" tone: "Fill 'er up boy. Hi Test!" Just a few yards away, a hippie hitchhiker stood by the freeway ramp. We had blown right past him while heading toward the gas station. Chip obviously had hardly noticed the shaggy fellow, ignoring him imperiously and paying him no attention whatsoever! When the hippie lad heard Chip order gas in his booming "command" tones, his ears perked up and he said, in reverence and awe, "That voice! I know you. You're the voice of my generation! My God, you're Chip Monck. You're the Voice of Woodstock." A smile slowly crept across Chip's craggy face, he jerked his thumb over his shoulder, and pointed to the convertible's backseat. To the hippie with the backpack, while never even looking at him, Chip haughtily ordered: "Get in!"

Chip was the most innovative lighting designer around. His skill in conjunction with his chill demeanor made him a desirable person to work with.

Bob See: He always treated people with the highest regard and highest respect. A lot of people wanted to work for him. He never lost his temper. If he did, he would do it in a very sarcastic manner. But never really scream at someone. He wanted to do the best job. I think his design and the way he operated the lighting designer, production management, he was one of the best in the business. He worked for the Stones for many years, and they produced something that was much different than anyone else. Not to say he was the sole person behind it, but I think he had something to do with it. I think in turn a lot of people tried to copy him.

Like everything else at Woodstock, the technical aspect of the festival was fraught with complications. The stage, for instance, was a huge source of issues.

Chris Langhart: The roof that had been provided was unable to hold any lights up because it never got up. They had a good concept of what it was going to be when it was done, but they had no concept of how it was going to be held up there in the intermediate stages of construction. Since it only got to an intermediate stage of production, they didn't have time to get it done, they just had to get it in a state where all the forces were balanced and it could just stay there. I suppose that they could have hung lights on it, but somehow they never felt that they could, so the whole job was done with follow spots.

Despite this, Monck triumphed.

Chris Langhart: There isn't a better follow spot operator than Chip Monck. He could do shows in his sleep. It was an easy gig for him to run the whole thing on follow spots. There were a lot of them, about twelve, and they were the biggest ones you could get at the time. Chip did a pretty good job with them, it wasn't a particularly bright situation.

Chip wasn't the only Fillmore fixture that John Morris brought to the festival. Joshua White—whose Joshua Light Show was a popular feature at the Fillmore—was supposed to do his magic behind the acts at Woodstock, though technical difficulties and the weather conditions severely limited his role.

Chris Langhart, technical director at the Fillmore and a professor at NYU, also joined the team at Bethel. Langhart had been involved in the Fillmore from the very beginning: his students had virtually rebuilt the whole theater. Originally, he was responsible for constructing the stage at Woodstock, but he had creative differences with founder Michael Lang.

Chris Langhart: I had a very sort of Saarinen-like tent thing in mind, very modern. Lang was looking for something very woodsy and log-cabin-like, but I didn't understand that when I created my designs. So Michael had a whole other architect team lined up to do the stage. I fell into doing everything else: the things that needed to be done to create the city.

And what did that entail?

Chris Langhart: Somehow, it fell into place that I would be dealing with all the parts of the festival that nobody else wanted to deal with—the toilets and the communications, and the supply of power and the performers' pavilion.

Among his various tasks was creating an elaborate network of underground pipes to supply clean water, light towers, the (in)effective fence around the periphery, a bridge for the performers to walk from the backstage area to the stage, and even a turntable for the stage so that one act could be setting up while another was playing.

Chris Langhart: The stage turntable was part of the concept from the get-go. I don't know where the idea for the turntable came from. It went for a while, but the casters started pulling out and jutting out at odd angles. It got to the point where it just wouldn't go around even with tons of people pushing at it.

If any team could have pulled off the technical aspects of the festival, it was the Fillmore guys. Remember, there was absolutely no precedent for Woodstock. With limited resources, limited time, and limited funds, Morris, Langhart, Monck, and Bill Hanley did the best they could. They took on roles that were above and beyond their original assignments. The founders would have been screwed without them.

Stan Schnier: I've known Michael Lang for a long time, I love him. I think he was and is a visionary. He thought up this incredible concept. But without the Fillmore team, guys like John, Joshua White, Chip Monck, Steve Cohen, John Chester, Chris Langhart, it is questionable what would have happened as far as presentation went. They all came through Bill Graham; without Bill Graham none of those people would have been there.

COUNTRY JOE MCDONALD

Another little miracle occurred soon after the Swami left the stage. An unexpected solo star was born. There was a critically acclaimed book about the post-Woodstock rock 'n' roll industry in the '70s called *The Star-Making Machinery* by Geoffrey Stokes. It detailed the behind-the-scenes machinations employed by record companies, publicity services, promotion departments, and talent agencies to create and sometimes cynically manufacture new stars. And as we all know too well these days, stars can be manufactured *American Idol*–style. But sometimes stars can still pop up from out of nowhere and take the world by storm. It happened to Elvis Presley. It happened to the Beatles. And it happened to several unsuspecting souls at Woodstock. One of them was Country Joe McDonald.

Country Joe and the Fish were a late addition to the Woodstock roster. They aren't even listed on the original posters and flyers advertising the festival. Booked less than two weeks before the event, the Fish were slated to perform on Sunday. It was just happenstance that Joe McDonald arrived early on opening night to take his own measure of the festival as an observer. It is even greater happenstance that John Morris, frantic to put acts on the stage to mollify the growing crowd, remembered a conversation that he had had with Joe in Europe a couple of years earlier.

John Morris: I was onstage, the traffic was backed up all over the place. I didn't have an act to put on. I turned around and on the side of the stage by himself was Country Joe McDonald.

Bill Belmont: John walked up to me and said, "Look, what do you think of having Joe doing a couple of tunes, four or five until we can get someone here?"

Joe McDonald: I was just there to watch the show. I got there really early. There was no traffic problem for me. I got up on the stage and watched Richie play. That was fun. Then John Morris came over with Bill Belmont and asked me if I wanted to start my solo career. I didn't know what the hell they were talking about, you know. The band was scheduled to play on Sunday. So Friday was an off day and Saturday was an off day, and Sunday was the day we're supposed to play. So I made a bunch of excuses about why I couldn't do it . . . I was looking for excuses to not go out.

Bill Belmont: I went up to Joe and said, "Listen, we're kind of in a bind. There's nobody to go on, we can't find anybody, a couple of people are showing up, but they're not going to be here for another hour and a half. We don't want the crowd to get restless.

John Morris: He and I had done a tour together in Europe a couple of years before and we had had a conversation about a solo act. He's wearing an army field coat, and I walked over to him and said, "You're about to start your solo career." I believe his words were "Are you outta your fuckin' mind? I don't even have a guitar!" So we found him a guitar.

Joe McDonald: It was an FG-150 Yamaha, really great acoustic guitar. I was lucky because it was a really great acoustic guitar and it was in tune.

John Morris: Then he said I need a capo. Now my musical involvement was not sufficient enough that I knew what a capo was. I thought he was talking about an eviscerated chicken that came in a plastic pack.

Bill Belmont: One of the guys in the crew yells out, "I have a capo!" So we had a capo.

Joe McDonald: Then I said, I can't play because I don't have a guitar strap. So they got a piece of rope and just tied the rope to the guitar, and then I ran out of excuses.

John Morris: I put my hand firmly on his back until the rope arrived, and then I put him onstage.

Joe McDonald: I said okay because there was really nobody else to play. I could see the logic behind it. I'm pretty agreeable. It had been some time since I had done a solo folksinger act. I went out there and I started singing. In '65, I was a folksinger, so it was a natural thing for me to stand and play the acoustic guitar and sing.

Bob Santelli: I spoke to Joe a couple of years ago about his performance at Woodstock, and Joe is as much a fan of the music as much as he is a performer in it. He told me how he couldn't wait for the festival to begin, he made sure he had a spot on side stage so he could watch all the performances, and how he was really excited to be there and to catch all the talent that was booked. And then suddenly he started hearing how this person or that artist had not been able to come yet, that they were stuck in traffic, that things were problematic. And of course, Morris and Lang were looking around to find someone to get out onstage to keep the festival going. To start getting the attention of the crowd onstage instead of elsewhere. Joe borrowed a guitar and went out there and performed, and it was probably the most important performance of his long career.

More than any other performer at Woodstock—with the possible exception of Joan Baez—Country Joe's career was about the marriage of music and politics.

Ellen Sander: Country Joe is very political. Joe McDonald is a political animal before he's even a musician, and he's a good writer, too, and so everything he did was political. He was also kind of a cynic. He had a certain persona.

Both music and politics had been very important to Joe since he was very young.

Joe McDonald: I was born in Washington, DC, but we moved out to California when I was three years old and that's where I've been pretty much my whole life. My mother was a housewife until the middle of her life, and then she became a politician. My father was a cowboy and a farm boy initially. Then he worked for the telephone company until I was about twelve and was self-employed after that. My parents didn't give us lectures about politics when we were growing up, but my parents were involved in the union and desegregation. So I grew up in that environment. Brotherhood and peace and that sort of stuff.

As for his musical career, that also began early on.

Joe McDonald: I started playing the trombone in grade school and then through high school. I was the president of the band and then the orchestra, and the marching band. I started playing guitar my senior year of high school and stopped playing the trombone and started writing songs. I had a little rock 'n' roll band then.

One of the songs that Joe wrote in high school was about a spaceship coming down from outer space and a monster coming out of the UFO and talking to the earthlings. He adapted it and changed the lyrics for a high school friend who was running for student body president. In the new version, which he performed at a school assembly, the alien told the students to vote for his friend, and you can probably guess the result: he got elected! So you could say that for Joe McDonald, music and politics were joined at the hip right from the start. It is therefore not at all surprising that Joe introduced a political element to the festival that no one else could approach. His musical education continued after he enlisted in the military.

Joe McDonald: Then I joined the navy and took my guitar with me and learned some Japanese folk songs and that sort of thing. It was like the Harry Belafonte kind of calypso folk song thing. Then I came back out of the navy to Southern California and went to college for, like, three semesters and I was singing folk music and writing some folk songs, protest songs. Then I moved up to the San Francisco Bay Area, where I've been since then, since 1965.

One could liken the responsibility thrust upon Joe to step out on that stage to perform solo in the same way that some individuals have it thrust upon them to learn to swim by being tossed into the ocean. Only this wasn't a sea of water. No, this was a sea of people—five hundred thousand strong—and following Richie Havens's high-energy, totally involving opening set proved to be a bigger challenge for Joe than he'd even had the time to imagine.

> **Bill Belmont:** You know, it's very difficult to go up there and sing songs that people are used to seeing with a band. Joe had never been on the East Coast. He had never been a solo performer, so there he was singing a bunch of songs that people kind of knew—at least "Flying High" and "Janis"—but there's a huge crowd and a sound system, and you hear one guy, and I cannot imagine what it sounded like on the hill.

> **Joe McDonald:** Well, I was torn between what I should do, because I didn't want to detract from the band set. Being pretty much the bandleader I was thinking as the bandleader. It was kind of a hodgepodge twenty minutes or something. When you look at the set, I sang the song for Janis. "It's Really" and "I Seen a Rocket" are songs with the same sound I had in high school. I reached way back for that one. I didn't have a defined persona as a single act. I didn't know what to do. But if you look at the film footage, no one was paying any attention to me by the end of "I Seen a Rocket." They were talking—kind of like a picnic.

That's when Joe had an idea. Woodstock was an event where most of the overtly political rhetoric was checked at the door. There were exceptions. (As we'll see, Joan Baez's gentle proselytizing about draft resistance was acceptable and tolerated; Abbie Hoffman's rant about John Sinclair and the nation's marijuana laws was decidedly not.) Joe took a different, daring, dramatic approach. It harkened back to his days in the marching band.

"Gimme an 'F'!"

> **Joe McDonald:** We would spell out the name of the team at sports events, so I figured that we should give a cheer for ourselves in that style, thus, "F-I-S-H what's that spell? FISH!" We recorded it like that in front of the "Vietnam Rag" song. Playing the Schaefer Music Festival in New York City the drummer got the idea to change fish to fuck and we did it for the first time there, and then after because it was such a hit.
>
> At Woodstock, I didn't know whether to do the fuck cheer or not. I didn't know. The fuck cheer was not that new, but I had never done it by myself before. So I walked away from the microphone to talk to Bill Belmont. He was there and nobody else from the band was there.

Nobody even responded when I left the microphone. So I said to Bill, "What do you think, should I do the cheer?"

Bill Belmont: I said, "I don't see why not. I mean, a song is a song."

Joe McDonald: And he said, "Nobody's paying any attention. What difference does it make? Give it a shot." That emboldened me and I stopped being nervous and I thought, You know, he's right. What do I care? I might as well have some fun here. Then I walked back out and then I did it.

Bill Belmont: So he turns around and starts it. And everything changed. At "Gimme an F" everyone knew what was going on. What happened next was in the movie.

What happened was pandemonium! In an instant, no one was partying or picnicking or talking among themselves. They were on their feet, fixated on the lone performer with the long hair in an army jacket screaming at them from the stage. There are so many reasons why Woodstock had to happen, and liberating the word *fuck* was just one of them. Today we call it the "F" bomb, and it can still get government-licensed over-the-air radio and television stations in big trouble with huge fines if it slips by the censor or the seven-second delay. Isn't it ironic that a word once forbidden to be written about or uttered publicly is now itself the subject of entire books and ubiquitous in American popular culture? As ridiculous as it all might seem today, even great artists and authors had to dance around the F word volcano in their work. The late Norman Mailer was persuaded by his publisher in 1948 to substitute the euphemism "fug" in his breakthrough novel *The Naked and the Dead* (leading to a delicious exchange with noted wit Dorothy Parker who greeted him when they met with the observation, "So you're the man who can't spell 'fuck'!"). But starting with the Free Speech movement at the University of California, Berkeley, the whispered F word got louder and louder with each passing day of the '60s. And if it could be said that "fuck" had a coming-out party, it took place at Woodstock on August 15, 1969.

Joe McDonald: I yelled "Give me an F!" and my response was "Oh, my God" because they all stopped talking, and they looked at me and yelled "F!" Then after being relaxed and feeling a little bold, I started to get nervous that they were looking at me. I mean, they were all looking at me. Then I had to continue. I'm not sure why, but obviously it was easier for me to do "fuck" instead of "fish" at that point. So I did "U" and they kept going. So by the time I finished spelling the word and asked them to shout the word, there was a rhythm established.

Ellen Sander: The cheer was a known thing and the whole audience responded, "What's that spell!" It was unbelievable, everybody was laughing so hard. And you know, when you're laughing and you're screaming, you've got a lot of oxygen pumping through your body; it does something to your metabolism, to your thought process, to your brain to have all that air coming through. It was great, a lot of people by that time had spent twenty-four hours there. So maybe their fatigue was maybe hitting them a little bit: a little bit hungry, a little bit thirsty, a little bit worried about the weather. And just to have that moment was one of many highlights of the day—the whole crowd screaming "fuck!"

John Morris: I thought it was great. What could you think? It was amazing. It's one of the most political moments in a festival that was not political. I don't care what anybody says. It makes me think: How did I grow up over the three days? Or how did I change? Something I'll have to sit down with a bottle of brandy and figure out someday.

Joe McDonald: It established a mood; a political and social credibility for the Woodstock generation. Prior to that the attitude was "Try and be polite about it" with protest music. To not try to be offensive.

Bob Santelli: You couldn't say "fuck." It was not like today. To have that happen was pretty, pretty wild. At that time that was the ultimate word you could use to demonstrate your anger, your frustration, your refusal to accept what was going on, because back then that was "the word," you might be able to say shit or hell or damn, but you certainly couldn't say that word. That word was absolutely top to bottom taboo.

Stan Schnier: Those were conservative times, to stand up onstage and say "fuck" in those days was unheard of. You just didn't do that, you couldn't do that, you wouldn't do that. I don't even think in The Village Voice they used the work fuck in those days, they put "f blank blank

blank." Maybe Jack Kerouac could write "fuck" in a book, but that was about it.

Bob Santelli: But at the time it wasn't like people were sitting in the Woodstock audience saying, "My God, did he just say what I thought he said?" because all rules all laws were left outside the gates. So that didn't disturb or shock people in the audience, but of course later on it was a pretty powerful expression and raised many eyebrows. It became an anthem. Not because of the word <u>fuck</u> or because of the cheer that evolved around the word <u>fuck</u>, but it was basically the attitude of the song.

It's impossible to talk about the meaning of "The Fish Cheer" without discussing the larger political backdrop of the festival. When the album came out in 1970, my colleague at WNEW-FM the legendary radio and television personality Zacherle put it on the air without screening it first. There for the whole tristate area was the fuck cheer in all its glory on the radio. It was obviously a mistake, and, other than saying "Oops!" the moment passed without repercussions. No fines. No congressional hearings. Just "Oops, we're sorry!" The music director, however, was instructed to slash the vinyl track with a razor blade on all subsequent copies of the album received so the offending word would not be heard again!

Bob Santelli: When you think of Woodstock and you think of Vietnam War songs, you think of Joe's performance there. It was legendary and it was important. It set the stage. It was one of the few times where politics was actually invited up onstage and actually embraced. Generally speaking, Woodstock was not about politics. It was not about things that were happening outside in the world; the bad things. This was about creating a new world, a new identity, a new nation, this Woodstock nation. It wasn't about trying to solve the Vietnam War or rallying and trying to send a giant message to the straight world and to the American government that we wanted the war stopped. And yet, Joe, in the way that only Joe could do it, was able to go up there and add an element of politics that was embraced. It was really one of the very few times in the festival where that happened.

Vietnam had been on America's mind since the Kennedy administration. It was originally presented as a group of US "military advisers" going over to help our ally France in its struggle to contain Communism in Southeast Asia. Though never declared a war as defined by the Constitution, by Lyndon Johnson's presidency, America's involvement escalated dramatically and US casualties soared to an alarming number. Opposition to the conflict mushroomed and was very vocal and widespread. The country was painfully divided in a way it hadn't been since the Civil War.

The nature of the protests emerged early on. Lines were drawn between old versus young, hawk versus dove, square versus hip, "My country right or wrong!" versus "Hell no, we won't go!" No generation before the baby boomers was big enough or bold enough to take a look at the status quo and say, "Er, no thank you." The tear in the very fabric of the country was horrific and painful. And it began to be reflected in all of the arts, but particularly in the nation's popular music. Song poets such as Bob Dylan, Phil Ochs, and Tom Paxton began to write what Dylan himself called "finger-pointing songs." Others such as Joan Baez and Judy Collins, through their choice of material, shined a flashlight on society's ills. These men and women were as much journalists as musicians telling their vast and growing audiences about poverty, injustice, racism, and warmongering on the loose in the land of the free and the home of the brave.

No issue revealed the country's widening chasm more than Vietnam. At the same time that this generation was embracing sex, drugs, and rock 'n' roll, it was simultaneously learning to endure the shock and trauma of assassinations, race riots, and police brutality. Those were the clouds hovering over Woodstock that had nothing to do with the weather.

Ellen Sander: The year before had been very tumultuous. There was a lot of violence in the country, and there was a lot of unrest, and so there was a yearning in the air, and I think that that yearning kind of found a home at Woodstock. I think the assassinations of Martin Luther King and Robert Kennedy, and the riots the previous summer at the Democratic National Convention in Chicago created a mood and set the stage for something like this. We boomers grew up in kind of unique circumstances, and we got hit with a lot of things that a lot of previous generations didn't go through. We had the bomb: when we were just schoolkids, we were confronted with the notion that the entire world could be annihilated and that the weapons to do so were in the hands of two superpowers that were very much antagonistic toward one another. That was never that far from your mind. And then there was the war in Vietnam, which we all thought to be an unjust, undeclared war; and there was a lot of antiwar activity and certainly that was a part of my life. I don't think anybody will ever know the answer to the mystery of why didn't Woodstock descend into chaos and violence—because all the elements for that were there—but instead it was a very peaceful thing. And people there at the time, we felt that it was kind of a destiny, that that would kind of be the path of the future—of peaceful cooperation, of a spirit of community, of tribalism, those things . . . It didn't quite go the way they expected [laughs] but at least for that weekend, we had it.

Stan Schnier: To me, Woodstock is about Vietnam. It's at a time when you have a whole generation of kids who are really traumatized by the war. There was a draft. If there was a draft today, America would be so different than it is. When there's a draft, the whole culture changes. And all this rah-rah-rah crap about our kids being off getting their heads blown off, it changes really quickly when it's your kid. With really poor people, there's a tradition of that, they might say, "This is heroic because Freddy's uncle did it too when he died in Korea." When I was that age, it deeply affected me. It was different. Jimmy Calpin, from Honesdale, Pennsylvania, a boy who I went to school with, got his leg blown off last week, and you're going next week. We had those terrible assassinations, and they pushed people together. The older generation were pro-military (though not my parents, who were both musicians—my dad just wanted to play music). But I came from a culture where all of our parents were from World War II, they had all fought the good war and that was a justifiable war. And the idea of the country going to war was a positive thing in their mind. Older people didn't question it; it was only kids. It's fascinating, it's not like any other time in modern history . . . so the music is just a reflection of that. The music didn't come first, the music is like an aftereffect. What do a bunch of scared kids do when they live in an environment where their parents don't understand them? To me, everything that's happened since then has been like a theatrical playtime makeup version of that.

Most of the songs about war in general and Vietnam in particular were deservedly dark and somber. They dissected the conflict with intelligence and seriousness of purpose. Some were better than others, but they all shared a visceral disgust with the very idea of armed conflict and dying or brutally wounded military personnel. Joe McDonald's song about the issue contained all of those emotions, but presented them in a brilliant, original, incongruous way. Much like Phil Ochs had raised eyebrows about citizen apathy in the face of urban crime, rape, and murder against the background of a raucous, barrelhouse piano in his song "Outside of a Small Circle of Friends," Joe placed his "take no prisoners" stance against the Vietnam War in the framework of a good-timey, music-hall singalong in his "I-Feel-Like-I'm-Fixin'-to-Die Rag." The result was mesmerizing.

Michael Wadleigh: I think Joe is a really intelligent, far-thinking guy. He certainly was way ahead of his time. I think that as a poet and a propagandist, which is what he was, he came up with a devastatingly good song that would make people really think. It's too obvious to write a song that says "stop the war, stop the war," "we must have peace," et cetera, but to come up with the lyrics he came up with was amazing. Especially the line, "Be the first one on your block to have your boy come home in a box." You'd think you could never write something that cruel and brutal. Certainly if you look back at the great Bob Dylan, Bob doesn't have lines that really address American parents. His songs are more eclectic, more out there. Joe wrote this mainstream song "1, 2, 3, What Are We Fighting For?" that was so much fun to sing. It spread all over America, then it spread through the world, and it was a great anthem.

Joe McDonald: You know, it was funny. It was an energizing moment. I kicked into my folk song singer mode: let's sing along. I knew what I was doing then. I need audience response to figure out what I'm doing usually. At least they have to look at you, clap, or something. The funny thing was, I really didn't think that they weren't singing along. When you're outside, the sound doesn't really carry. I couldn't hear them. I couldn't see them because there were so many people. It wasn't until I saw the film that I realized that they were singing. So I harangued them, "How do you expect to stop the war? So many of you fuckers out there sing along. I want to hear you sing." And they sang. It was amazing.

Bob Santelli: By 1969, things had gotten to such a point, the war had been with us for so many years and so many young men in particular had been impacted by the threat of the draft, people who were normally somewhat tolerant on the outside of Woodstock. Now these people came into Woodstock and did the "fuck" cheer with such enthusiasm and spirit that it was almost as if it were an emotional release of all the tension and stress about what they had just left behind—about going back home on that Monday and finding a draft notice in the mailbox. Today, the cheer wouldn't raise an eyebrow. And of course, it's not just the word, it's the meaning behind the word.

John Morris: Joe was totally antiwar. Joe was an activist person who intellectually couldn't stand the Vietnam War. And he saw an opportunity and took an opportunity to get his feelings across to other people. I thought the cheer was a statement of where we were. And I thought it was totally appropriate.

Ellen Sander: "The Fish Cheer," it wasn't just about comedy. It was about politics, it was about sexual revolution, it was about defiance, and it was about fun.

Joe McDonald: I was completely alone. In the three days of the music, all those performers, I was the only one known as a military veteran and the only outspoken person writing outspoken political songs against the war. Later on, Joan Baez did come up and sing "Drugstore Truck Driving Man," but that's from the point of view of a pacifist who won't fight the war. My point of view was completely different. The fuck cheer was not anti-soldier, it was pro-soldier, and I'm the only guy who was walking point on that.

"The Fish Cheer" caused several repercussions for Joe in the wake of the festival.

Stan Schnier: Right after Woodstock, we were in Worchester, Massachusetts, and he was standing onstage and the state police walked out on the stage from either side in the wings and they arrested him for obscenity. And that was a big case; that went on for years. He had William Kunstler represent him—it was a freedom of speech thing.

Mike Wadleigh: There were a number of very famous court cases involving Woodstock. One that went all the way to the Supreme Court, at that time, and even now, Country Joe McDonald's song could not be played on the radio where you hear a half a million people screaming, "Fuck!" That was simply not allowed. But we won. I testified and other people did. The argument was, as Joe so eloquently put it, what's more obscene, having your boy come home in a box or that word? It was part of his artistic expression. But that was not what was protected. Political free speech is what was protected.

Comparisons were made at the time and to this day between Country Joe and Muhammad Ali about their very different but equally bold and effective ways of registering their disagreement and disgust with American involvement in Southeast Asia.

Joe McDonald: I like the comparison between me and Muhammad Ali because Muhammad Ali could kick your ass. And I could kick your ass musically. I mean, he kicked your ass in the ring, and I can kick your ass on the stage. But in his personal life he also walked the walk. He's a black man. He was drafted. What I did at Woodstock didn't necessarily make the communists happy. I didn't like the communists. I didn't like the capitalists. I didn't like the authoritarian figures. I bring with me a certain credibility, which I think had been absent on the stage in pop music to that point. People had a reputation for being drunk, or maybe they were cowboys, or whatever. There weren't many of us. Muhammad Ali paid a price for his visible stance, and I paid a price for my visible stance—being ostracized, not being box office.

We asked Joe to elaborate on the idea that he wasn't box office.

Joe McDonald: You couldn't go around doing that. It was kind of against the law but not against the law, and people respected me, I think, but they didn't want to be associated with me. I became like an instant living legend. I was well known before that. But, that was a moment of "boom!" My solo performance and my appearance in the film made me someone to be feared, someone to be loved. It traveled to Vietnam. Soldiers learned it. It was a political tool. It created my career—the persona I have now. It played its role in the politics and the culture of America and my generation and the Vietnam War in a very important way. And that's great. It made me an important person and well loved by an audience that I wanted to reach—the counterculture, the socially aware rock 'n' roll, Aquarian Age audience. What I'm not happy about and I feel bad about is that I was never included in the commercial box office group. But I was absolutely prepared for that moment, and it launched me into a whole other dimension. It's been a great trip, and it ain't over yet.

There was a symposium about the *Woodstock* movie a couple of years ago in Los Angeles and Joe attended.

Joe McDonald: Just recently, I went and watched the film again. In Hollywood, we had a big screening with a cleaned-up digital soundtrack, and it's still a great movie. But it's funny, if you take me out of the movie, in a way you have VH-1.

At that very symposium, each panelist on the stage was handed the microphone to give a brief synopsis of his or her role. Some of the descriptions were anything but brief, some might argue even self-aggrandizing. When the mic was passed to Joe, he picked it up, and said only three words for his self-description, then passed it on to the next panelist: "Gimme an 'F!'"

Perfect!

JOHN SEBASTIAN

J once cohosted live broadcast coverage of a Bob Dylan/Grateful Dead concert at Giants Stadium in the Meadowlands of New Jersey. It seemed as if more than half of the audience was attired in tie-dyed clothing of one sort or another. My colleague Dave Herman asked me to describe what we were seeing for the listening audience, and all I could think of to say was that it looked as if someone had broken into John Sebastian's closet.

As well as things went with Richie Havens, chaos continued to reign backstage. Sweetwater had yet to arrive. Tim Hardin was still in hiding. Logistics demanded that one man or one woman with an acoustic guitar would be the best bet to get something going out there onstage. Joshua White had a bird's-eye view of the frantic juggling act around him.

Joshua White: They didn't have their shit together, not the performers, but the technicians. They just completely got jammed up. The first thing they put out there was solo guitarists, and this is all during the day and I was setting up the light show. I was literally up behind, observing on my platform; the screen wasn't hung yet, so I was staring at these performers and looking out on this field, which was filling up with people way beyond anyone's expectations. So they just had to get somebody onstage.

At this point in his life and career, John Sebastian was mounting a solo comeback after three very busy and, in John's phrase, "moderately successful" years with his Rock and Roll Hall of Fame band, the Lovin' Spoonful.

John was a born and bred New Yorker whose father, John Sebastian, was a successful classical harmonica player. John remembers picking up the instrument as a toddler, but then giving it up for a while.

John Sebastian: I guess I was about five the first time I stopped playing harmonica because I had been playing before then, but then at five, I suddenly became sensitive about being identified as, "Oh well, you're gonna be just like your father, right?" And thank goodness, my father gave me a lot of backup on that and said, "Now look. You know as well as I know that you're a completely different character and you're gonna be very different." And, of course, he was right. But it also encouraged me later at about fourteen when my father gave me an old acetate of Sonny Terry, and I listened to this and said, "Gee, this is completely different than what I've identified with the sound of a harmonica. And how is he doing that?" And I had to discover cross-harp and find out exactly what blues harmonica playing was all about. It was very different than what I was used to and eventually I became the only blues harmonica player in New York. And I also played guitar, that was my first instrument, but I couldn't get arrested on that because there were eighty million guitar players! So the harmonica became my bread and butter for a few years.

John became the hired gun on literally dozens of albums recorded during the folk boom by artists such as Judy Collins and Tom Paxton. But he also soon realized the benefits of stepping out of the background into the spotlight.

John Sebastian: I went to camp and fell in love with somebody who played autoharp and so I wanted to immediately become the most traditional of folk artists. Simultaneously, I met Lightning Hopkins at a television program my father was doing . . . and that, combined with listening to "A Whole Lotta Shakin' Goin' On" and Link Wray on the radio, made me want to sort of be a composite character . . . mulching the whole thing together.

Often grouped with the other folk-rock pioneers of the era—Bob Dylan, Roger (Jim) McGuinn, John Phillips, et al.—John quickly dismisses the credit:

John Sebastian: I've always hated the term. It sounds so sort of slapped together. I just look at it as American music, and American music is a continuum. At the time the Spoonful started—before I had written any songs—we were taking jug band tunes and sort of putting bigger engines in them. That was sort of our approach—electrify a few jug band tunes. But, I don't know, "Summer in the City," that's not folk rock.

Starting with "Do You Believe in Magic?" in the fall of 1965 until "She Is Still a Mystery" in the fall of 1967, the Lovin' Spoonful placed ten Top 40 singles on the US charts, seven of them Top 10, and one of them (the aforementioned "Summer in the City") a Number One single in the summer of 1966. Internal strife related to a drug bust splintered the group in 1967, and John left the others (who struggled on for a while as a Sebastian-less Spoonful) to go solo in 1968. None of this takes away from the Spoonful's role as one of the premier American bands reclaiming rock 'n' roll in the post–British Invasion years. But here too, Sebastian dismisses the notion of the Spoonful as a successful group.

John Sebastian: Well, first of all, by modern terms, the Spoonful was hardly successful. In those days it looked wonderful and, in fact, when you hear records on the radio and this was a Number One record for the Spoonful, people think, "Well boy, that guy must—must—he gonna die rich." Well, the fact is, is that in those days Number One records were very often seven hundred thousand sellers and so the Spoonful was maybe popular by those standards, but what happened shortly after the Spoonful's demise, rock 'n' roll turned into big business, and the Spoonful never really were able to cash in on that. But we did have a wonderful time, and I think maybe the reason for our success was simply that we had the songs, we had done our homework, we put in the time in the clubs so that we were a tight band. And although we didn't have the publicity of a lot of the American bands that were contemporaries of ours, I think that we were the premier American band at the time of the British Invasion.

At least Richie Havens knew, one way or the other, that he was scheduled to perform. But what about John Sebastian? He went to the event strictly as a civilian. He intended to enjoy the sights, the sounds, the ups, the downs, the "highs" and the lows of Woodstock. Instead, in a flash (and admittedly he was experiencing lots of those!), he found himself center stage, stoned out of his mind, a kaleidoscopic Day-Glo spectacle in specs, attempting to entertain half a million fellow travelers. John was in the process of getting his life and his music and his first solo album in order when he decided to attend the much-ballyhooed Woodstock Festival as a spectator. Here's how it happened:

John Sebastian: Alright. So let's start at the beginning. You want to know what's up with this Woodstock thing and how did it happen? All right. I think I probably wouldn't have gone to Woodstock if it wasn't for Paul Rothchild, ever the scenester, ever a guy who knew what was gonna be the happening thing next week. He calls me and says, "So are ya goin' to Woodstock?" I go, "What? What Woodstock?" He says, "You gotta go. This is gonna be a festival. It's supposed to only have ten or twenty thousand people, but a lot of people are showin' up at this. I can tell from when all the people I'm callin' are goin'. So, you know, this will be a great thing." Well, I went to the Albany airport and was almost discouraged out of going because there weren't any planes available, but through the wonders of pre-9/11 life in the '60s, you could wander anywhere in the airport and I'm passin' by a window when I see a guy loading a helicopter. And I look closely, and just then the guy turns to me and looks at me. I go—it's Walter Gundy, my friend from Greenwich Village, who now road manages the Incredible String Band. I actually didn't know that part, but he yells to me, you know, "Come! Come!" I open the door out to the—to the tarmac and he says, "Look, you're tryin' to get to Woodstock?" I said, "Yeah. There's no nothin'." He said, "No. Nothin' is goin'. The only way you're gonna get there is to get in this helicopter right now." So I don't even have a guitar with me. "Okay. Great. I'm in." So I landed in the middle of the scene.

Billy Altman: I remember John Sebastian's tie-dye outfit. He helped put tie-dye completely on the map at Woodstock.

John's colorful garb and beatific smile caught the eye of stage manager John Morris.

John Morris: John Sebastian was another accident. He was not booked on the show. I believe that it was during Richie that I looked backstage and walking down the street, tie-dyed from head to toe, carrying a guitar, with these little round glasses was Sebastian.

John Sebastian: I wasn't on the poster. Nobody intended for me to play. I was there strictly because this was the most happening thing that had gone on, and I wanted to be there and see it. I wanted to be a spectator. Because all my friends were backstage, I ended up backstage.

John Morris: And I said to somebody, "Go get him and bring him up here." They went and got him and I said, "I need a big favor. You gotta help me. Can you perform?" And he went, "Sure man, cool!" And he went out there and did it.

According to Sebastian, Morris wasn't the first guy backstage who had the idea to have him play. It had started to rain and another acoustic act was needed.

John Sebastian: People began to go, "Oh, great! When are you playing?" And I'm, "I'm not playin'. I don't even have a guitar." Well, it just so happened that my old pal Timmy Hardin did have a guitar and was there. I get summoned into the war room there in the center of the backstage area. And Chip Monck, the voice of Woodstock asked me, "Look, it's raining. We're havin' trouble with the sound system. We're afraid to put an amplifier on the stage. We're figuring we could keep this audience's attention if we had a guy with one guitar who could hold 'em. You're elected." So I go to Timmy and I say, "Timmy, I need a guitar." He lends me a Harmony Sovereign (Phonetic). This is the great workhorse guitar, ah, for people buying instruments for under $60. Ah, so with that instrument and a slight buzz, I went on in the rain and, as it happened, the rain had stopped by the time I finished.

The (tie) die was cast. Sebastian would perform. Chip Monck did the honors:
"Please welcome with us—John Sebastian!"
And out he walked onto the stage.

Thank you. I don't know if you can really tell how amazing you look, but you're truly amazing! You're a whole city! I've been out in California and . . . I've been living in this tent. I had the tent for about four days, and I met this lady that does tie-dying. So she taught me how to do it, and I got sheets and I put them up on the inside of my tent. And it's soooo groovy to come here and see all you people living in tents. A cloth home is all you need if you got love, I tell ya. This is . . . this is a tune about . . . rainbows, I guess.

If there could be such a thing as a tie-dyed song, it's the new one that John performed on the Woodstock stage (it's also in the movie and on the album), "Rainbows All Over Your Blues":

> And fish out your blue suede shoes
> I'll paint rainbows all over your blues

In addition to "Rainbows," John performed two other new songs that would appear on his 1970 debut solo album (*John B. Sebastian*) called "How Have You Been?" and "I Had a Dream." He also did one of the Lovin' Spoonful's greatest hits, "Darling Be Home Soon."

At the point where he tried to leave the stage, he conferred for a moment with Chip Monck, then strolled back out to the microphone to do an encore, but not without his typical John Sebastian enthusiasm:

Oh boy. This is really a mindfucker of all times, man! I've never seen anything like this, man. I mean, like there's Newport, right? But they owned it. It was something else. Wow! Just love everybody all around you and clean up a little garbage on the way out and everything's gonna be alright. Yeah man, and Chip—my friend Chip—he's . . . You're doing so well, man . . . he says to look out for the fence too, man. You have to look after the fence. You know. Like the press can only say bad things— unless there ain't no fuckups. And it's lookin' like there ain't gonna be no fuckups. This is gonna work.

I'd like you to hear a tune about . . . I guess, about those discussions I was talkin' about [that] I seem to have had in so many small circles of friends around living rooms, around pipes when there were no rolling papers. When they were selling no papers on the street. When we weren't walking around this big green beautiful place and not being afraid.

I'd like to sing you a song. Actually, I'd like to dedicate it to . . . there's a cat, and I really don't know his name, but I remember that Chip said that uh, that uh, his old lady's just had a baby. And that made me think, Wow! It really is a city here! But this is for you and your old lady, man. And uh. Whew! That kid's gonna be far-out!

As they did with many artists, they rearranged some of John's dialogue in the film and on the soundtrack, but it was at this point that John launched into another song from his last days with the Spoonful—"Younger Generation."

John Sebastian: You react to the crowd that's in front of you. Somebody comes and says, "There's been a baby born. Try to sing the right song." So that was it. I said onstage what I felt, which was that this was an outgrowth of six people sittin' around a low-slung coffee table smokin' pot. Now it was just huge. But it was totally the same arrangement. That's part of the reason why the camaraderie that was felt at that festival existed—the generation had already been drawn together by musical forces, and by intoxicants that were, if not wildly illegal, at least illegal enough that it created a little bit of a community in the process of passing the stuff around. Both things [the music and the drugs] play heavily, I think, into not only the creation, but the mood of the weekend.

"Younger Generation" was a great choice under the circumstances, but unfortunately, John totally forgot the lyrics midway through and needed the crowd's help to finish it up. I asked about this moment recently.

John Sebastian: Personally speaking, I feel like I ended up doing myself a great disservice in retrospect because I was very much a member of the audience that weekend. I'd been living in the mud for two days participating liberally in the psychedelics of the era and, by the time I got onstage, I was just about as stoned as I'd ever been. And the fact is that, although it was very much in keeping with the mood of the weekend, I have sung and played better almost any time, including when you wake me up in the middle of the night. So in a lot of ways I'm sorry that that performance had to go that way. I wish I'd had a little more warning.

Despite this, John acknowledges that he'll always be connected to that performance for as long as he lives and beyond.

John Sebastian: I felt like Woodstock was me and I was Woodstock. You couldn't get one page of a book in between me and that crowd. I felt very, very much at home. Here on the stage were so many of the friends that I had made in this wonderful climb that I'd had this opportunity to make. Now I was friends with all of these people and at the same time when I looked out in the crowd, if I didn't see the actual people I knew from Greenwich Village, everybody looked like the same people from Greenwich Village—it had that Greenwich Village atmosphere of a completely multi-culty kind of a festival atmosphere. And there wasn't any reaching over the spotlights or anything in that game at all. I have said at various times that the pattern usually is, the smaller the venue, the more intimate—the more the detail of expression you can get across. I can't say that for Woodstock, because Woodstock was huge, and I still felt tremendous, tremendous detail in—in what I was able to get across.

But things happen for a reason, and at that moment in the festival, a tour de force performance wasn't necessarily what was needed anyway. Besides, not all observers felt Sebastian was so bad.

Michael Wadleigh: John was flying fairly high. He was such a psychedelic person himself. I suppose you could say that that "Younger Generation" was a flower child song. It was such a sweet song, and gets sweeter the older we are. I'm a grandfather now, as he went through the ages of people, the connections we have through generations, it was an irresistible song, the sweet way that he sang it.

Critic Billy Altman assesses John's participation this way:

Billy Altman: I got there when John Sebastian was playing. I was a giant Lovin' Spoonful fan, so seeing Sebastian was just perfect for somebody like me. The Spoonful were such a fun band and for me, being in a jug band at the time, they were a great example of that whole kind of good-time music. Sebastian was a great writer and performer. He was a very engaging, friendly, personable performer. People like him and Richie Havens were really perfect for the first day because they were so positive and very good at being able to be on a stage by themselves in front of a big crowd. I thought his set was great.

John Morris: It was John. It was sweet . . . and it was absolutely necessary at that moment. I was not listening for musical quality, I was listening to hear something coming over the PA. And he did beautifully.

SWEETWATER

This is the story of what might have been for a number of artists who were scheduled to appear at Woodstock, but didn't: Iron Butterfly, the Jeff Beck Group, and the Moody Blues. They were on the posters and in the media ads, but fate intervened for all three.

The Moodies were invited and considered attending but never signed a contract for the date. Since they were not touring at the time, when they realized that it would cost them far more to get to the concert than what they were offered to play, they ultimately turned down the gig.

As for the Jeff Beck Group, it was another case of internal combustion. The band was falling apart during the course of its 1969 US tour. Shortly after pianist Nicky Hopkins departed, the group splintered apart, and their appearance at Woodstock was scratched. Ironically, Nicky Hopkins ended up playing at the festival anyway with the Jefferson Airplane.

The best story about a phantom Woodstock appearance is the one about Iron Butterfly. And who better to tell it than John Morris.

John Morris: Jeff Beck never showed up. They never came. And Iron Butterfly sent me a telegram. And I hated it. I said, "How did this get here?" They sent me a telegram saying, "We will arrive at LaGuardia. You will have helicopters pick us up. We will fly straight to the show. We will perform immediately, and then we will be flown out." And I picked up the phone and called Western Union, and got a cooperative lady at Western Union. And it said:

F or reasons I can't go into.
U ntil you are here
C larifying your situation,
K nowing you are having problems
Y ou will have to find
O ther transportation
U nless you plan not to come.

If you read that on a telegram, the first letter of each sentence reading vertically says "FUCK YOU!" And the lady who was doing it worked it out with me, and she didn't realize what I was doing. Well, she did because I said I want to send an obscenity and we worked it out between the two of us. And that's what we sent them.

Perhaps another group would have been better off if they never got to perform at the festival instead of just being late. Sweetwater was another one of Woodstock's soap operas—but not for the usual reasons. Their troubles began even before they got there, just goin' up the country. The group's decision to travel to Bethel by tour bus proved to be a disastrous one, simply because they got stuck in the massive traffic jam headed toward the festival. This was long before mobile phones, and even before the CB (citizen's band) radio craze of the '70s. A call from a pay phone on the way did get through to the production office alerting the promoters of their situation and setting in motion the chain of events described earlier that got the festival going.

Though they were scheduled to open the festival, three acts and a swami had done their thing before Sweetwater was fully prepared to perform. They earned the distinction of being the first band to take the stage at Woodstock that Friday afternoon.

Sweetwater started out in 1968 at a coffeehouse called the Scarab in the vicinity of Los Angeles City College. A loose contingent of musicians who called themselves Jaywalker and the Pedestrians was playing there when a seventeen-year-old Glendale High School senior named Nancy Nevins walked into the club and sang a soulful version of "Sometimes I Feel Like a Motherless Child," a traditional Negro spiritual that dates back to slavery days. Blues and rock icons have adopted and adapted it to express deep feelings of pain and despair leavened with a glimmer of hope for those times when you *don't* feel like a motherless child. Coincidentally, Richie Havens reached back for this one from his gospel choir days when he was constructing his "Freedom" finale on-stage at Woodstock.

Nancy Nevins's version clearly impressed the patrons, staff, jaywalkers, and pedestrians at the Scarab, and plans were quickly put in place to start a new group called Sweetwater and to install Ms. Nevins as the lead singer. In a nod to the flower power, navel-gazing affectations of the time, she altered the spelling of her first name to "Nansi" (since changed back to its original spelling).

At a time when rock 'n' roll was flexing its muscles, experimenting with new sounds and styles and pushing the limits of what rock could be, Sweetwater had a lot going for it. In addition to Nevins's strength as a vocalist and the band's black, Caucasian, and Hispanic personnel, there was a very eclectic approach to the group's instrumentation. Fusing blues, folk, jazz, and rock, Sweetwater relied less on the ubiquitous electric guitar and more on instruments such as the cello, congas, and flute. The result was a very pleasant mixture of genres that got the group noticed and playing some high-visibility gigs on the West Coast from early on. A female lead vocalist with otherwise male-dominated progressive-rock musicians was in vogue with groups such as Big Brother and the Holding Company with Janis Joplin, Grace Slick's Great Society, and the early Jefferson Airplane with Signe Anderson (later replaced by Grace Slick). Sweetwater fit right in opening shows and sharing bills with the rock aristocracy.

Warner Bros./Reprise arrived with the big company record deal, and it looked as if the group was on its way. FM radio jumped on board giving the band a loose national network of airplay and exposure. The album did not yield a hit single, did not make it onto the nation's Top 100 album charts, and sold only moderately, but it did earn them an invitation to Woodstock, which could have been a magic bus express ride to stardom. But it wasn't. Here's a whole bunch of "maybes." Maybe if they had arrived on time; maybe if they had opened the festival; maybe if they were in the movie; maybe if they had appeared on the soundtrack—things might have been different. But they weren't. And the cruelest trick of fate of all was still to come just a few months later.

On December 8, 1969, Nancy Nevins suffered severe, traumatic, incapacitating injuries in an automobile accident on the Ventura Freeway while driving to Silver Lake. After just missing a pileup on the rain-slicked road, Nancy pulled over only to be rear-ended by a drunk driver.

She was comatose, brain damaged, and completely lost the use of one of her vocal cords. After six throat operations and years of mental and physical rehab, she began to put her life back together. There was a failed marriage and some troubled times, but there was also a college degree in American Studies, a master's degree in English, and a new career in teaching. She continued to love music, and returned to performing, sometimes with a refurbished version of Sweetwater.

But back in 1969 and 1970, things were looking pretty grim for Sweetwater. They limped along without Nevins, even managing to put out a second album in 1970 called *Just for You,* working with some vocal tracks she had recorded before the accident, then a third titled *Melon* in 1971. However, the writing was on the wall, and Sweetwater folded its tent shortly thereafter.

For those who were not in the audience at Woodstock, the film was viewed internationally as a definitive record of the festival. Like some of the other bands that were cut, the group is basically a forgotten entity.

Mike Wadleigh: One thing I want to set you absolutely straight on: there have been many questions through the years about why certain groups are in the movie and certain groups aren't. We absolutely could have put anyone we wanted to into the movie. It was not because they didn't give us their permission. It was certainly not because certain acts weren't Warner Brothers acts.

Our contracts with both Warner Brothers and the organizers said I could do whatever the fuck I wanted to do. Believe you me, I did it. We did have voting sessions. We did have a lot of altered-state and unaltered-state viewings, and I very much listened to people's reactions to certain groups. I would've loved to put in one number from every single group. I had a lot of respect for the festival organizers who had selected those groups. But I'll tell you, I hardly remember Sweetwater, it just didn't hold up.

Except for the inevitable Woodstock update profiles, that could have been the end of the story. In a strange turn of events in 1999, a screenplay about Sweetwater's saga was chosen as the subject matter for the first ever VH-1 made-for-cable TV biopic called *Sweetwater: A True Rock Story.* Instead of resurrecting the group and giving their story a happy ending, the film ended up adding insult to injury. *Time* magazine's review is typical.

Some things are worse than burning out or fading away, such as this risible rock biopic. VH-1's first original movie turns the story of the first band to play Woodstock into a schlockadelic mystery tour of ham-fisted period reminders: characters actually say, "You messin' with her trip?" Felicity's Amy Jo Johnson works valiantly with this fame-booze-downfall story, but some things are just better left to Where Are They Now?

BERT SOMMER

.

This one is personal.

He wasn't the best-known artist to appear at Woodstock. In fact, he was muscled onto the bill by virtue of being managed and produced by one of the promoters. But even if he was there because of his connections, he deserved to be there because of his talent. Over the years, I established personal and professional relationships with many of the performers at Woodstock, but this one was a real friendship.

Bert Sommer.

Just the mention of his name still brings a big smile to my face, and even that has a little bit of irony attached to it because "Smile" was one of Bert's best songs, and the one he chose to close his Woodstock set with:

> Smile, 'cause we all need one another,
> And it only takes a song to understand.

Bert understood.

I was a fledgling disc jockey at the most important FM rock radio station in New York City, if not the country, when I discovered a 33⅓ rpm LP that landed on the turntable in the music library at WNEW-FM, where we used to listen to new releases in consideration for airplay on our shows. Each DJ was allowed to choose his or her own music, and we could define our personalities not only by the things we said, but also by the things we played.

The album was called *The Road to Travel* and the cover featured the biggest Afro on the palest white man that I had ever seen! And the leadoff track was the best ode to postcoital lovemaking that I had ever heard entitled "And When It's Over." I played it relentlessly on my shows at NEW and Bert (as excited as any new artist is when they first hear their song *on the radio*!) called to thank me. We hit it off immediately. I had seen him in his role as Woof in the hit Broadway production of *Hair,* and he had also put some time in with the '60s group the Left Banke, replacing the band's lead singer after their big hit "Walk Away Renee" in 1966. Michael Brown, the Left Banke's principal songwriter, has said of Bert:

> Working with Bert was truly like working with a genius. Bert taught himself everything. He would play piano without thumbs early on, just four fingers on each hand. We wrote many songs together, and I also had a great time playing with him live onstage in his early career. Bert was very intelligent and very perceptive. He could see through anything. He zeroed out the machinery of relationships and society. He was an independent thinker. His blue eyes would be ablaze when he talked. A remarkable person.

Remarkable, but also somewhat jinxed. You might even call him the Rodney Dangerfield of rock 'n' roll. He got no respect—certainly not up to the level that he deserved. For years after his *Hair* and Woodstock exacta, he would self-deprecatingly joke, "Yeah, that and a token could get me on a New York subway ride!"

Bert took the Woodstock stage at 8:20 p.m. on August 15, 1969, just before sunset. He began his set with a song from the debut album called "Jennifer," written about one of his costars in the LA production of *Hair,* singer Jennifer Warnes. You may know her from her many appearances on the old *Smothers Brothers Comedy Hour,* or her own recordings over the years, including the Number One hit single duet with another Woodstock performer, Joe Cocker, "Up Where We Belong."

Not surprisingly, Bert's set included a showstopping moment—his cover of Paul Simon's "America" that was going to appear on his next album *Inside Bert Sommer.* He dared to take out Paul's comic relief line about the couple on the bus "playing games with the faces." It only served to make the song even more poignant and powerful than Simon and Garfunkel's original. Simon himself has stated that it was one of the best covers of any of his songs by anyone.

Bert also wrote a song at and about the festival, which became a modest hit for him in 1970, called "We're All Playing in the Same Band," but he was never quite able to take his recording career to the next level. He did, however, achieve another measure of acting fame playing Flatbush of Kaptain Kool and the Kongs on *The Krofft Supershow* in the mid-'70s.

Bert died of respiratory failure on July 23, 1990, at the age of forty-one. I was working at K-ROCK in New York at the time and played "Same Band" in his memory:

> *We're all playing in the same band.*
> *There's enough guitars for you and me.*

He never gave up on the Woodstock dream. If he were with us here today forty years after his hippie hat trick, I could easily imagine him saying, "Yeah. *Hair,* Woodstock, and 'We're All Playing in the Same Band.' That and a Metrocard could get me a New York subway ride!"

BERT SOMMER

TIM HARDIN

Tom Law: Tim Hardin was a great friend. Another guy who died of a heroin overdose. He wrote a lot of great songs, "If I Were a Carpenter," "Lady Came from Baltimore," "Reason to Believe." He wrote all those in the house I grew up in, in the Hollywood hills. At Woodstock, he was out of it. He was junked up.

I know this will come as a shock and surprise to many of you, but there were drugs at Woodstock—all different kinds and many of them. Even in the airspace above the crowd, narcotics were evident. Like many of the musicians, Alvin Lee of Ten Years After arrived to the stage by helicopter.

Alvin Lee: I was actually hanging out of the open side of the helicopter. And this guy made me put a harness on because I kept leaning out. And I was sort of hanging out of this door, over all of these people, and there was an incredible smell of marijuana. Which I thought about afterwards and I thought, Well, how could that be, because the helicopter blades are pushing the air down? But of course, there were acres of people and the air, the helicopter's sucking <u>in</u> air at the top. It actually was happening. So I was well away before we landed.

One of the smartest decisions the authorities made that weekend was to ignore the more benign narcotics on the premises, particularly marijuana. Long a favorite of jazz and blues musicians in the early twentieth century, marijuana, to mix a metaphor, was easily injected into the bloodstream of Woodstock Nation. Oh, it was around before that weekend all right, but always covert, surreptitious, and under the radar. At Woodstock, grass grew in stature faster than anything the folks at Lawn Doctor could ever have imagined.

Exhibit A: Jerry Garcia in the *Woodstock* movie holding a joint up right before the camera and exclaiming, "Exhibit A—marijuana!"

Exhibit B:

Henry Gross: There were fifty million pounds of marijuana consumed at Woodstock, and not one reported case of glaucoma.

That's the lighter side, the funny side, of drugs at Woodstock. There was, to be sure, a darker, more malevolent and dangerous side as well. One of the deaths recorded at the event was directly caused by a drug overdose. And there is a very good reason why one of the medical facilities at the site was nicknamed the Bad Trips Tent, and that is because there were so many "bad trips" linked to the use of psychedelics at the festival. Who could ever forget Chip Monck's exhortation to the crowd over the PA system.

Chip Monck: The warning that I've received, you might take it with however many grains of salt you wish, that the brown acid that is circulating around is not specifically too good. It is suggested that you stay away from that. But it's your own trip, be my guest. But please be advised that there's a warning, okay?

Odd phrasing, for sure, yet a terrific reminder that there were risks and consequences to face for the liberal use of illegal substances at Woodstock, or anywhere else for that matter. Prices were paid for it that weekend, and prices continued to be paid in the days, weeks, and years that followed. That too is a part of the legacy of Woodstock.

In fairness, there were many more less threatening reasons to visit the med tents than drug usage. The single largest number of reported injuries involved cuts and bleeding from bare feet around the festival grounds. But there certainly were enough bad trips and nonfatal ODs to have Woodstock serve as a cautionary tale against unbridled drug use and addiction.

There are so many sad stories to tell about some of the performers who appeared at Woodstock that it's difficult to know where to begin. Perhaps Tim Hardin is as good a place to start as any. We already have a picture of him in our minds refusing to be the opening act and instead hiding out under the stage to wait until dark before he made himself available to go on.

Tim Hardin was born on December 23, 1941, in Eugene, Oregon, and he died on December 29, 1980, in his apartment in Los Angeles, California (a much less noted music maker fatality than the murder of John Lennon twenty-one days earlier). The LA coroner's office rendered its judgment on January 26, 1981: "death from acute heroin-morphine intoxication due to an overdose." Not many were surprised by it. Greatly saddened, but not surprised.

Tom Law: In 1965, I found him in LA, petrified, coming down off junk. I rescued him. I didn't know Tim from Adam at the time. A friend of mine had called me from New York and asked me to check on him, take care of him. He was literally scared for his life because he'd ripped off these guys in New York and fled for LA. I roomed with him for a while, he came up to my house and got straight. Then he started hanging out with the wrong people, and he got back into doing drugs.

Tim inherited his musical acumen from his parents. Both studied music and earned master's degrees in the field. His mother was an accomplished violinist, and his dad played in jazz bands before settling into a career as a mill worker. Tim began playing guitar as a student, then singing in the Eugene High School choir. He decided against going to college, choosing instead to enlist in the Marines. That choice, he once told an interviewer, was "a legal loophole that allows the prisoner to sign himself into another prison—from parental care to the military." He also confided to interviewers that his addiction to heroin began while he was in the service.

After completing four years of active duty, he returned to the States and headed for the folk music scene that was percolating in New York's Greenwich Village, where he impressed and became friends with peers such as John Sebastian.

John Sebastian: The first time I heard Timmy Hardin, I said, "This guy is a genius." Timmy came into the Village in about 1963 or '64. My house was one of his first stops, because I knew everybody he knew. Tim had heard my playing at Fred Neil's shows.

What was Hardin like as a person?

John Sebastian: My first meeting with him really characterized Tim and his incredible self-confidence. He showed up at my house the day before we were to do a recording session together. He said to me, "John, I think you're great, and tomorrow you're going to be even better because you'll be playing with me." Now this was in an era when everybody was trying to subvert their ego. It was the beginning of the hippies and peace and love. But Timmy was incredibly aggressive and extroverted, but he was able to back it up with tremendous strength as a songwriter and player. And he was right—I never did play better than I did at that session. A large part of Timmy's presence was his involvement with heroin.

Erik Jacobsen, Charles Koppelman, and Don Rubin, the same team behind the rise of Sebastian's Lovin' Spoonful, took over the reins of Tim's career and got him a deal with Verve-Forecast Records. His first single, "How Can We Hang On to a Dream," was released in February of 1966, followed by the album *Tim Hardin I* in July. It was a fully realized "official" debut recording. (Tracks he had recorded a couple of years earlier came out on Atlantic in 1969, infuriating Tim and his creative team.) Credit for the confessional singer-songwriter movement that dominated the early '70s is often heaped upon Joni Mitchell, James Taylor, and Carole King, but it really began in earnest in the mid-'60s with Bob Dylan, Laura Nyro, and particularly Tim Hardin.

Despite Hardin's reputation as a bad boy, because of late and sometimes incoherent gigs, John Morris decided to give him a shot at Woodstock.

John Morris: He was, rest his soul, gone. He was one of the people who, but for circumstances which they brought on themselves, could have had a career that went forever. We didn't know that, but his Woodstock appearance could have been one of the biggest things that ever happened to him. Everybody loved Hardin. He was a great folk artist. But he was wasted; those things just mounted up against him. He didn't do a good performance. He didn't capture the people. Sebastian did and had a whole new career.

If Woodstock was not Hardin's finest hour as a performer, as it was for so many others, he had only himself to blame. The monkey on his back—check that—the *gorilla* on his back made that inevitable. Though filmed and recorded, none of his material made it onto the original *Woodstock* recordings or into the movie. But in film outtakes of his performance that have survived, he looks pale, disheveled, and more like a death mask of himself than the handsome, robust man whose images adorned his early album covers. His live performance of "Carpenter" had none of the authority or nuance of the original recorded version. It's unfortunate because for many of the budding rock intelligentsia who went to Woodstock, Hardin's appearance was initially a real selling point.

Billy Altman: He was a little edgier than most of the other performers on that first night, but he was a tremendous songwriter and musician. He was somebody I really wanted to see. He had been ostensibly part of the later part of the folk movement, people like him and Eric Andersen in '64 and '65. But he was a bit removed from the time when people knew who he was off the top of their heads. So I think his playing at Woodstock was supposed to be part of his comeback.

Bob Santelli: I was a huge Tim Hardin fan, and I was a guitar player and played all his songs. I loved the way in which he blended jazz and folk music and elements of rock. He sounded so unique. When I heard he was playing Woodstock, I remember thinking, Jeez, I'd love to see him, but outdoors it's gonna sound weird because he was so much of a club act. For him to do well, intimacy was very, very important. I remember hearing rumors that the guy wasn't all that well because of drug use, but I had never seen him up to that point. I recall distinctly that was one of the reasons I wanted to go to Woodstock was to see Tim Hardin. I ultimately wound up seeing him in a college in New Jersey, and I sat five feet away from him in a tiny club, and it was the most disappointing performance I had ever seen because I loved the man so and he was so messed up. He was one of the few big mistakes at Woodstock. He should have never been invited to Woodstock because his music never would have worked even if he had been completely straight and on top of his game. That music would have not gone over well no matter how well it was performed. It was just a bad bill for him. And it's unfortunate that he couldn't overcome that, because playing in front of so many people, if he did manage to pull it off, I think it would've done great things for his career. But people in the music culture totally respected him, especially in New York. And of course he was living and hanging out in Woodstock as well, so he was a natural person to invite.

Too far gone for his performance to make the cut, he does make an appearance in the film version of the festival.

Michael Wadleigh: He was very stoned. The problem with his performance was that he was ripped out of his gourd and didn't perform well. I put in that little thing of him because I thought his comments about technology were funny, Japanese motorcycles, and people doing chants and so on. It was a chance to make fun of the flower children and the motorcycles. It was a social comment. His set was hopeless.

He survived some of the other marquee Woodstock drug casualties by a few years, but it all caught up to him by the dawn of the '80s. The list of deaths by drug of performers who appeared at the festival reads like a who's who of progressive rock: Hendrix, Joplin, Moon, Hardin, Garcia, et cetera. So, can a distinction be drawn between "good" and "bad" drugs at Woodstock? I'm tempted to say that there is a huge chasm between moderate, recreational drug use versus severe addiction and substance abuse of any kind. I'm certainly no expert. But how can anyone ignore the body bags piled up in the years since the festival and filled up with drug casualties who could be described as some of the best and the brightest that this generation had to offer?

Marty Brooks: Walking back to the car, I saw someone shooting up. That was the first time I had ever seen someone using heroin, and it shocked me. Shooting up seemed like a violent act to me. It didn't seem like something someone who preached "peace and love" and living a natural, nonconsumerist life would be doing. Perhaps "hippies" weren't perfect.

On the twentieth anniversary of Woodstock, Mickey Hart of the Grateful Dead told *Life* magazine:

TIM HARDIN

People are using a lot of funny drugs now. Psychedelics were what was going down then. Society took a drastic turn in the years following Woodstock. Heroin, speed, and cocaine came in. People weren't seeking a higher consciousness, but a lower. They started getting twisted. These are paranoid drugs; the motives for doing them are destructive. But I had my music. That kept us real focused.

RAVI SHANKAR

Where did the idea of a rock festival come from anyway? In its earliest days, the music traveled to the audience, not the other way around. Busloads of acts with hit records crisscrossed the country doing one-night stands, then moving on. "Sock hops" at high schools hosted by local DJs were another way for this new music to be seen and heard. High-profile, influential DJs such as Alan Freed and Murray the K could set up shop at a big movie theater during a holiday week and present a laundry list of pop attractions six or seven times between the films being shown from early in the morning until late at night.

Slightly older and more sophisticated musical forms such as folk and jazz had already established a festival atmosphere for themselves.

Bob Santelli: Since 1945, literally thousands of music festivals have occurred. Increased prosperity at home permitted more leisure time, and the widespread use of the automobile eliminated most travel woes. Jazz, bluegrass, country and western, folk, blues, and classical festivals were common and often repeated annually. The Newport Jazz Festival in Rhode Island and the Monterey Jazz Festival in California were highly successful festivals in that idiom. The Fiddlers Convention in Union Grove, North Carolina, and the Ann Arbor Blues Festival in Michigan stimulated rich and energetic reactions to their respective musical genres.

Meanwhile, as rock 'n' roll matured, it followed the examples established by these other musical models. One man in particular restructured the whole idea of a rock concert and how this music could and should be presented to a large audience. Instead of record hops or short performances by a large number of recording acts, Bill Graham pioneered the presentation of lengthy performances by a couple of headliners in moderate-sized halls for a two- or three-day period.

The leap to a festival setting was a no-brainer. The landmark event for this type of presentation was the three-day Monterey International Pop Festival in June of 1967. First conceived as a profit-making venture by a couple of local promoters, the idea rapidly evolved into a nonprofit fund raiser to benefit music education nationally. A core group of five artists and producers—Lou Adler, the Mamas and the Papas, Terry Melcher, Johnny Rivers, and Simon and Garfunkel—each put up ten thousand dollars to finance the idea, and invitations to the party started going out to the cream of the crop of 1967 musicians. The event was a huge success, launching the careers of Jimi Hendrix and Janis Joplin, introducing the dynamism of the Who to an American audience, and giving the great Otis Redding the crossover success that he so richly deserved.

The goals of the musicians were lofty ones. I remember speaking to Paul Simon about it a couple of months later and this is what he told me.

Paul Simon: Well, the Monterey Festival was an incredible success. In the three days of performing in the stadium and on the fairgrounds, there were about one hundred thousand people. There wasn't one bust. There wasn't a fight. There was just an incredible time for performing and for meeting people. I don't think it's ever been done in the history of the music business like that. It's a nonprofit organization. It netted a quarter of a million dollars . . . I was voted fifty thousand dollars for New York. That money is going into a guitar project. I got fifty thousand from Monterey and I got the promise of guitars from Fender Instruments, and we're going to go into slum areas and give guitar lessons for free and we're going to give the guitars away for free, using the people in that area to teach it so that the money stays right inside. In other words, we're not gonna have white cats coming into Harlem to teach; we're gonna keep the money right in Harlem. We're just gonna give it to 'em and let 'em teach and give the stuff away for free. That's just one of the things. That's just a pilot project. If it works here in New York, it'll be put into effect in San Francisco and Chicago, Los Angeles and Detroit.

Not all of the festivals after Monterey were so altruistic and public-spirited. Most were conceived as commercial ventures. We already know that Woodstock was a "free concert" only by default—only because the genie got out of the bottle before the toll takers were in place! But none of this explains the almost mythical, mystical drawing power of these events.

Bob Santelli: The first difference involves the age group that attended the rock festivals. Never before had such a large proportion of a music festival audience been so young. Another very important element in the rock festival tradition, which was uniquely different from other music festivals, was the widespread use of drugs. The final factor that distinguished rock festivals was the sheer number of people they attracted. With the post–World War II baby boom babies coming of age, the youth culture was at its height. When summer came and school let out, there were a very large number of eager, restless kids ready to heed the call when the promise of a rock festival beckoned.

And heed the call they did! Even if it meant enduring all of the harsher elements that went along with the setting of an outdoor gathering.

Arthur Levy: I thought, Oh, an outdoor festival. There would be chairs, it would be organized. I had no idea it was going to be sitting on a blanket on a rolling hill. From the rain Friday night, it was going to be sitting in mud piles. I thought it would be civilized. There was no precedent for Woodstock on the East Coast except for Newport. There had been small country music, or bluegrass festivals, things like that . . . but the idea of a big festival was unknown.

In addition to Newport, there had been other festivals: Atlantic City Pop, Monterey Pop, Miami Pop, and the various smaller festivals on the East and West coasts.

Bob Santelli: There was a festival just prior to Woodstock called the Atlantic City Pop Festival. A number of guys in my band and a number of my friends went down to Atlantic City Pop Festival, which was basically a lot of the same people that would play Woodstock, but it was at that time that I began to really zoom in on the fact that this festival was going to be big. And would dwarf not only Atlantic City Pop Festival but also virtually all the other festivals that had come before.

There were other unexpected characteristics that distinguished the Woodstock experience from all of the other festival experiences.

Arthur Levy: The West Coast festivals were more rustic. I went to Newport every year from 1965. That was the first time I went, and that was the year Dylan went electric. You had a motel room in town, you went for the concerts where there were chairs set up, fences separating the chairs, it was really organized. There was a certain formality to Newport that had to do with city fathers and mothers who sanctioned the festival to happen. It was a classy festival. It started out as a jazz festival before it was a folk festival, which was formal. People came in nice clothes.

These other ways of doing things were clearly on the mind of many of the rock aficionados who attended Woodstock.

Arthur Levy: Since 1965, Newport had been incorporating more and more nonfolk music: blues bands, some rock 'n' roll, the Chambers Brothers, the Blues Project, and by 1969 B.B. King and Johnny Winter. Because of that there was a connection between Newport and Woodstock.

Billy Altman: One of my big recollections from Newport was that Jethro Tull played early on. And on their first album they had done a tribute to Roland Kirk, they had done his song "Serenade to a Cuckoo." I remember Ian Anderson giving this impassioned spiel about being inspired by Roland Kirk. And then Roland Kirk came out about an hour and a half later and did "Pinball Wizard," playing three horns at the same time. It was like, "Okay, you want to do a tribute to me? Then I'll do a rock thing." And it was this unbelievable version of "Pinball Wizard," which had just come out then. It was fairly astonishing.

Woodstock managed to widen the musical horizons even further with its inclusion of more international acts, one of them being Ravi Shankar.

Ravi Shankar: If Monterey was the beginning of a new movement or beautiful happening, I think Woodstock was almost the end. We had to go by helicopter from the motel where we stayed many miles away, and landed just behind the stage. I performed with Alla Rakha accompanying me on tabla, in front of an audience of half a million— an ocean of people. It was drizzling and very cold, but they were so happy in the mud; they were all stoned, of course, but they were enjoying it. It reminded me of the water buffaloes you see in India, submerged in the mud. Woodstock was like a big picnic party and the music was incidental.

For all the star power of Woodstock, it was completely missing any real presence by the holy trinity of '60s rock 'n' roll. Though in hindsight, it was clear that it was an event no self-respecting musician of the times would want to miss, there wasn't a Beatle, a Dylan, or a Stone to be found anywhere near the site. But in Ravi Shankar, Woodstock did have one of the Beatles' teachers.

Bob Santelli: Most of us knew nothing about Indian music. We probably wouldn't have been interested in Indian music at all had not the Beatles introduced the sitar and other components. Ravi Shankar's credibility really extends from George Harrison and the other Beatles who had gone to India and had expressed interest not only in the music, but also in the philosophical offerings that the culture of India gave to the West so he comes with instant credibility.

The Indian influence began to seep into their music, and the sitar made its presence felt as early as the *Help!* soundtrack and *Rubber Soul* album, but even more notably on both *Revolver* and *Sgt. Pepper's Lonely Hearts Club Band.* "Within You, Without You" seemed shoehorned onto *Pepper,* and the addition of a slight laugh track at the end of it always seemed to be a wink and a nod at George's obsession with both the culture and the instrument.

In those days, as the Beatles went, so went much of popular music. Pretty soon then, the sitar, that fretted string instrument with a gourd at one end and a long neck on the other, began popping up on major hits and album tracks by a wide variety of recording artists. Just a partial list: "Paint It Black," by the Rolling Stones; "Judy in Disguise (with

Glasses)," by John Fred and His Playboy Band; "Cry Like a Baby," by the Box Tops; "Green Tambourine," by the Lemon Pipers; "Paper Sun," by Traffic; "Turn Down Day," by the Cyrkle; "Monterey," by Eric Burdon and the Animals; "Hooked on a Feeling," by B. J. Thomas; and "Signed, Sealed, Delivered," by Stevie Wonder. Donovan used Indian instrumentation on many of his singles and album tracks. And another group that appeared at Woodstock used the sitar extensively in their music—Mike Heron and Robin Williamson of the Incredible String Band.

It isn't often that one single individual has that widespread an influence on such a broad spectrum of popular music, but when it comes to sitar use in rock 'n' roll—all roads lead to Ravi Shankar. He was born on April 7, 1920, in Benares, United Provinces, British India. He apprenticed with the great Indian sitar master Baba Allauddin Khan. His first public performance took place in 1939. His studies didn't end until 1944, just about a year after George Harrison was born.

Ravi is *very* serious about his music. He knew instinctively when a Western musician was taking sitar studies seriously versus dabbling with it as a novelty. After performing at the Monterey International Pop Festival in 1967, he paid a visit to San Francisco's Haight-Ashbury district and made this observation:

Ravi Shankar: I felt offended and shocked to see India being regarded so superficially and its great culture being exploited. Yoga, tantra, mantra, kundalini, ganja, hashish, Kama Sutra? They all became part of a cocktail that everyone seemed to be lapping up.

George Harrison learned firsthand how serious Ravi could be and offered this telling anecdote in his autobiography, *I, Me, Mine:*

George Harrison: The first sitar lesson was interesting in that it was so nice to find somebody who was such a master being able to start from scratch with a beginner. One thing that happened said a lot. The telephone rang and I put the sitar down, stood up, and went to step across the sitar to go to the phone, and Ravi whacked me on the leg and said, "The first thing you must realize is that you must have more respect for the instrument." . . . It is all part of the discipline, and it is true, you can't appreciate anything if you have no respect. I never was into those people smashing up their guitars anyway. That was just rubbish.

Not that Ravi didn't have a sense of humor. Quite the contrary. I will never forget attending the afternoon show of George Harrison's Concert for Bangladesh at Madison Square Garden in New York City on August 1, 1971. Ravi was the first act, and George introduced him and urged the crowd to be patient and respectful. Ravi and his accompanists noodled around for a bit on their instruments. When there was a pause in their tinkering, the audience burst into applause. Ravi leaned into the microphone and with a big smile said, "Thank you. If you appreciate the tuning so much, I hope you'll enjoy the playing more. Thank you!"

After Monterey Pop, Ravi was a regular on the Fillmore and festival circuit, which is how he and his management formed an East-West bond with John Morris.

John Morris: Jay K. Hoffman, who was Ravi's manager, was a friend. And I'd worked with Ravi at the Fillmore a couple of times. Actually, Jay caught me in the balcony of the Fillmore during one of Ravi's shows, lulled fast asleep. But it fit. It worked. It was new and it was something that nobody knew about. You know, it wasn't bass, drums, guitar. It was great music. Ali Akbar Khan, the drummer, tabla player was just fabulous. And so was the sitar. None of us knew what the hell a sitar was. And we were learning during that five- or six-year period of time. The other thing too was that Ravi's presence, Ravi's heart, and persona have always been so strong and so good and so positive that he makes people fall in love with him.

Billy Altman: There was a whole aspect back then of just going to hear people play and you would let the music wash over you. You would just sit there and listen. Ravi Shankar was always great for that. He would be able to impart a peaceful feeling to people. Friday was such a different day than the rest of the festival. They were expecting fifty to one hundred thousand, and now you have five or six times as many people showing up. And it was a great fit to have that peaceful influence.

Stan Schnier: I think I told you that there were two groups that when they played the Fillmore, we'd all yell, "Yeah!" We'd come and rip the tickets and then go sit in Bill's office because there was absolutely nothing we had to do because the crowd was so peaceful. One was the Incredible String Band and the other was Ravi Shankar. It was the same crowd. They'd burn incense and drop flower petals all over the floor.

At Bethel, the flower petals were soggy and the incense got snuffed out because of the raindrops falling during Ravi's set. But it certainly didn't dampen the determination of the musicians or the enthusiasm of the audience.

Bob Santelli: Ravi Shankar was a festival veteran. He was almost like Mr. Rock Festival, but he didn't play a note of rock music. All those people who on the surface might not have been interested in Indian music or raga music all of a sudden you heard Ravi Shankar and, wow, it had the intensity and power of rock music. Although it was done in a very spiritual way that lent a sense of spirituality to the stage at least for a little while at Woodstock. I remember seeing Ravi Shankar several times in the '60s and '70s. I was not a particular fan of Indian music, but I was drawn to the stage. The music was hypnotic. You would use it to enter a meditative state. It disarmed you and it allowed you to only imagine what this music stood for for so many hundreds of years and only to imagine the intricacies of this music. It was compelling, it was magnetic, and it fit. Would it fit today at a festival? I don't know whether kids would be as tolerant of it because it went on for a while. But it was certainly music that fit into the overall spiritual objectives of Woodstock and the other festivals as well.

MELANIE

Billy Altman: Melanie was great. A real singer-songwriter, very emotional, peaceful, and positive. So many of the Friday artists gave off such a positive vibe. "Beautiful People" is a song she played at Woodstock that was about this generation anyway. So there you have a nice dovetailing of a song that is about the very audience she's singing to. That was a really nice snapshot of the moment.

Look in the dictionary under the words *flower child* and you're likely to find a picture of Melanie. In fact, *The Hippie Dictionary* defines the phrase thusly: "A person who has reverted to a simpler, more natural way of life. Someone with flowers in their hair, either actually or figuratively. Usually a peaceful, nonviolent person."

Melanie Safka was born on February 3, 1947, in Astoria, Queens, New York. Subsequently, she moved with her family to Boston, Massachusetts, then to Long Branch, New Jersey. Following her high school graduation, she attended the American Academy of Dramatic Arts. That's where she met her true soul mate, Peter Schekeryk, who became her mentor, publisher, producer, manager, her still-husband, and the father of her three children.

If someone had been commissioned to write a song about the audience at Woodstock, they might very well have called it "Beautiful People." But the fact is that a song with that title already existed. It had been written by Melanie Safka. Following in the footsteps of one-named singers such as Dion and Cher, Melanie recorded her debut single for

Columbia Records and, while not a big enough hit for the label to commit to a whole album, it did get her a lot of airplay on the nation's "new groove" radio stations, and even an appearance on *The Tonight Show* with Johnny Carson. Her unique lyrics, idiosyncratic voice, and charming stage presence proved irresistible and guaranteed her a place on the stage of the testosterone-driven music industry of the late '60s. How big a stage that would turn out to be took everyone, including Melanie, by surprise.

Melanie: I was in Europe. My career really started over there for some reason, and I was doing a film score with the London Symphony Orchestra in England. Now, before I went to England, I had met Artie Kornfeld and Mike Lang—because we just happened to have offices in the same building—and I heard about these three days of peace, love, and music. I thought, Oh, that sounds so nice. I want to do it, okay? And they said, "Sure, kid"—and I was there. And I didn't even know if I should really go back to do this because I was in London, in the same studio with the Rolling Stones, and yeah, it was very big stuff. But something told me to go. Peter stayed in England, and I went by myself. And my mother drove me to Woodstock and we hit some traffic.

The aforementioned traffic . . .

Melanie: I thought, Oh, it must be an accident, and oh—now I'm going to be late. So I made some phone calls and I found out, "Oh no, don't go there; it's at a different place." So I went to this motel and I walked in the door—and there in the hotel lobby is media from—everywhere in the world!

Ellen Sander: We got to the Holiday Inn and there were a <u>lot</u> of people there. I got settled in my room, took a shower, and started wandering around. I went to the hotel bar, and there were all of these people that I knew there from the music business, and musicians, and they were kind of just milling around. We were getting various reports that there were large crowds and so everybody was kind of eager to go.

There were members of the Jefferson Airplane, Jerry Garcia, other members of the Dead, Janis Joplin. There was a big card game going on. People would sit down and play for a while. I remember Jerry played for a while. Pretty much it was just kind of a party in the bar.

I remember I got a fistful of quarters, five dollars' worth of quarters or something, and played "Hey Jude" on the jukebox over and over. Everybody started singing it.

Myra Friedman: Everybody was there. The Who. The Jefferson Airplane. Grateful Dead. I remember somebody at the jukebox playing "Hey Jude" over and over again, and I also remember the guy at the desk. People would go to him as a joke and he would announce over a megaphone "Call for Mick Jagger!" . . . He was <u>not</u> there. Everybody was doing it. They were just being nutty.

Melanie: There's Janis Joplin in the hotel lobby, slugging her Southern Comfort, surrounded by media and cameras—big giant microphones, that I had never seen in my life, and—and cameras—and she's talking, and I'm thinking, Oh my God! What is this? What does this mean? I had never performed for more than five hundred people. So here I am, and somebody comes up to me and says, "Okay, get in the helicopter," and I went, "B-b-b-b-but, my mother?" And they said, "No, only band members." I didn't even have the savvy to say, "This is my manager." I just said, "Oh, bye, Mom." And I never saw my mother again for the entire three days.

It was only when she was above the crowd that she had some sense of what to expect onstage.

Melanie: I looked down from the helicopter at this and I thought, How can I do this? Who's gonna listen to me? I mean, I was so terrified from the moment I saw the crowd of people, and I didn't really know anybody there.

Once the helicopter landed, production shuffled her backstage.

Melanie: They showed me to a little tent—it was a very little tent, with an earth floor, and I neglected to get or they didn't give me the artist pass. Sometimes I'd wander too far from the artist area and I would get thrown into the crowd, then I'd have to sing a few lines from the only song that Rosko was playing on WNEW-FM which was "Beautiful People." Then they'd let me go back to my little tent. I developed this hacking, horrible cough—and Joan Baez heard me coughing from the big-deal artist tent—and she sent over hot tea. That was my Woodstock moment.

The backstage area was another one of Chris Langhart's logistical responsibilities. The modest tentlike structure sat behind the stage across a small dirt road. Melanie made her way to the stage via a short wooden bridge that crossed from the artists' area over the road and to the stage. Richie Havens was performing when she made it to the stage.

Melanie: Richie Havens was singing "Freedom." I waited there all day. Every once in a while somebody would come up and say, "You're on next," because I had an easy setup: one guitar and a mic. Then they'd come back and say, "No, you're not." All day long, "Yes you are," "No you're not." Back and forth. So my cough got worse and I drank more tea. That was my day. And then it was night and it started to rain and the announcer made some kind of announcement about lighting candles. I think some people from the Hog Farm had passed out candles. By the time I went out, the whole hillside was starting to light up with candles, and it just looked like a hillside of magical fireflies or something. At first I was in complete terror. I remember walking this plank to my doom, my certain doom. I thought, This has to be the end of me, and I mean, I really did leave my body, I was in such terror. And I finally rejoined myself, I think, for the second song.

If it was painful, at least it didn't last long. Melanie sang "Beautiful People" and "Birthday of the Sun," and left the stage with cheers and hugs and the undying appreciation of the organizers and the audience. And perhaps, most important of all, with the inspiration for a new song from the experience that would become one of her biggest hits, signature songs, and a bona fide anthem about the festival, "Lay Down (Candles in the Rain)," which went to Number Six on the American singles charts in May 1970.

Melanie: It happened immediately afterward. I was so relieved that it was over and I did it and it was wonderful and people were hugging me, and I was hugging people, and it was so great. I wrote about this religious experience that I had with the rest of humanity.

"Woodstock" by Joni Mitchell, and "For Yasgur's Farm" by Mountain are the two other long-lasting odes to Woodstock, but Melanie's song crystallizes the mystical undercurrents of the festival.

Melanie: Because I knew it was a spiritual experience. And I called [the great gospel choir] the Edwin Hawkins Singers, and they were on the same label as I was, and I said, "Listen, I have this song that we have to do together." Edwin Hawkins said, "Oh, does it have Jesus in it?" And I said, "No." Anyway, I actually had the nerve—I can't even believe I did this—to go to where they were rehearsing in Oakland, California. I went to the school gymnasium and I sang them, by myself, the whole thing of "Candles in the Rain"—and I said, "This is the part you'll come in on, 'Lay down, lay down,'" and I'm singing, and by the end—they were singing with me.

Whatever your belief system or nonbelief system, there is such a thing as spirit in this world. School spirit, community spirit, patriotic spirit, even the spirit of rock 'n' roll. Melanie's spirit has truly fused with the spirit of Woodstock and is, indeed, inseparable from it. That is why she never sits still for any revisionist history that denies or alters its existence.

Melanie: A lot of the people are cynical about it. There was so much promise that didn't get fulfilled. There's a tendency to say, "Well, that wasn't a big deal. We're on to something else." But my feeling is that something very important did happen. And I'm really happy to be part of that. I don't enjoy looking at the things that make it ridiculous, that try to make it less than what it actually was. It was a spontaneous coming together, and it was as close to a religious gathering as I have ever known.

MELANIE

ARLO GUTHRIE

Myra Friedman: He was adorable, he was real. He meant what he said.

Arthur Levy: He reflected the crowd. The crowd identified him as one of their own in terms of age and hippie lifestyle. There may have been other hippies in some of those bands, but Arlo was the quintessential hippie.

"Hippie-speak" wasn't invented at Woodstock, but it certainly reached its late-'60s zenith there. Subsequent exposure in the movie sent its colloquial charm and societal significance all around the globe and made it an international phenomenon:

"Qu'est-ce que c'est 'groovy'?"

On the first night of the festival, Havens and Sebastian could have been the Funk and Wagnall's of Woodstockian syntax. But as this excerpt from his set shows, the Shakespeare of hippie-speak, the undisputed heavyweight champion of "slang gone cosmic" was Arlo Guthrie.

Yeah, it's far-out, man! I don't know, like, how many of you can dig how many people there are, man . . . like I was rapping to the fuzz—right—can you dig it? Man, there's supposed to be a million and a half people here by tonight! Can you dig that? New York State Thruway's closed, man! Yeah . . . a lotta freaks!

Arlo looked stoned whether he was or wasn't, sounded stoned whether he was or wasn't, and acted stoned onstage at Woodstock most certainly because he was. He'd be the first to admit that he had no business performing up there in the condition he was in. Like everyone else that night, he had no idea of when he'd be called to the stage, so he partook liberally of the substances available.

> **Arlo Guthrie:** I remember being there. And I remember there was nothing to eat or drink, it had all been ate or drunk. And I was thirsty. But there were a hundred or somethin' cases of champagne in the back that they had saved for the end of the third day or somethin'. Well, we started attacking that! I think I drank about a case or two before we went out, and I was totally gone!

While the unscheduled-to-play John Sebastian and Country Joe solo "dropped in" that first night, Arlo Guthrie, who was scheduled to perform, literally "dropped in" to play his set.

> **Arlo Guthrie:** I walked out there and they had a big hole in the middle of the stage 'cause they were gonna turn the stage around and set up the guys in the back while the guys in the front were playing. Well, the hole never worked, and they never turned the stage around. But they didn't tell me about the hole, so I walked out there and fell right into a six-foot hole. You know how it is sometimes when you're feeling like that—I just walked through the wood and came out the other side—I just kept going. And I walked out and I played, and, ah, I forgot what I played.

Fortunately, we remember. He played a very short set with a lot of personality.

> **John Morris:** He had "Alice's Restaurant" out, and, again, his performance was about personality, about his soul. Because a lot of these people, they have good souls, they did what they did because that's who they are. And Arlo came out there, and he was funny, and it was raining and he got everybody to sing with him and did it in the spirit that is Arlo Guthrie.

Arlo Guthrie: I know I did "Coming into Los Angeles," but the one on the record, the one that you see in the movie, is <u>not</u> the "Coming into Los Angeles" that we did. That's the one that they took from another recording somewhere and snuck it on there—which is why you never see us playing in Woodstock 'cause they couldn't synch it up. They always have pictures of people smoking dope or something like that, you know. That was a shame too, because they took the worst possible recording of some terrible night we did somewhere in the city, and stuck it on there, and I was always horrified at that.

I think we can see from the content of "Comin' into Los Angeleeeeze" ("Don't touch my bags if you please, Mister Customs Man") how the song came to epitomize Arlo's brief moment in the Woodstock spotlight, but he brought to his set some other interesting elements as well. He was the second artist after Richie Havens to perform a Bob Dylan song. Six years his senior, Dylan used to babysit Arlo for Woody and his mom Marjorie. One of these babysitting jobs took place at the famed Newport Folk Festival.

Arlo Guthrie: He just kept walking me around saying, "Hey, this is Woody's kid," or something.

Already known as much for his comedic ramblings as his music, Arlo next launched into a virtually inscrutable fable about a bear in the woods and a Cub Scout troop, but it hardly mattered. The euphoric "gather 'round the world's largest campfire and listen to my improbable story" atmosphere of the evening left the crowd docile, happy, and clamoring for more.

Bob Santelli: He was the perfect hippie. He has his father's sense of humor. Back then, not a lot people knew his name, but they knew "Alice's Restaurant." If you got to see the film, you got to see what a kooky, warm, fun-loving kind of guy he was. But of course, he had come with tremendous pedigree. His father of course being Woody Guthrie. Not a lot of seventeen-year-olds or nineteen-year-olds sitting in the crowd at Woodstock knew that. So Arlo was up there on his own terms and based on his own musical merit.

Arlo's gifts for music and storytelling were predestined. The oldest son of Woody and Marjorie Mazia Guthrie, a professional dancer with the Martha Graham Company, Arlo's official biography claims that he was born with a guitar in one hand and a harmonica in the other. The American musical lineage that begins with Woody Guthrie moves along a well-traversed path from the 1930s right up to this very moment and includes such hallowed names as Pete Seeger, Bob Dylan, Roger McGuinn, and Bruce Springsteen. Working-class words set to simple tunes addressing all manner of social, political, environmental, and interpersonal issues have always been grist for the mill of American music and musicians with a social conscience.

What was it like being the son of such an extraordinary man?

Arlo Guthrie: I think it's hard to sometimes separate the fact from fiction—or the truth from legend. People have been trying to do that now for a number of years—especially concerning early folksingers. I think my dad's legacy is probably not yet set—it's not written in stone, yet. It's one of those things that's still being argued on paper, and I like that. I don't particularly care about the difference between truth and legend, so I am not a stickler for what the true facts were. I don't think the truth can be known anymore. The truth about the past can't ever be known, as far as I'm concerned, but you can know what's true in the present.

Playing music around the house for his talented parents was one thing, but standing up in public and playing for the first time presented a completely different challenge. He remembers it vividly:

Arlo Guthrie: When I was a kid, I used to go down to Gerde's Folk City—my mom used to take me, actually, down to hear whoever was singing—and that's where I first heard Sonny Terry and Brownie McGhee, and probably Judy Collins. I remember Ramblin' Jack Elliott and a bunch of folks, including Cisco Houston. One night, Cisco was playing down there, and I decided I had to go see him—and I wanted to go real bad. I got my mom to drive me down there, and we sat around, and Cisco was playing, and in the middle of his show he decided that he was going to ask me to sing a few songs. I remember I could feel it coming, and I looked over, and sure enough, he was

ARLO GUTHRIE

85

asking me to go up there and sing. I went up and borrowed his guitar and started playing.

How did it go?

Arlo Guthrie: I was absolutely devastated by the experience of everybody looking at me, and, of course, I couldn't really sing. Maybe the last few years of my life I started actually singing, but that night my knees were going crazy, and they were totally out of rhythm to what I was play-ing, and it was a devastating experience. But everybody was very kind and applauded me very politely. I did about three of my dad's songs— "Talkin' Blues" and maybe "Pastures of Plenty" and something else—but, I can't remember now. It was fairly exciting.

When Arlo first began playing music in 1967, it was impossible to discuss him without referencing his father. But this identification was short-lived.

Arthur Levy: He got it out of the way early in his career. Yes, he was Woody's son. No, he sounded very little like Woody. No, he wrote very little like Woody. All those contrasts and comparisons and differences and similarities all got taken care of very early in his career. By the time he was at Woodstock, no one was talking about Woody. In that very short period of time between "Alice's Restaurant" at the end of '67, and Woodstock in '69 he became his own man.

In 1967, Arlo became a pop culture sensation at Newport with his eighteen-minute, twenty-second talk-song about Thanksgiving, littering, Officer Obie, the draft, and a restaurant called Alice's.

Arlo Guthrie: One time I got invited to go to Newport actually to play, and this was a big deal. And they stuck me out in some afternoon crowd. I went out to play "Alice's Restaurant," which I had just sort of fin-ished writing. I remember I was standing out in the middle of the field somewhere on a little platform and it was hot, and it was sweaty, and there were a lot of people there—and I broke four strings in the middle of "Alice's Restaurant"—I ended up playing on two strings for the last chorus or two, I couldn't believe it—no one ever breaks four strings— but that's how it happened.

Despite the tough circumstances, Arlo and Alice made an impression.

Arlo Guthrie: I got a big response, and they asked me to come back and sing it again somewhere—I forgot where the second time was—and I sang it there. And at the end of the festival, I think it was Pete Seeger convinced me that I ought to sing it onstage, and I did. It was the end of the festival, it was the last night there, and I was the last thing to happen. I sang "Alice's Restaurant" in front of more people than I ever imagined in my life—and people came out with me to sing it. I forgot who was there, maybe Joan Baez, Judy Collins, Pete Seeger, and a bunch of other folks and we were all singing "You can get anything you want" together at the end of the thing, and I felt like this is where I belong.

Arlo had just turned twenty-two when he took the stage at Woodstock.

Arthur Levy: He was only two years into his career at that point. He represented for many of us, this anyone-can-do-it philosophy. It wasn't a complicated act. He wasn't a complicated performer. And it felt like, yeah, anybody can do this, and I mean that in an extremely complimentary way. He made it seem easy. He made it seem that you didn't have to be an artist of the level of Joan Baez to be a performer. You could be an artist who was loose and natural and childlike and kind of high. It made it much more common.

Arlo made a similar observation about the generation of performers who have succeeded him.

Arlo Guthrie: Right now we're seeing a resurgence of interest in certain kinds of music that my father would have appreciated. There are a lot of other people, some of whom are still around—like Pete Seeger. And there were a whole group of people who really made it their business to show us all that you could sing, even if you weren't a "real" singer. You could play music if you weren't a "real" musician. You could have fun and in doing so, you could change the way people think about things. And I think that's fact.

Arlo almost didn't make it to Woodstock and might not have gone if he'd known how big the New York State Thruway–choking crowd was going to be.

Arlo Guthrie: We had some hesitation about going there because—people don't remember—but back in 1969, every time over fifty people got together, there was riots, and cops would come and hit you and everything, and it was disaster time. So we weren't sure when we heard that there were gonna be a hundred thousand people at a festival that maybe it's gonna get out of hand and it's gonna be a big drag. But we decided to go anyway, and, of course, by the time before the gate even opened there were eighty thousand people before they'd had time to even collect any tickets. So we didn't have any idea how big it was gonna be.

With a head of curly hair rivaling Michael Lang's and a baby face of stoned insouciance, he was the mirror image of the audience he faced. He was the instant poster child for the event. His appearance, words, and demeanor overshadowed his musical performance.

Arlo Guthrie: Nobody remembers the music. They all come up and say to me something about the New York State Thruway is closed and there's a lot of freaks or whatever. There are young kids who that's a big deal for them somehow or other. I don't know.

The filmmakers behind *Woodstock* included Guthrie's now-iconic remarks about the New York State Thruway in the final cut. These moments in the film are certainly a playful jab at Guthrie and the blissed-out hippies he represented. When the film was screened, many audiences had a similar response to his appearance:

Dale Bell: Some people laughed when we wanted them to laugh, especially when Arlo Guthrie says, "Hey, the New York State Thruway is closed . . . That's real cool, man!" He would get ridiculed. There would always be this "Come on, Arlo, what are you talking about?"

This portrayal undercut Guthrie a bit.

Bob Santelli: He has this tremendous musical pedigree, but that didn't really come out at Woodstock. He comes across as this fun-loving hippie who's goofy and laughs and has this kind of cool relationship with marijuana and just thinks the whole thing's a gas. There's a deeper side to Arlo that people at Woodstock didn't see and eventually would come to see as his music becomes less hippie-esque and more meaningful in the manner in which he recalls his father's talent. He started by taking "City of New Orleans," Steve Goodman's great song, to the top of the charts and then as he goes into the '70s right up into today. Arlo Guthrie is truly Woody's son. It's something that most people didn't see at Woodstock.

Though the legacy of his Woodstock performance might not be the thing Guthrie is proudest of in his career, he knew right away that the festival itself was of great significance.

Arlo Guthrie: The moments you are aware of being in a historic event are few and far between. Most history is determined from hindsight. But we knew at that time that we were in a historic moment. Most historic moments, whether they are viewed from inside or from hindsight are disasters—diseases, floods, famines, earthquakes, wars. The chances of you finding yourself in a historic moment that is not a disaster is also fairly rare. So the odds of finding yourself in a historic moment that is not a disaster, where you know it's a historic moment, are astronomical! That's what it was like. It was wonderful and breathtakingly exhilarating!

JOAN BAEZ

Joan Baez: Woodstock was drugs and sex and rock 'n' roll. Woodstock was Janis "coitus interruptus" Joplin and Jimi "genius" Hendrix, and the gorgeous sweating chest of Roger Daltrey of the Who. Woodstock was Country Joe McDonald and Dirty Sly and the Family Stone gettin' HIGH-YUH! Along with a half a million people. Woodstock was rain and mud, GIs in disguise, and cops cooking hot dogs for hungry hippies. Woodstock was white ladies of the lake emboldened by the roadblocks set up between the golden city of freedom and their sororities, pulling back their river-rat hair with the lake dripping from their pretty elbows, not really unaware of the cameras grinding away on the shore, focused on their lovely breasts. Woodstock was Wavy Gravy and his Hog Farm. Woodstock was two babies being born and three people dying. Woodstock was a city. Yes, it was three extraordinary days of rain and music. No, it was not a revolution. It was a Technicolor mud-splattered reflection of the 1960s. Woodstock was also me, Joan Baez, the square, six months' pregnant, the wife of a draft resister, endlessly proselytizing about the war. I had my place there. I was of the '60s, and I was already a survivor. I sang in the middle of the night, I just stood up there in front of the residents of the golden city who were sleeping in the mud and each other's arms, and I gave them what I could at the time. They accepted my songs. It was a humbling moment, in spite of everything. I'd never sung to a city before.

She was young. She was beautiful. She was radiant. She was also six months' pregnant, preparing for life as a single mother because her activist husband, David Harris, was serving time in a federal penitentiary for draft resistance. Her name is Joan Baez, and she had been "the Folk Madonna" of American popular music for almost a decade.

On arriving at the site, Joan was as startled and befuddled by the size of the crowd and the scope of the event as anyone. She inquired, "Who's on?"

"A guy named Bert Sommer," a Woodstock staffer replied. "I think Timmy Hardin's going on next."

"The order just went 'kerplooey'?" she asked plaintively.

The answer solidified her status as the primary jewel in the opening-night crown, "You close anyway. You're closing!"

Joan diffused the nervous excitement in the air with a quip, "Okay. Maybe there'll be a few more people here by then. I don't like a little puny gathering like this."

In that one simple sentence, she refuted what she considered to be one of the greatest misconceptions about herself that has followed her around for her entire career: that she doesn't have a sense of humor. Her seriousness about causes probably does mask her biting wit, but all one needs to do is listen to her dead-on impression of Dylan in her version of "Shelter from the Storm" to realize that this woman has the capacity and the wisdom to laugh at anyone, at anything, at any time, including herself.

Mike Jahn: When Abbie Hoffman announced his plans that they were going to protest at the Democratic National Convention in 1968, Joan and I were in the front row. She was amazed by the whole thing. Abbie read off a list of all the performers who were going to be there, giving free concerts. As we know, only MC5 showed up. One of the bands who was supposed to be appearing was Primitivo and the Tit Squeezers, which Abbie just made up. She thought that was pretty funny.

Of course, her appeal went way beyond her sense of humor.

John Morris: She was a lot of things. She was the queen. Totally acknowledged as the queen. Everybody loved her. I mean, I was totally in love with her. I worked with her in England afterwards. I had worked with her at the Fillmore before. I adored Joan. And she was the perfect person to end it on because everybody was wearing down that first night.

"In-your-face" politics was not suffered gladly at Woodstock. But Joan Baez was given a veritable "get out of jail free" card to sweetly deliver her antiwar, antidraft sentiments to a field full of potential draftees.

In addition to being a genuine star, Joan was also just one of the people and didn't seek any special treatment.

Wavy Gravy: I remember that Joan Baez came to where we had set up the free kitchen with a big sign that said "fried lice" and the giant papier-mâché hog floating in space. We had a free stage there. As if we needed a free stage. It was all free stage . . . But nobody recognized her because she had her hair cut. So she's waiting in line in the rain for her turn. I couldn't believe it. She couldn't say to somebody, "I'm Joan Baez, what are you thinking?"

You cannot discuss Joan Baez without talking about her politics. She was the first white performer of note to bring attention to the civil rights demonstrations in Washington. She boldly stood for what she believed and was blessed with a unique instrument to get her message across.

Michael Wadleigh: Here was a woman who understood what the times were about. She was a real leader, and still is, by the way. She's an amazing political and social person. You wanna talk about voices, you don't often hear a voice like that. When she sings "Swing Low, Sweet Chariot" a cappella, with such power, confidence, and skill that she does, she can blow away anybody of any race of any gender with the instrument she has. She told me, she just has the gift. She doesn't have to work hard, train hard or whatever, the voice was there. Of course, I'm such an admirer of how knowledgeable she was about the political movement.

Darkness had fallen. The first unexpected storm of the weekend had dampened Ravi Shankar's set of exquisite, exotic Indian music. The evening's flow halted until the rain had subsided enough to allow the music to continue safely.

John Morris: Chip Monck lit the living daylights out of her. And she was this beautiful woman. Chip's method of doing lighting was to take their energy and push it even harder. And he was a brilliant lighting designer—the best ever in rock 'n' roll. And with Joan, it was purples and roses and blues, and working with the songs which he knew like the back of his hand—and he just made love to Joan with the lights. It was beautiful.

Joan Baez took the stage at around 2:00 a.m. She spoke softly, addressing the five hundred thousand people in front of her as intimately as she did an invited group of guests at one of her backyard barbecues in California.

Joan Baez: I'd like to sing you a song that is one of my husband David's favorite songs. And let me just tell you that he's fine . . . and [patting her six months' pregnant belly to the applause and cheers of the crowd] . . . we're fine, too! David was just shipped from the county jail, which is very much of a drag, to federal prison, which is kind of like a big summer camp after you've been in county jail long enough. And they shackled his feet and they shackled his hands and they shaved his head and all that jazz, and he's perfectly good-natured about the whole thing. And the last time I saw David, he was smiling as usual and we had waited a long time for the federal marshals to come to the house and pick him up, and, as it turned out, they could have picked him up anywhere after the tenth of July, and they waited until after the sixteenth so probably any noise about David would have been buried in the moonshot.

So anyhow, I was in touch with the federal marshals and I said, "You know, just let us know when you're coming and stuff, and I'll give you directions 'cause we live up in the hills." And they were too proud to take the directions, so they were two and a half hours late. And they pulled into the yard, and we had a big party going on and people with beads and hair and really looking happy and having a good time, a lot of cameras, a lot of action. And these poor federal marshals didn't look very happy at all. And they said, as a matter of fact, that they had gotten a little lost, and I thought to myself, I wonder if you know how lost you really are? [laughter and cheers], but, anyway, they were just doing their job. So I saw them driving off down the wrong side of the road, and one of the girls who works with the resistance had put a big ole . . . "Resist the Draft" sticker on their bumper and that's the last I saw!

This was low-key compared to some of the antiwar speeches Baez was known for.

John Morris: Joan had the War Resisters League, where if you paid Joan, you paid part to the War Resisters League. They were the Berkeley anti-war performers who had an audience and made use of it in a way that wouldn't turn you off. I mean, there was a thing about Joanie which I must admit I've said a couple of times myself, much as I adore her: "Shut up and sing." Because she would tend to go on and do a long antiwar diatribe. But she didn't at Woodstock, because the situation didn't say that to her.

Instead, at Woodstock, Joan chose to make an impression through music rather than speech.

Arthur Levy: She probably realized that this was an audience that was not that familiar with her. This was not her standard Carnegie Hall or Town Hall audience. I think she wanted to make a lasting comment that they would remember, politically. She was not going to waste an opportunity to make a social and political impression on them. She succeeded in doing that.

The look of this tiny, pregnant woman, dwarfed by the stage and the amps and the sound towers and the crowd, is totally mesmerizing. This is before the age of jumbo video monitors above the stage magnifying the performer and the performance. Yet a million eyes are focused intently on the dot at center stage, unable to break the magnetic attraction.

In honor of David, she launched into the traditional organizers' folk ballad, "I Dreamed I Saw Joe Hill Last Night." The crowd ate it up.

Michael Wadleigh: "Joe Hill" is an old song about the labor movement, which Joan felt was connected to her husband David in jail who had been brutalized by people, and the civil rights workers who had died in the South. It was going back to the roots, going back to many years before Woodstock. I thought it was a good idea. I liked the feeling of it, a ballad like that.

Arthur Levy: Joe Hill was a Swedish immigrant who came to America in 1910, who joined the Wobblies, the IWW—the International Workers of the World. And he was a songwriter. Because he was a high-profile songwriter, the anti–labor union forces framed him on a murder rap in Salt Lake City in 1914 and railroaded him into an execution the following year. He became the first martyr of the labor union movement. It was a long-time staple of Joan's sets and it was David Harris's favorite song.

The lovable, unflappable Ms. Baez ambled through a dozen rain-splattered songs including the aforementioned "Joe Hill," the Edwin Hawkins Singers' "Oh Happy Day," Tom Paxton's "The Last Thing on My Mind," and the great civil rights warhorse "We Shall Overcome."

> **Arthur Levy:** For her, "Joe Hill" and "We Shall Overcome" would be the high points because it was her getting to sing the songs that mattered to her in this struggle she was experiencing. Joan has never been one to waste an opportunity, or take an opportunity lightly. Here she was performing to the biggest audience of her career and it was important to play those songs.

Her sister Mimi had been widowed when her novelist husband, Richard Fariña, died tragically in a motorcycle accident. She sang "Sweet Sir Galahad"—the only original song in her set—in honor of her sister. "Sweet Sir Galahad" is one of the only songs that ultimately makes it onto the officially released Woodstock concert soundtrack recordings and sounds as pure and pristine and lovely today as it did on that August night in 1969.

Little remembered is Baez's duet with West Coast singer-songwriter-musician Jeffrey Shurtleff. They sang Gram Parsons's and Roger McGuinn's "Drug Store Truck Driving Man." An activist colleague of Joan's, Shurtleff introduced the number.

> Hello to all friends of the draft resistance revolution in America. Good evening. I hope it stops raining. One thing about the draft resistance that's different from other movements and revolutions in this country is that we have no enemies, and it's one of the beautiful things about it. And to show that our hearts are in the right place, we'll sing a song for the Governor of California—Ronald "Ray-Gun." Zap!

Also included in Joan's set is a Bob Dylan song "I Shall Be Released." The Dylan-Baez relationship was a tricky one.

Arthur Levy: They were lovers for a brief window of time. He lived with her at her cottage in Carmel. Which when she got married to David Harris, the first thing that David Harris did was make her sell the cottage. I think part of that was because he wanted her to move to the Struggle Mountain commune where they lived. The other part was I think that there was too much of Dylan wrapped up in the cottage in Carmel and he wanted Joan to be away from that. But Joan and Dylan were together. She did enormous good for Dylan's career, which for the next forty years, either he has rejected acknowledging or acknowledged it so magnanimously.

What was the crux of the problem?

Arthur Levy: He went to England in the springtime 1965 and took her along. And she expected that he would introduce her to his new audience there the way she had introduced him to her audience at the start of his career. And he turned his back on her. He never introduced her at any of his concerts. He treated her shabbily. It broke her heart for a minute. Luckily, she had her own concerts scheduled, which were sold out—she had a huge following in England. She had nothing to worry about in terms of that. But she was looking for him to return the favors that she had done for him for the past two years, but he just turned his back on her. She was very hurt. She didn't record any songs by him for the next three years. Then she goes to Nashville in 1968 and records a whole album of Bob Dylan songs. After having had this enormous public falling-out with him in '65.

In the end, Dylan left her personally and professionally in the dust of his "wandering boot-heels." She confided to me many years later how traumatic that all was. I asked her if she was conscious of the exact moment that the balance of power had shifted.

Joan Baez: That's what was so hurtful. None of us likes to give up any of that power, no matter what anybody says. You don't like letting go of power or esteem or whatever that baloney is, and so I <u>was</u> conscious of it. It was a big shock. When we were in Woodstock and some girl, a weary pilgrim type, came over to the table and I was infuriated because she was flirting with Bob— Well, they're supposed to be asking <u>me</u> questions, you know, and I hadn't run into this. And I was not the least bit happy with someone being as famous as I was. I wanted, with humor and all the rest, to express that.

I asked Joan about the fundamental differences between her and Bob.

Joan Baez: Bob and I don't have anything in common. We were together. We were put together by people's ideas of us and, in some ways, we worked that out and lived that out and had some fun times. I would say, "What is it that's different?" and he would say, "Well yeah, I know exactly what it is; you think you can change the world, and I know nobody can change anything." Well, there's going to be a limit to what kind of a relationship I can have with somebody who really feels that way. I think what may be lacking in this society is not necessarily being serious about people or being serious about ourselves but people being serious about something. I think that for your life to have meaning, you have to be serious about something. There are lots of musicians who are serious about their music, and I appreciate that, but I'm not that deeply into the songwriting process or the musical process. When I'm serious about music it's when I'm singing from the stage—but, I've felt many times if there's a discussion in a room about social issues, I'm much more drawn to that, than, say, a discussion by musicians about music. That doesn't really interest me very much. And so all of those things are involved in what would make a really sustaining relationship for me. Somebody's got to be serious about something. These are the ones that last.

Dylan, as we know, didn't make it to Woodstock from just up the road, but Joan came from clear across the country to do it. Her mother accompanied her. Joan's poetry, her prose, her panache, her passion, her polish, and her politics made her a natural choice for an invitation to the Music and Art Festival. She almost didn't do it, however, because her hard-bargaining manager Manny Greenhill held firm to his demand for a five-figure fee for his client. They agreed in the end to a price of ten thousand dollars, putting the pregnant superstar in the upper reaches of the Woodstock payroll, and worth every penny of it and then some for what she brought to the party.

The final song from Joan's set was her show-stopping a cappella version of the gospel classic "Swing Low, Sweet Chariot." Her soft as velvet, sharp as a razor sweet soprano voice cuts through the raindrops, slices through the night air, and cuts deeply and movingly into the hearts of the weary pilgrims before her at the end of their first long day's journey into night. Dale Bell, the associate producer on the *Woodstock* film, arrived while Baez was singing "Swing Low."

Dale Bell: To me, ironically, the one piece that stands out in the middle of that entire crowd was the single voice of Joan Baez, which was playing when I arrived. She sang "Swing Low, Sweet Chariot" and we were shooting at the time. That piece, when we finally got it edited, to me was as essential and seminal as all of the noise the Who, Jimi Hendrix, Mountain, Jefferson Airplane—they were all good and diverse in their own way. But the pure vocal strength and magic of Joan Baez was incredible. It was absolutely incredible.

She ended the night by playing "We Shall Overcome" as an encore. We have referenced the spiritual elements that were draped over almost every aspect of the mythological Woodstock experience. Perhaps none was as well received or more comforting than the folk Madonna's goodnight prayer to the assembled multitude.

John Morris: I think what we said to the audience afterwards when Joanie finished was, "Good night. Curl up next to your brothers and have a pleasant evening." She was the lullaby so that they could make it through that night.

Saturday

FOUNDERS, QUILL,
THE KEEF HARTLEY BAND,
THE INCREDIBLE STRING BAND

Tom Malone: Friday night's show ended late and we stayed up all night on the hill, as it was too dark to find our way back to the car. With the break of dawn illuminating the hillside, we awoke to find the population on the hill greatly reduced and open space before us. Seizing the opportunity to move closer, we picked up our trusty tarp and moved down the hill a few hundred feet closer to the stage and we put our wet sleeping bags on the wooden barrier wall between the stage and the crowd to dry in the sun. After establishing our new location, it was time for me to feed the troops. Two would hold the spot on the hill while the rest of us went to the car to cook breakfast, which consisted of pancakes and Kool-Aid.

Before we jump headlong into the second day of music, let's take a step back and meet the movers and shakers who set the Woodstock juggernaut in motion.

John Roberts: This started out as a lark entirely. We came to the idea of writing a sitcom about two young men with a lot of money who get into business adventures. The only problem was that we didn't have enough business experience to come up with episodes. So we decided to solve that problem by taking out an ad in the Wall Street Journal: "Young Men with Unlimited Capital Looking for Interesting and Legitimate Business Ideas."

John Morris: Michael and Artie's lawyer, Miles Lourie, had read an ad in the <u>Wall Street Journal</u> saying "Young Men with Unlimited Capital Looking for Interesting Investment"—it really was an ad in the paper. And they met with John and Joel, but what they really wanted to do was open a studio in Woodstock, and John and Joel had a studio on Fifty-seventh Street, and they didn't really want another studio.

Joel Rosenman: In January of 1969, Mike Lang and Artie Kornfeld came to see John Roberts and me. They had an idea for a retreat recording studio in New York, and from that little idea Woodstock somehow happened eight and a half months later.

John Roberts: Miles Lourie had a couple of young clients named Mike Lang and Artie Kornfeld, who wanted to build a recording studio in Woodstock, New York, and thought we should meet because we'd have things to talk about.

Michael Lang is the face of the Woodstock founders to this day.

Ellen Sander: Michael had blond curly hair like a halo. He had a very kind of, oh, like, kind of a Michael J. Pollard face. He just had a sweet face. He was the quintessential hippie.

John Morris: "The curly-headed kid" [laughter]. We named him that early and it stuck! He had an interesting energy. He was very hip, of the era, a bright kid who had vision and saw that this could be turned into a festival and could make sense. There had been festivals before. What Michael wanted to do was to put on a three-day outdoor music event, and that's what we made happen.

Ellen Sander: Michael is a radiant soul; he was very gentle and a supremely intelligent person. He just is the kind of person who, when he walks into a room, you turn around and you look at him and you go, "Wow, who's that?" because he just seems to radiate something very appealing and very, very sweet. And I could see why musicians and creatives would gravitate toward him. I had no idea he was into production of this scale.

Michael Lang: I had been thinking about doing a series of concerts in Woodstock. And I had mentioned it to Artie. We used to kick it around every now and then, and then we got the idea of opening a recording studio up there, because it was such a good area for that. Bands liked it, and there were a lot of people living there—the Band and Janis Joplin and her band and Dylan and parts of Blood, Sweat and Tears—just lots of different producers and a lot of musicians coming in and out. Part of the plan was to have a rock concert to help promote the new studio.

Joel Rosenman: Within a very short period of time, we had enough written material to look at so we knew conclusively between ourselves that [the recording studio] was not the kind of project that we wanted to get involved in.

Michael Lang: One evening, we thought, Well, what if we did it all at once? And we thought, Well, it would probably be a good idea to do this festival, I remember at the time, and the studio also, and one sort of evolved out of the other, and make it a yearly event. Great way to kick it off, and it was also a great way to sort of culminate all these smaller events that had been going on for the past couple of years. Just get everybody together and look at each other and see what we're here about.

Joel Rosenman: It was that little addendum to their project proposal that caught our eye. I remember saying to John, "This is really a yawn, don't you think?" And he said, "There's no way that we would want to get into this project." And I said, "But you know the idea of having a concert with those stars. Why don't we just skip the studio idea and just do a big concert? We could make a fortune." And he said, "This is not what they're proposing." And I said, "Those guys will go for anything." I was wrong about that. They fought tooth and nail because they had already been to a couple of concerts. They knew what a rocky road you had to travel. They knew how difficult it was to get through a rock concert with your wallet and your hide intact.

Artie Kornfeld: And it just sort of came together. Michael talks about "How did it all happen?" He says, "Talking with Artie." And I would say that's how it happened. Talking with Michael and Linda [Kornfeld's wife]. I always feel Linda had as much to do with it as Michael or I. I was the music business guy, and Michael was the hippie, and Linda was in the middle. She was the spirit. When people say they never knew what was going to happen, if you ask Michael—this was before Joel and John—or if Linda was alive, we knew what was going to happen because we guessed. People would come. We talked about rain and what would happen. It would probably be a free concert because you never could control a crowd that big. And what the political ramifications would be. And we talked about how it would have to be nonpolitical to be political. And how we would have to deal. That was basically talked out that night, that first night, probably behind some Colombian Blond.

John Roberts: As it happens, the night before these guys came to see us, I'd seen the movie <u>Monterey Pop</u>. I had just been struck by the energy and the beauty and the music and the excitement of that particular event. I said to Michael and Artie, "You mean sort of like a <u>Monterey Pop</u>?" and they said, "No, no, no, nothing like that; you know, nothing big like that; just a little, a little thing, maybe a couple of thousand people." And Joel and I talked about this for a while and said, "You know, we really like this rock party idea a lot better than we do your recording studio, so why don't we do that instead?" And they said, "No, come on, we really want to do this recording studio." And we said, "Okay, fine, we'll do the rock festival first, we thought of then as a party, we'll do the party, we'll charge admission and we'll use the profits to build a recording studio—and since they had nowhere else to go—and they have about as much credibility as we did, which is to say none at all—they said, "Sure, that sounds fine to us." So that's how Woodstock was born.

Thus, the four began organizing the unprecedented event. Little did they know it would change the way rock 'n' roll was viewed by millions. They were an unlikely team, two squares, and two hippies. They had their run-ins and inherent conflicts.

Michael Lang: I guess my job, aside from assembling this band of men and women, was to mumble at the authorities to get us through this. John and Joel were either adventurous enough or crazy enough to join us, and the four of us went off to assemble this little event. It went on to have a profound effect on our lives and other people's lives.

Midway through Friday, Artie Kornfeld, Mike Lang, and John Morris had conferenced about the current state of the festival. The fences were down. People were getting in for free. The sheer population of the festival was overwhelming their capabilities. It was still about the music. It was still about entertaining. But it was no longer about making money. The priority of the festival founders was to avoid total pandemonium.

Artie Kornfeld, as captured in the *Woodstock* film, seemed pretty relaxed about the whole thing.

Artie Kornfeld: It's worth it. Just to see the lights go on last night, man. To see the, just to see the people stand up, man, it makes it worth it. It's, you know, I mean, I feel there, there will be people that, you know, there's people out there that like really don't dig it. Very few of them there. But you know, it really is to the point where it's just family, man.

Family or no family, someone had to foot the bill, and it certainly wasn't Artie Kornfeld. Joel Rosenman and John Roberts, the men responsible for fiscally backing the festival, were not nearly as groovy about the whole thing.

John Roberts: I think if I'd been privy to that conversation when it took place on August 17, 1969, I would have been pretty ticked off about it. We were the financial partners—we were the ones who were charged with cleaning it up, and paying all the bills, and making sure that all the lawsuits were taken care of afterwards. Since Michael and Artie didn't really have that much of a financial stake in it; in fact, they had no investment in it personally—they were profit participants—we felt, you know, that they were less than helpful and responsible about the aftermath.

Of course, the financial reality of the situation was the last thing on the minds of the folks laid back in Yasgur's field, gearing up for the second day of music. As we saw from the juggling that produced the opening-night order, the Woodstock lineup card was by no means etched in stone. It was clearly a case of necessity being the mother of invention. From the originally designated start time of 4:00 p.m. Friday to the actual closing time of 10:30 a.m. on Monday, traffic, weather, logistics, money matters, and old-fashioned music business clout were the real determining factors of this rock 'n' roll variation of who's on first. For all its peace-and-love trappings, Woodstock was firmly grounded in business, and very much beholden to the show business grid in place at the time. Woodstock would smash this paradigm to smithereens and render it irrevocably obsolete in its aftermath.

Hard-nosed agents and managers looking for the best billing, not to mention the dollar bills that they could get for their clients (and themselves, of course) ruled the day. There was also a lot of "It's not what you know, it's who you know" going on. As we've seen, Bert Sommer got the gig because of his association with Artie Kornfeld; Santana was there purely as a result of the clout of Bill Graham; and Saturday's opening act was there strictly through a connection with festival organizer Michael Lang.

Arthur Levy: Quill was one of the bands that were booked by Mike Lang's company, Amphion. That's why Quill was there. They were the opening band on Saturday. They are probably the only band of the whole weekend that was not a nationally known band. They were a Boston band. They had a record out. Their drummer was a famous guy named Roger North. He invented the North drum, which was a curved drum. Those drums became very popular with rock drummers. Curved tom-toms. They never really got their due. I roadied with them for about a week after college. They were kind of jazzy blues–based. They had some pop songs. They sounded like a lot of the other Boston bands at the time—Beacon Street Union and Far Cry. You know, that kind of bluesy psychedelic, stretched-out, jazzy, sometimes modal sound. They were a great band.

Quill was indeed a Boston-based band and a regional attraction along the Northeast corridor. Lang knew their manager from his Florida head shop days and conspired with him to put Quill on the bill for a couple of reasons. One was precisely because they were still largely unknown, and Michael was cocky and prescient enough to believe that an appearance at Woodstock (and hopefully in a movie about it) side by side with all the giant, headline, established recording stars scheduled to be there could be the launching pad to instant fame and fortune. (He was right, of course, but that band turned out to be Santana, not Quill. In the words of Maxwell Smart, "He missed it by *that* much!")

The second reason to have them around turned out to be a bit more successful. Lang called on Quill to quell growing community opposition and fears about the festival by "volunteering" them to do a series of free concerts at local prisons, hospitals, and mental institutions leading up to the big weekend. The band itself ranked this "minitour" among the weirdest it had ever done. Rock audiences at the time were often described as crazy and out of control, but Quill actually did a number of shows for audiences that were composed of people who were certifiably insane or convicted outlaws.

As quietly as Joan Baez had put the crowd to bed about 2:30 a.m., a voice came booming over the PA system midmorning startling the slumbering mass and paving the way for Day Two of music. It was Mel Lawrence. Not used to speaking to a mass of people that large, his first "Good morning!" pinned the VU meter on the soundboard into the red and startled the horde. Sheepishly, he reapproached the microphone and said, "Sorry about that. Let's try that one again . . . Good morning." And the sleeping giant in front of him returned polite applause. "Thank you. Listen, last night was incredible, and we just wanted to let you know that everything's okay. No hassles. We're going to have another groovy day today and into the night and tomorrow!" [*This time a roar of approval from the crowd.*] "We've gotta keep this place livable so we can prove to the rest of the world that we can make it together in peace and in comfort. And we're gonna do it, too!" [*Another roar, as if on cue.*]

Everything's okay? No hassles? That's not how the late John Roberts remembered it:

John Roberts: One of the things that concerned me the most was Governor Nelson Rockefeller, the governor of New York at that time, called me on the phone and told me he was thinking of sending in the National Guard, and I had to practically beg him not to do that. I said, "You know, what's happening here is utterly peaceful, and if you send in young people with rifles, I can't vouch for what's going to happen. So, why would you do that?" And he said, "Well, alright, than I won't; but if anything goes wrong it's entirely on your head." Spoken like a true politician. I said, "Thanks, Gov, I'm twenty-four years old—you know, I guess I'll have to live with that for the rest of my life."

John Morris: I'd already been on the phone with Nelson Rockefeller's chief of staff earlier in the morning, who wanted to send in the National Guard to clear the place out. We almost had an Attica. They went, alright give us a couple of minutes, and they called us in a couple of minutes and said, "Alright, go with it." Now they were digging themselves a gigantic financial hole, but they along with Max stood up and said, "This is what it is. This is what we have to do."

Asked directly how close the National Guard scenario came to reality, Morris replied emphatically:

John Morris: It was too goddamn close to happening. They panicked in Albany. They thought it was a bunch of dope-soaked hippies who were going to tear the place apart. In those towns, there were a number of people who were afraid that there was this horde that was going to come up over the hill and rape their daughters and eat their cows. Or rape their cows and eat their daughters. And I mean cannibalism. There was a fear. There was a tremendous fear if you look in the footage of <u>Woodstock</u> of the people who say "These kids are great. They're really nice. They're helping." Whatever. Or the people who went and got shotguns, and sat on their porch. Rockefeller's people said we are going to close down the area. We are going to surround it with National Guard and clear it out. And I went, no, you're not. What you're going to have is a gigantic massacre, which doesn't make sense. And I believe I talked, there were a number of phone calls going back and forth for a couple of hours and very early in the morning. I said you wanna do something right here? You want to help the people or these kids who are in your state, or are quote-unquote in your control? Send us medical supplies. Send us stuff that helps us to deal with it. The roads are locked up. I can't get artists in. What I'm doing now is hiring every helicopter I can lay my hands on. Now I don't believe you would give me National Guard helicopters to do that, but support us, and help us.

Fortunately for all, the Guard was never called in. Meanwhile, back at the stage, some prerecorded albums were blasted through the sound system for the cleanup. Then, about a quarter after twelve, real live music was ready to start up again. Quill took the stage, and while technical difficulties prevented their complete performance from being filmed, there is footage of the group handing out maracas and other percussion instruments to audience members in the front rows in an attempt to jump-start the massive crowd and get them back into the good mood, good vibrations, and good behavior that had been ignited the night before. Quill did their best, but couldn't get their or the crowd's mojo workin' and served basically as an appetizer for the headliners coming up later on the main menu including Creedence Clearwater Revival, the Grateful Dead, and Janis Joplin.

There was also another problem. It had been hot on Friday afternoon and evening, but it was *brutally* hot on Saturday afternoon with humidity through the celestial ceiling. That combined with the reality of hundreds of thousands of bodies packed into the same space in close proximity to one another—each one practicing varying degrees of physical hygiene—created a virtual bowl of human soup. And not necessarily a tasty one either! Let's put it this way: BO at Woodstock did not stand for "box office."

And body odor wasn't even the worst olfactory offense at Yasgur's farm. The toilet facilities were woefully lacking. The actual number of people present so overwhelmed the planned-for number of Portosans available that another very human, very noxious odor became a huge problem for many of the attendees. Harriet Schwartz was a nineteen-year-old employee of Warner Bros. who made the trip to Bethel on Friday afternoon after work and encountered all of the logistical difficulties that you can imagine just in the effort to get there before the music stopped on Friday night. But there was an even bigger obstacle to overcome by mid-afternoon on Saturday.

Jim Marion: There were endless delays on the stage, and we were getting pretty bored. Of course, we had been completely blasted for twenty-four hours. It didn't take long for our blankets to be covered with mud. As the beer warmed up, we gave a good bit of it away to our neighbors, then sat on the empty cartons. Beside the scent of burning joints, my primary olfactory memory of Woodstock was the smell of urine. I recall it rained a couple of times briefly, and we were concerned about the content of the runoff we were sitting in. The area where we were sitting really stank, and we had been polite enough to use our empty quart bottles as "recycling receptacles." For most of those around us, there really was nowhere to go since we were basically landlocked by others.

Harriet Schwartz: If you had to go [to the bathroom] at Woodstock, you probably would have been better off, pardon the expression, to go in the woods. But there were no woods. So, yeah, they were terrible, and it was because these portopotties, or whatever you call them, there was no way they could handle the influx, shall we say, of what they had to handle. So by the time you could get anywhere near one, and you did have to stand on line to get to one, your eyes were tearing. Your throat was closing. It was the most horrific stench I have ever smelled in my life. And once I got done with what I had to do there, I literally had to walk around to clear my head a little bit because I thought I was going to fall down . . . If you didn't love your neighbor, you were in a lot of trouble, because your neighbor was right at your elbow. They say a half a million, some say even seven hundred thousand showed up at Woodstock—the numbers fluctuate a lot. But I can tell you, we worked our way to fifty feet from center stage. It took us almost all of Saturday to do it, but once we did, that's where we stayed. And of course, the closer you got to the stage, the less room there was. It was like a mosh pit—<u>worse</u> than a mosh pit. So I was literally like an accordion. I would sit, my back would be on somebody else's knees, and somebody else's back would probably be on my knees. If you don't love people that are around you, you're in a lot of trouble. But everybody there generally was sweet, loving, caring. We were all in the same boat together. We <u>had</u> to be.

And maybe that really was one of the saving graces of Woodstock. But it certainly wasn't the best circumstances for a performer to go out there and entertain the crowd, particularly the lesser-known attractions who took the stage early on Saturday afternoon.

Jim Marion: We had heard the words "free concert" enough to know that this wasn't going to be the orderly show we'd expected. Nobody seemed to know who had played or when anyone would play again, so we found our way back to where we'd pitched our tent; picked up another one of my friends; grabbed some blankets, binoculars, and two cases of quarts of Schaefer beer; and headed back to the stage. It was probably early afternoon when we got back to the stage area, and, boorish as it probably was, we started weaving our way through the mud and sprawled-out bodies in an attempt to get closer. I think we felt, as ticket holders, that we had some innate right to be assholes and move closer, stepping on a number of people. We finally saw a small opening about three hundred yards from the stage and plopped down with our blankets and beer. A band was playing during this time, and my friend, a blues fan, said it was former John Mayall drummer Keef Hartley. I couldn't attest to that since the sound was awful and most of the crowd around us seemed comatose. After my beer consumption, herb consumption, no sleep, and sitting in the increasing heat, I promptly fell asleep.

At the end of Quill's set, another act needed to be put in front of the sweltering lions. That act happened to be the Keef Hartley Band. Keef had solid credentials in the English rock scene evolving from the light pop rock of the early British Invasion to the heavy blues-rock influence that had taken hold by the end of the decade. Hartley earned his stripes with John Mayall's Bluesbreakers, plus a stint with another group called Artwood (formed by Ronnie Wood's brother, Art. Get it? *Artwood.*) I distinctly remember discovering the Keef Hartley Band when I arrived at WNEW-FM in July of 1969. There was no playlist, just a rack of LPs in a bin behind me. The first random grouping was labeled NA, which stood for "new albums." Sitting somewhere in there was the new release by the Keef Hartley Band called *Half-Breed*. The cover art caught my eye, and the brassy, blues-rock caught my ear. I had just read their name in the commercial for Woodstock mentioned earlier, and I decided to play the title track of that new album on my first show at the radio station. I took a copy of it home with me to listen to the rest and remember thinking to myself, Yeah, these guys are definitely festival worthy. However, the band did not fare well at Woodstock. Part of it was the climatic conditions described earlier. But another part was definitely the chaotic stage logistics. Hartley's guitar player Miller Anderson described the situation to journalist Dmitry M. Epstein.

Miller Anderson: It all happened so fast. It was a new lineup of the Keef Hartley Band, and we were very underrehearsed . . . We did not play well, as we could not use our own equipment. We used Santana's gear. It was a missed chance for the band.

So far, Saturday was so-so. And, to complicate matters further, there was also some leftover business to take care of from the night before. One of the groups scheduled to play on Friday—the Incredible String Band—never made it on due to fears about playing electric instruments in the rain. The group's representative at the time, Joe Boyd, known today as a record producer and author of the well-received book about his experiences in the music business called *White Bicycles,* looks back at the decision not to play on Friday night as one of their worst. He told the Incredible String Band fanzine *Be Glad:*

> **Joe Boyd:** What happened then was I said, "You don't know what's going to happen—you may never get onstage," but they wanted to wait for the rain to stop and so someone else went on—Melanie—who triumphed in that slot and wrote "Candles in the Rain" about that exact moment! We talked to John Morris . . . who was a friend of mine, about the logistics of where we could pick up on the following day . . . and it sort of haunted me, that moment, because I should have pushed—just dragged them bodily to the stage and said, "Forget the amps, just play acoustically." It might have been wonderful, it might have been a great triumph—we might have been in the film and on the record, the whole thing! We ended up going on the following afternoon . . . in the baking sun. People were ready for something heavy and loud and they came on and just—died!

Group member Rose Simpson echoed Boyd's recollection to *Be Glad.*

> **Rose Simpson:** He should have just said, "Get on that blessed stage and you play, shut up moaning about getting wet, and get up there," and we should have done it, we were silly not to, he regrets it I know. The String Band would have had a different history if we had. One of our big mistakes really. I can see why we did it. We were a bit miffed really, it was just unpleasant, it wasn't very nice being in the wet and cold, hungry and not knowing how the hell we were going to go anywhere next.

It is said that the Incredible String Band was the only act that appeared at Woodstock not to be called back to the stage for an encore. Given the cards they were dealt, this is quite plausible. They were mellow, they were esoteric, they were progressive . . . and they were boring. I know this dismissive review will upset and outrage their still rabid fan base, but the fact is that they were simply the wrong group, in the wrong place, at the wrong time. It may have all worked just beautifully in a small air-conditioned theater setting such as the Fillmore East, but in that baking cow pasture in Bethel, they were more like the Not So Incredible String Band. A real shot in the arm was what was needed to salvage the day and kick-start Saturday afternoon at Woodstock into high gear.

SANTANA

Jim Marion: Our tent was at least a mile from the stage area. It was pitched in somebody's backyard, the occupants having fled. Most of the tents were geographically well removed from the stage area and spread all over creation. I'd also say that most of the attendees didn't even have tents, having come completely unprepared for what ensued. Once you were able to situate yourself in the stage area, you didn't leave. There were a lot of delays in the shows, and technical glitches, so the mood of the crowd early Saturday was a bit dicey. There was a lot of "downtime" for the audience, some of whom didn't move for three days!

It was Saturday afternoon. The heat, food and water shortages, sanitary problems, and sheer boredom and overcrowding were beginning to take their toll. If the promoters lost the goodwill of the audience, they would have lost everything. This hippie house of cards would get blown away faster than the fuzz on a dandelion, and even faster than the money in John Roberts's and Joel Rosenman's respective bank accounts.

Rescue came from an unlikely, unpremeditated source—a man and a band named Santana. But before we tell his story, you need to know about the man whose influence got him on the bill.

One of the most unique and colorful stories in all of rock 'n' roll history is that of Bill Graham. Born Wolfgang Grajonca in Berlin, Germany, in 1931, Graham was a Holocaust survivor who arrived in the United States with a group of Jewish orphans and was raised in a foster home in the Bronx. He chose the Americanized name William Graham from a phone book because it matched the initials of his birth name. He was drafted into the army and served his adopted country in the Korean War earning both a Bronze Star and a Purple Heart. He flirted with a show business career in the Catskill Mountains of New York State, but switched gears to concert promotion when he moved in the early '60s to San Francisco, where he found himself in the thick of the Bay Area's progressive-rock revolution. Combining a forceful personality with tremendous business acumen and showmanship, he rose to the level of top rock concert promoter in the country. And though not officially involved with Woodstock, he strode like a Colossus at the event leaving huge footprints in the mud at Yasgur's place.

Without Bill Graham, Woodstock would have been an entirely different beast. It may have not happened all. He was the father of the modern music industry. At the first Fillmore, out in San Francisco, he helped launch acts like the Grateful Dead and Jefferson Airplane. The scene was entirely different before Graham made his mark.

John Morris: Before Bill Graham, it was Murray the K and these DJs hosting group shows that radio stations put together. When he opened the Fillmore West, it was of course the place for all the San Francisco bands to happen and to begin. He created that. The first major concert in San Francisco was the Trips Festival, which Bill did because he was asked to as a benefit for Ken Kesey and a whole bunch of other people. He just looked at it and said, "This makes a lot of sense. There's a lot of money here. Somebody needs to put it together and organize it."

Bill had been a student of the Actors Studio. Possibly because of his theatrical background, he brought drama to the music.

John Morris: He turned it into a theatrical business, or a theatrical presentation—add lighting, add curtains, add staging, promote it as a show.

His flair for booking was unlike anyone else's.

Stan Schnier: If you look at the way Bill Graham booked shows, that's where all this comes from, because only Bill had that—I don't know if it was brilliance or luck—he would put James Brown on the bill with Pearls Before Swine, and no one ever did that before, no one ever did afterwards. But for a little window of time, he was willing to put any-body with anybody if he thought it was interesting. And we know the obvious results: people like B.B. King suddenly got to play for white kids and they were in shock.

This was, of course, pre-Woodstock, when acts were just a few thou-sand to book. But Graham demonstrated that there was an audience and that they were willing to spend money for the music they wanted to hear. People like Michael Lang were paying attention. Graham founded the Fillmore East in New York, just off the NYU campus, and brought the music scene he had built out west, to the East Coast.

John Morris: I talked him into coming to New York—because the stuff that was being done in New York was all very ad hoc, very much of a mess. And there was no production to it.

Jim Marion: My friends and I had been attending rock concerts since 1966, and, after it opened in early 1968, we'd become "Fillmore rats" at the Fillmore East, which was our gold standard for concert venues. Every week, I'd look for the advertisement in the Sunday New York Times entertainment section, to check the upcoming Fillmore shows.

Feared and revered throughout the industry, Graham had created a new way of seeing music. And he did it with soul.

John Morris: My contribution to Graham was that I had a theater back-ground and had done technical and had actually tried to be an actor once. We wanted to put production values into it.

Bob See: He had a certain production value that I never saw with any other promoter. He felt that the performer was important but that all the things surrounding the performer were equally important. Whether it be how to dress your set up, whether it be the environment the per-former performed in. He was very intent on making the Fillmore East a theatrical event, not just this get 'em in, do this, do that.

A role model, a tyrant, a pioneer, Graham revolutionized the business and left a mark on everyone he worked with.

SANTANA

John Morris: There's no such thing as a general impression of Bill! [laughs]. Bill was a dynamo. I would say the thing about Bill if you were going to try to sum him up is that he was a person who could never find the peace and happiness he wanted. But without him, there would be no rock 'n' roll business.

Stan Schnier: He was really astute, he was incredibly aggressive, he was unbelievably competitive. I mean, if you were trying to compete with him, he would squash you. Chet Helms out in San Francisco was promoting a little show. Bill just, like, steamrolled him. Bill said, "You think you're gonna book so-and-so? Fuck you!" He tied everything up. He was aggressive, hungry, hardworking. That's all he did.

Joshua White: Bill, because of his age and his wisdom, and who he was, he could straddle both worlds. He had no problem. He was a Holocaust survivor. He had no problem adapting. He adapted to being an American, he adapted to being a kid from the Bronx, he adapted to being an underemployed actor in New York, and he adapted to being a member of the San Francisco mime troupe. He adapted at every step because that's what survivors do. Bill managed to be the one person who could adapt to both the business reality of the scene and still be able to stand up to the performers. And these people were very crazed. They played beautifully, but they were filled with anger. And the person who was willing to stand up and deflect those angers was Bill.

Stan Schnier: I thought that Bill Graham was it. I was close to my father, so I don't know if you could say he was a father figure to me, I'm not a psychologist—but my roommate and I just absolutely adored Bill. We thought he was the greatest thing in the world because he would stand in the office and he would tell people like James Brown and Chuck Berry, "Fuck you! You fucking show up on time or you can go fuck yourself," and "You'll never work for me again, I don't give a shit! You get the fuck onstage . . . when I say eight o'clock, I fucking mean it!" And he'd scream and everybody else there would say, "Whoa, Bill, that's Chuck Berry." And Bill would say, "I don't give a fuck who you are!" So we always thought that was great.

And sometimes his tactics led to blows:

Stan Schnier: One night some Hell's Angels came in the front door and they said, "We want to come in for free." And I said, "Well, nobody gets in here for free unless Bill says you can come in for free." "Yeah, well, we're coming in. Fuck you!" and I said, "Well, hold on a second," and I said, "Hey, Bill, these guys want to come in for free." Bill said, "No way." And the guy said, "Yeah, well, fuck you, man, we're coming in for free." "The hell you will!" And the guy took out a big chain from his motorcycle and he whacked him, and he broke two or three of Bill's ribs.

There was a lighter side to Graham, a celebratory side.

Bob See: We were doing the Chambers Brothers and they used to have a cowbell that they used to bang and during one of their songs ["Time Has Come Today"] Bill got the cowbell and was there on the side of the stage, and Bill came through and he was pounding on the bell with everybody else. He would get into the enjoyment as an audience participant as well as being there and dealing with putting it all together.

Graham's instincts reached an extended family of musicians that included a soon-to-be rising star. Carlos Santana was born on July 20, 1947, in Autlán de Navarro, Mexico. His father, his grandfather, and his great-grandfather were all musicians, so Carlos's destiny was sealed at a pretty young age. He began by playing violin but soon switched to guitar and learned his craft in the saloons and brothels of Tijuana.

Moving to San Francisco in 1966, he fell in with a group of musicians playing a fiery brand of African and Latin music mixed seamlessly with American rock 'n' roll. The original five-man ensemble featured Carlos on guitar, David Brown on bass, Gregg Rolie on keyboards, Tom Frazer on rhythm guitar, and Rod Harper on drums. They called themselves the Santana Blues Band not because Carlos viewed himself as the center of it, but because the musicians' union required each local performing unit to name a designated leader. Carlos accepted the assignment reluctantly. As the group evolved, "Blues Band" was dropped from their name, and a couple of personnel subtractions and additions were made. Gone were Frazer and Harper, and added were percussionists Mike Carabello and José Chipito Areas as well as a new young drummer from the Bay Area by the name of Michael Shrieve.

SANTANA

Michael Shrieve: I had already seen Santana, and I really liked them. They said, "We're thinking about getting another drummer and we heard you play your sound really good. Can we get your number?" And I said, "Sure." They took my number and I didn't hear from them. There was a studio in San Mateo, which is a city in between Redwood City and San Francisco, where I used to hustle studio time for whatever group I had going. One night I went in there and as I was walking in, literally walking in the door, Doc Livingston, the drummer of Santana, was walking out. They had had a fight. A couple of the guys remembered me. They were recording their album—they had been signed. They remembered me, they asked me to jam, and at the end of the night they took me in the side room and asked me if I wanted to join the band. So I said, "Let me check my schedule." They drove me home. They followed me to my parents' house and I woke my folks up and said, "This is where I get off. I know you've been expecting this." So they took me up, and I took my place on the couch in the Mission District, and we got started.

The precise chemistry of the group was essential, and they made every effort to integrate Shrieve into the balance.

Michael Shrieve: So they scrapped the album and we started doing some live dates to work me in. It was a real natural thing. We did a lot of rehearsing. I learned really early that the rehearsals were really intense. That's why I say it wasn't a hippie thing, because if you made a mistake they were all over you, you know, making fun of you, talking about your momma. It wasn't like, "Oh yeah, that's beautiful, man, whatever." It wasn't like that. I mean, you had a Mexican, a Nicaraguan, a Puerto Rican, a militant black, and two white boys from the suburbs. It was intense, but I loved it. It was really great. We rehearsed really hard, and then we'd go over to the Fillmore, 'cause we could always get in for free and check out to see if there was something we could learn from the band—and if not, we'd look at the pretty girls.

Initially fans weren't that welcoming to the new player.

Michael Shrieve: I remember playing at the Fillmore for the first time with them, and there was actually booing because they were getting popular and the audience thought, Where's the drummer? After I did a drum solo I got a standing ovation. Then I felt it was good. So that was the way it happened.

Everybody knew everybody in that thriving San Francisco rock scene so it's no surprise that reigning rock impresario Bill Graham took a shine to Santana from the get-go. Bill claimed in his autobiography that Santana was the only band to headline the Fillmore West without having made a record. Graham also wrote in the liner notes for Santana's box set:

> For as long as I can remember, whether I was alone or with others, I've had an insatiable romance with Latin music. When I got into rock 'n' roll, people like Michael Bloomfield and Paul Butterfield introduced me to the world of B.B. King and Bobby "Blue" Bland, the Staple Singers and Muddy Waters, thus began an affair with the blues. So when I heard Santana that very first time at the Fillmore, it was as though these loves had mated and borne a child. Through the years, I've seen and felt the evolution of this band, this sound, this spirit. It's mature and yet forever young; full of innocence and guilt, passion, and tranquility. The essence of Santana provokes my sensuality. It allows my heart to soar, and commands my body to move. That's the highest that any artist's expression can take me.

Joshua White: Bill has an enormous love for Latin music. From his days in the '50s in New York, he couldn't wait to put Mongo Santa Maria on the bill. He went up to Spanish Harlem to listen to music. In the end of his life, when he was too rich and too bored, he dabbled in acting, and there is a scene in Bugsy where you see Bill Graham tangoing in the background. He just loved Spanish music more than anything else, and for good reason, because it was amazingly bright. I have a little bit of this because there was a whole Latin moment in the '50s when I was a kid where we all danced the mambo and knew who the artists were and listened to Symphony Sid on the radio and appreciated it. Santana was the perfect band for Bill because they were young, he could mold them, and they were not spoiled, and they played fucking amazing Latin music, unbelievable Latin-based rock. And the leader was a great virtuoso musician.

That certainly explains personally, professionally, spiritually, and emotionally why Santana became such a big chip in Graham's Woodstock negotiations.

SANTANA

Bill Graham: It was obvious to me that [the Woodstock organizers] were rank amateurs who were in way over their heads. But anybody who would've tried what they were doing would've been a rank amateur. Because it had never been done before. These people had very little or no experience in either public assemblage or presenting music. They had no reason to be nervous about me or what I might do to their festival, but they did come to me. We talked on the phone, and then there was a meeting in a loft somewhere in New York.

It was very clear what our relationship would be. I would tell them the bands that I thought would help them whom they hadn't yet thought of themselves. If there were bands they had chosen that they wanted me to comment on, I would. They were having trouble with some bands and they wanted to use my name and say that I was involved.

I knew they had Chip Monck doing the staging so I could vouch for their personnel. I was not running the operation so I could not guarantee what would happen, but I said they could use my name. In return for Santana being put on the show on Saturday night. During prime time. Which was difficult. I didn't want them on at seven in the morning or three in the afternoon. Because Santana still had no album. People on the East Coast had heard of them. But never really seen them before.

Bill Belmont: The person that was doing most of the talking and most of the booking and most of the negotiating was John Morris. John did almost everything. Michael Lang appeared to be a principal only later on as the summer wore on. In May, Santana went back east for their first eastern trip.

Bill Graham: Michael Lang called me and he said, "Bill, we're doing this and we've got this place upstate and a lot of bands are reluctant to come in." I was telling them who they should book and on the other end, I was telling agents and managers that this was okay to do. That it could work. But I was never involved in any of the negotiations that went on.

Carlos Santana: Of course, it was Bill Graham. Bill was approached by Michael Lang to help him out because he certainly had experience putting concerts together. And Bill had a fascination and an obsession with us, like he did with the Grateful Dead. He said, "I'll help you, but you've got to put Santana on." "Who's Santana?" They didn't know us from Adam, you know? So he stuck to his guns and they let us play.

John Morris: I had gone to California, and I saw Santana, and I said, "Oh my God!" The music is fabulous, the people are fabulous, the drummer is unbelievable, and the guitarist is just killer, and he's not the lead singer—that's pretty interesting. Then I saw them a couple of times over the weekend, and I said to Bill, "Who's their manager?" and he said, "They don't have one right now," and I said, "You're out of your mind. You've gotta get 'em." He did later, but he didn't then. And I got on the phone and I called two people that I knew pretty well, Jac Holzman at Elektra, and I called Clive Davis, and I said, "Get on a plane and come to San Francisco. I have just seen the most exciting act I've seen in ages." Clive came and listened and signed them. I wanted Santana. Bill wanted Santana. I wanted the Grateful Dead. Bill wanted the Grateful Dead, so it's entirely possible that there were maneuverings there.

Bill Belmont: The only way Graham could give them the Grateful Dead was if they took Santana, and that's how Santana got on the bill for twenty-five hundred dollars. Michael Lang was like, "Who the fuck is this band anyway?" It's true that John knew the band and liked them, but Graham forced them on as a way of solidifying the Grateful Dead.

Michael Shrieve: All these festivals were going on. And then we heard about Woodstock. But nobody knew us, really. And Bill Graham finagled us in there. If it wasn't for him, we wouldn't have been on. We had no record out, but we were touring and we were playing with all the big groups like Chicago and the Airplane and Janis Joplin and Big Brother. We were good. We were holding our own.

Carlos Santana was conscious of being an unknown among giants.

Carlos Santana: It's always a compliment to be on the same stage with Jimi Hendrix and Sly Stone, Ravi Shankar, Richie Havens, and of course everybody else. To me, it was a supreme honor.

However, he was confident in Santana's ability to stand out.

Carlos Santana: I'm not trying to sound cocky or anything, but anybody else, I felt, we could give them a good run for their money. But Jimi and Sly were just on a whole other level—kind of like Michael Jordan. We knew that they had different kinds of spirits hovering around them. In other words, it wasn't just Jimi Hendrix's fingers playing that guitar. He had different kinds of spirits and ghosts around him. And I knew that. But everybody else—I felt that we could give them a good run. I just felt that we were equipped to deal with their audience. See, at that point we had been opening up for Janis Joplin in Chicago. And Paul Butterfield. And we saw how the band was taking the audience. They would boo us because they wanted to hear more Johnny Winter or Janis Joplin or Buddy Miles, but as soon as we played, they went, "Oooh! More!" All of a sudden, the women started discovering spiritual orgasms. They started dancing and their eyes rolled back to their ears. And they were laughing and crying and dancing at the same time—pretty much like a Grateful Dead concert. So we had confidence that we had brought something else to the table.

They took the stage, and Michael Shrieve looked out over the biggest crowd he had ever seen.

Michael Shrieve: I was an ex-surfer, and it was like standing at the ocean. As far as you could see, except for the horizon, were people. It was difficult to relate to. It was almost too much. Later I learned, after being in Santana and playing big concerts, that it became more frightening to play in smaller clubs because now you had intimate contact. They were saying that this was the biggest crowd that had ever been for a concert. I'd be lying if I didn't say it was intimidating.

And as for the performance?

Jim Marion: My friend, who had seen Santana earlier in the summer, woke me up for their set, which was one of the better performances that we saw. It brought the crowd to life. I spent most of the set with the binoculars on drummer Mike Shrieve, who was incredible.

John Morris: They were great. Really great. I had an advantage. I was up onstage, and I could look back at the audience, so I could see that these guys were just knocking them dead. They were hitting it out of the park. I was just very happy. I was right. Graham was right. Clive was right. All sorts of people were right. And at that point, we knew that this was a major, major event.

At first, the Woodstock Festival seemed like it'd just be another stop on the Santana tour. But it soon became obvious that this was something very different.

Michael Shrieve: The promoters, Michael Lang and John—all those people had their work cut out for them. Everybody was running around. And we were not supposed to play until later in the day. We'd go on and off the stage and walk around. It was a scene that although it's been talked about as if it was magical and beautiful, it was a mess, too, because they weren't prepared for this many people. Nobody knew that this was going to happen. This was definitely the culmination of the hippie nation, and everybody was into it, saying, "Yeah, look, we, we did take over the world. These are our numbers. And the music represents it, and we're coming together now. This is a force to contend with."

Carlos Santana: It's always a <u>high</u> and a <u>highlight</u> to remember the sound. I remember the sound before it came out of my fingers, then I heard it come out of my fingers into the guitar strings. From the guitar to the amplifier. From the amplifier to the PA. From the PA to a whole ocean of people—a mountain—a whole ocean of people, and then it comes back to you. You never forget that. That's where I discovered my first mantra. Most people know by now that I was totally peaking on mescaline, because they told me I didn't have to play until two o'clock in the morning or something. They lied to us. As soon as I took it and started totally flashing, it was two o'clock in the afternoon. So that was the first time I repeated my first mantra, which was, "God! Please help me stay in time and in tune!" I just repeated that mantra.

When Santana finally took the stage Saturday, no one was prepared for the sound they made.

Marty Brooks: On Saturday, with the sun shining, we walked back down the main road to the concert site. We didn't have any food with us, so we skipped breakfast. On the main road, behind stage right was a large boulder. That boulder became a meeting place, and we walked out there several times during the show. One time while we were out there, we heard an incredibly intense and exciting sound coming from the stage playing a type of music that I had never heard before. I said,

"We've got to get back on the grounds and see this band!" It was Santana and for me, they were the highlight of the festival.

Ellen Sander: I had never seen Santana before and I grew up in New York. I had never really appreciated Latin music, although it was certainly around. I mean, it was music that Puerto Ricans listened to. Latin music was around, but I never really listened to it. José Feliciano was my only exposure to Latin music at that point, and he wasn't that Latin.

Bob Santelli: You talk to people who had been to Woodstock, you hear [Santana] on the soundtrack, you watch them on the film, and you can see what a powerful performance they turned in. One of the best at the festival. And that was completely unknown to a large majority of people who were at Woodstock.

Ellen Sander: Santana's sound is very rhythmic and uplifting and very fully orchestrated. And it was very different from most of the mainstream rock 'n' roll we'd been listening to. It was just a very refreshing thing.

Michael Shrieve: The experience was exhilarating and exciting, and we did feel a connection with the audience and felt that, in watching them, the rhythmic stuff that we were playing made a real immediate connection with the people. I'm not just saying it was myself or the rhythm section. It was just that it was kind of rhythm-based music. And a lot of the instrumentals were very different than a lot of the music that was at the show and different than the music that was going on at the time, and it connected to large groups of people.

Michael Wadleigh: They were fantastic. To me the lyrics were unimportant. They were an international band, they were really multiracial and multisound with their conga drums, a real world group. An incredible performance. Michael Shrieve gave an unforgettable drum solo.

Michael Shrieve: But the thing about Santana was we played in a semicircle. We played to each other. We didn't think of ourselves as entertainers. We thought of ourselves as musicians who really tried to get something happening. We're a tribal sort of band, with the rhythm. We played African music, we played Latin stuff. The whole groove thing was based off of more African. And it worked that day. It was working everywhere we played. That day happened to be filmed, and that day happened to turn into a movie. And when we were done with the last song, the people went nuts.

The band members weren't necessarily pleased with everything in the set that day.

Carlos Santana: Not too many people fared well that day, or those three days because a lot of people had electricity problems. Actually, we lucked out, or I lucked out, because by the time we did "Soul Sacrifice," I was more coherent. The first stuff—I don't even want to hear it! I was really, really stoned or high or both.

Santana's debut album was still a month away from wide release and distribution, but it did serve as the template for the material that they performed at Woodstock. Opening with the first track on side one of the album, "Waiting," they didn't keep the crowd waiting any longer as they ripped through four other tracks from the disc including "You Just Don't Care," "Savor," "Jingo," and "Persuasion." It was the next song, however, that established Santana as the baby superstars at Woodstock.

Michael Shrieve: It was a tough set for us. And fortunately, this song, "Soul Sacrifice," came out okay because we really wondered about a lot of the rest of it. It wasn't until years later that I heard some of the other stuff and it didn't sound so good.

Though their success was inevitable, their appearance at Woodstock was the event that really launched them. Their appearance in the film, and "Soul Sacrifice" on the album are among the most popular. Their careers had changed forever.

Stan Schnier: There is nothing in that movie that comes close to the energy of Carlos Santana. It was like an out-of-body experience to see these guys. They were really, really young, and it's just all fire. I personally just have never seen anything that raw and in your face, ever. I've never seen other bands play with that much piss and vinegar. It's the time. Again, it's one of these convergences, but it is amazing, there's something about Carlos Santana at that time that was just on another planet. I might be crazy, maybe you wouldn't agree with me, but the energy of that performance was just beyond anything else that was going on.

Bob Santelli: Not surprisingly, by the end of the year, if my memory serves me well, Santana's first album was number one or close to number one on the album charts when Columbia released it.

Carlos Santana went to see the film for the first time with Jimi Hendrix's then-girlfriend, Devon Wilson.

Carlos Santana: She took me to see the screening of the movie. Jimi had seen it the night before, but he had left that day to go to Hawaii to play that Rainbow Bridge concert. And she said, "Jimi was really high on you guys!" "Really?" "Yeah. Wait 'til you see your part." "Okay." And we went to see it and it was a real flash to be in the company of Sly and Jimi, and actually be able to hold court. To captivate people's attention is not easy.

As for many of the Woodstock goers, the festival's significance goes beyond the lineup of performances.

Carlos Santana: The hippies shared whatever they had—food, carrot salad with raisins, tents, a joint—how they shared everything. Four hundred fifty thousand, or however many people were there, it was a living organism of people. A lot of people saw the mud, a lot of people saw the ugly things, but this is what I saw. I can only give you my vision of what I saw, and what I saw was a true harmonious convergence. It was the beginning of consciousness revolution on a mass scale. People who changed the war in Vietnam. People who changed the universities. People who altered and challenged the consciousness of this country— challenged Nixon, challenged everybody. If it weren't for them, we'd probably still be in Vietnam!

CANNED HEAT

Dale Bell: The festival itself was a trip back to the garden. It was inherent in the lyrics. People were talking about going back to green. Going back to the environment. Going back to the garden. Getting away from the city. Getting away from the war. Coming together. Living together as family. An open-marriage kind of concept was prevailing at the end of the '60s and early '70s. This whole concept of getting back to the garden. Where I think today a lot of the music and lyrics really hearken back to the movement that initially began in California with John Muir in the 1800s. It certainly prospered throughout California with its legislation and policies. The first national parks were declared out here by Teddy Roosevelt and John Muir. Thor Heyerdahl wrote his book <u>Kon-Tiki</u> in 1951, where he sailed across the Pacific and discovered pollution in the oceans. Rachel Carson wrote <u>Silent Spring</u> in 1962. There was real talk about the environment and what we should do about it. Eliminating pesticides was step one in the process, but there were many other components of trying to go to green. <u>Woodstock</u> embodied and gathered together a lot of those concepts. We know for sure the first Earth Day took place just one month after <u>Woodstock</u> opened. They had to be planning it way long before this . . . but when Gaylord Nelson and Denis Hayes, the two founders of Earth Day, saw what happened in August of '69, a peaceful gathering of five hundred thousand people, they thought to themselves, you know, it might be possible to create a special day to celebrate the earth. I know this was their thinking, and we were responsible for being able to demonstrate that. I'd like to think those of us who made the film may have helped a little to create that conversation.

Certainly, the Hog Farm's approach to the festival echoed this sentiment. Wes Pomeroy, who was overseeing security on site, delegated responsibility to the Hog Farm. He provided them with armbands to identify themselves.

Wavy Gravy: I don't remember who asked us, but they said how many armbands are you gonna need for this? And Ken Babbs of the Merry Pranksters who drove all the way across the country to be involved, said, "Well, how many people are you expecting?" "About a couple hundred thousand." And he said, "Well, that should be sufficient." Everyone turned kind of white. We settled on a couple hundred. We kept printing them up with a potato. Whenever we went into the audience, we had about twenty armbands, and if we saw someone act responsibly, we gave them ten. In that way, at the end of the festival, a lot of people were taken into our community. Like Janis Joplin said, "If you've got any food left, share it with your brother and your sister. That's the person on your left and the person on your right." People learned about sharing and what it was all about.

Michael Wadleigh: Looking at the film, you can clearly see that Woodstock wasn't about material values. You look at that simple, wooden, unpainted stage with no backdrop and you see these performers come on in rags, and they're some of the greatest performers of all time. Talk about going gentle on the land, you talk about low carbon footprint. That was one of the lowest you could possibly imagine. A lot of people walked and hitchhiked just to get there. People just weren't into the production effort that subsequent festivals have gone into.

For Mike Wadleigh, a song that was particularly representative of the green sentiment at Woodstock was Canned Heat's "Going Up the Country." In 1969, the rock 'n' roll tree grew a brand-new branch that harkened back to the country and western half of its roots. Dylan released *Nashville Skyline* with that new "country squire" voice. Poco was born. Rick Nelson's Stone Canyon Band was thriving. And Canned Heat captured the whole bucolic sensibility with their hit "Going Up the Country."

Michael Wadleigh: Canned Heat is just one of my favorites . . . I loved that group. They were musicians' musicians. They were known as the best good-time-boogie band ever. Very, very much a part of the Woodstock generation. They were loved by everybody. Everybody's favorite people. Hite is just so friendly. And then the fan comes onstage and he gives him a cigarette and a hug. It was really in the spirit of Woodstock. They were friendly and really a part of the audience. I used a couple of songs about camaraderie and friends.

The mere mention of a group's name conjures up an image. With Canned Heat, it's probably "Boogie Band" or "Good Time Music." While both of those are accurate appellations, they only tell a part of the story. Canned Heat was a consortium of collectors, fans, and scholars. The group formed in 1966, centered around a trio of true rock 'n' roll personalities: Bob "Bear" Hite, Henry "Sunflower" Vestine, and Al "Blind Owl" Wilson. (The group was clearly big on nicknames: future members included Adolpho "Fito" de la Para, Harvey "the Snake" Mandel, and so on.) Evolving out of a mid-'60s jug band, Canned Heat made a sharp left turn into the blues and never looked back.

They took their name from an obscure 1928 song called "Canned Heat Blues" by Tommy Johnson. And if you're looking for a drug reference in the nomenclature, it's certainly there. Johnson was writing about the venerable cooking fuel Sterno, which, if used carefully, provided the "chef" with a cheap high in the era of Prohibition. Used carelessly, it could result in blindness or even death. Johnson himself died, ironically, of alcoholic poisoning related to abuse of the substance.

Canned Heat embraced the masters of the genre and lovingly recreated and updated the music of Howlin' Wolf, Muddy Waters, et al. Some critics dismissed them as popularizers more than purists, but others lauded their efforts. The jazz bible *Downbeat* magazine wrote:

Technically, Vestine and Wilson are quite possibly the best two-guitar team in the world and Wilson has certainly become our finest white blues harmonica man. Together with powerhouse vocalist Bob Hite, they performed the country and Chicago blues idiom of the 1950s so skillfully and naturally that the question of which race the music belongs to becomes totally irrelevant.

Further distinguishing Canned Heat from their competitors was their ability to put hits on the American and international pop charts: "On the Road Again" and "Going Up the Country" in 1968/69, and a cover of Wilbert Harrison's "Let's Work Together" in 1970. Audiences didn't seem to take sides with the "popularizer" issue. They just bought the records, flocked to the shows, and got off their asses and danced. By the time Woodstock rolled around, Canned Heat was a favorite on the festival circuit and, like Janis, Jimi, and the Who, were veterans of the landmark Monterey International Pop Festival in 1967.

It is often said about one pop band or another that they are bigger than life. In the case of Canned Heat, it rings true. The late Bob "Bear" Hite earned his nickname with a big, bushy black beard and a three-hundred-pound-plus frame. The late Al "Blind Owl" Wilson *was* partly blind and had a Kermit-the-Frog-like voice just as Kermit himself was gaining popularity. The Heat was as much fun to watch as they were to listen to, which had been borne out by their appearance in the film *Monterey Pop.*

John Morris: God rest Big Bear Hite. One of the greatest bar bands in the world. You know you're happy when you're listening to Canned Heat. They were good and they just . . . they got you going. They made you feel good.

The group was at the height of their powers in mid-1968 when *Downbeat* once again proclaimed their greatness to readers in this review:

. . . probably the best band of its type in the world today, playing with a power and conviction, and generating an excitement which has been matched by only the finest of the Negro bands in this idiom, early post-war blues music. One would, in fact, have to go back to the great innovators of the genre . . . Muddy Waters, Howlin' Wolf, John Lee Hooker, Elmore James, Little Walter and the like . . . to find groups comparable to Canned Heat in mastery, ease, and inventiveness.

Much is made of the fact that Woodstock was only Crosby, Stills, Nash and Young's second gig together. This is largely due to Stills and Crosby's very public comment about it from the Woodstock stage. You remember. Something about being "scared shitless." Well, there was an equally auspicious though less heralded "second or third appearance" scenario at the festival, and it involved Canned Heat. In late July, internal squabbling within the band led Henry Vestine to quit just when the group was scheduled to play two shows at Fillmore West. Mike Bloomfield filled in for one of the shows but had no intention of becoming a full-time group member. Chicago musician extraordinaire Harvey Mandel, who had worked with legends such as Barry Goldberg and Charlie Musselwhite, and was almost Mick Taylor's replacement in the Rolling Stones in 1976 (Ron Wood got the gig instead), filled in for Vestine at that second show, was offered the position full-time, accepted it, and headed east with the band to fulfill a couple of dates in New York State. First up were two shows at the Fillmore East, followed almost immediately by a festival gig somewhere upstate.

Bob Hite told *Sounds* magazine in 1974: "We've always just fallen into something within a couple of days and then just gone out on the road and played. Sometimes it's shown it and sometimes it's been incredible. The Woodstock performance, which although there were a couple of tunes which weren't too good—'Going Up the Country' was one of them—there were some which were killers, stone killers. And that was with Harvey Mandel who had only been with us for one set before we'd done Woodstock and that was just a big jam. We all just like to play music."

Although Mike Wadleigh loved their music and what they stood for, he did not include any footage of the band in his first cut of the film *Woodstock*. "Going Up the Country" itself was featured, however. Though the band's performance did make it into the director's cut many years later, the release of the original Canned Heat–less *Woodstock* in 1970 did little to boost their careers. In May 1970, Harvey Mandel left Canned Heat to join up with John Mayall's legendary Bluesbreakers. And the real death knell for Canned Heat as we knew them came with the suicide of Al Wilson on September 3 at the age of twenty-seven. (The same age, by the way, that you hear about more often connecting the deaths of Jimi Hendrix, Janis Joplin, and Jim Morrison.) Hite died of a heart attack on April 5, 1981, and Henry Vestine passed away in Paris, France, at the end of a European tour by some configuration of Canned Heat in name only on October 20, 1997.

If Wilson and Hite had survived—if the group's visually arresting, musically satisfying, and energetic and charismatic performance had not been left on the cutting-room floor of the original documentary—I think Canned Heat's legacy would shine even brighter than it does. We'll never know. It remains just another one of those tantalizing Woodstock unanswerables.

MOUNTAIN

From the moment Santana began playing on Saturday afternoon, the sounds kept getting louder and the acts kept getting bigger—both literally and figuratively. The "heavyweight" jokes about Canned Heat and Mountain just beg to be told, but that would only diminish the real impact that both groups had on the music world. Nevertheless, if Bob Hite's girth was solid proof of how sturdy the Woodstock stage was, an even greater test of that fresh plywood's resilience was waiting in the wings. The relatively new group Mountain featuring Leslie West and Felix Pappalardi was about to take the stage. This was only their fourth appearance together, but both had extremely impressive résumés.

Felix Pappalardi is best remembered today as the producer of Cream and as a founding member of Mountain, ultimately (much like Cream) a power rock trio often credited as creators of the then-nascent brand of American hard rock called heavy metal. (The phrase itself comes from the lyrics of Steppenwolf's huge 1968 hit "Born to Be Wild"). Pappalardi's credentials go all the way back to the folk boom of the early '60s. He was born in the Bronx in 1939, and studied music lit, conducting, orchestration, trumpet, viola, and bass guitar at the University of Michigan before making his way back to New York and the burgeoning music scene in Greenwich Village. He told *ZigZag* magazine in 1971:

Felix Pappalardi: The thing that brought me down there in the first place was that all the best musicians I'd ever heard were down there and living within a twenty- or thirty-square block area of one another.

I started just going down there at weekends, then got to staying there overnight, and finally left home and stayed there forever it seems like. To begin with, I was just playing guitar and singing, then I played a six-string Mexican bass called a <u>guitarrón</u> behind people like Tom Rush and Tom Paxton. I teamed up with John Sebastian and various other people, and we became studio musicians for Elektra and Vanguard, as well as accompanying people like Fred Neil in the clubs. It was a great period of time for me. I loved it.

Felix tried his hand at producing and, not surprisingly, found that he was very good at it. His plum assignment was being chosen to produce two of the most groundbreaking and successful progressive-rock albums of the mid-'60s—Cream's *Disraeli Gears* and *Wheels of Fire*. His reputation as a producer offered him the opportunity of working with a wide variety of other artists including the Youngbloods, for whom he produced the durable hippie anthem "Get Together." He also produced a couple of sides for a regionally popular Long Island–based group called the Vagrants, which centered around a literal mountain of a man named Leslie West.

> **John Morris:** The three-hundred-pound psychedelic canary. That's what he used to be known as . . . Leslie and I go back to one of the first concerts I ever did. I did a thing on Long Island at the Mineola Playhouse, and they were late, and I was on the stage announcing that they weren't gonna come and that I'm really sorry, and all of a sudden I look up and there is this three-hundred-pound tackle running at me with feathers all over the place—a leather shirt—goes into a knee-slide, wraps his arms around my leg, and says, "Man! Mr. Man! Please let us play, Mr. Man! We're late, but we wanna play! Please Mr. Man!" and Gary Kurfurst, their manager in those days was a good friend, and of course, Felix Pappalardi was just an amazing player and person. And their music was just really good.

Leslie West is as good a storyteller as he is a guitarist. And what a story he has to tell:

> **Leslie West:** A few years passed by. My brother Larry and I were in this group called the Vagrants. Then we had this producer named Felix Pappalardi that did our single, and my brother says, "You know what. Listen

to this group." And I look at the back of the album. It says, "Cream produced by Felix Pappalardi." I said to my brother, "Wait a minute. Is this
the same guy that produced the Vagrants that produced this group?"
He says, "Same guy." I said, "How come we don't sound like Cream?"
He says, " 'Cause we suck! You didn't practice when Mommy told you to
practice." I said, "You're totally wrong. I practiced five, six, seven minutes
a day for three weeks!"

Next up came one of those mind-blowing, life-altering epiphanies:

Leslie West: Well, when I went to the Fillmore to see Cream, my brother
gave me the brilliant idea, "Let's take some LSD . . ." It was great acid,
but when the curtain opened and I heard Cream, I went, "Oh shit! We
really do suck!" So I practiced. And I practiced. And the reason that I
ended up playing guitar the way that I do is because I was in love with
Eric Clapton. Eric Clapton was to me the best, him and Jimi Hendrix,
but especially Eric Clapton. I saw this group Cream and I didn't know
"What's the guitar? What's the voice? What's the voice? What's the guitar? How? God! This is incredible!" It changed my life. It changed my life
so that I got to play with people that no way in the world would I ever
have gotten to play with.

Certainly, Felix Pappalardi was one of them. The relationship that
began with the Vagrants continued when Leslie decided to leave the
group and go it alone. Felix was brought in to produce his debut solo
album called *Mountain*. By the summer of 1969, Felix began playing
bass in concert with Leslie on lead guitar, N. D. Smart on drums, and
Steve Knight on keyboards. That was the quartet booked to play Woodstock, and the group did not disappoint. The alleged reason for having
a keyboard player was so that they would not be compared unfavor-
ably to Cream. There is also an assertion, which I could not verify, that
fellow Woodstockian alumnus Bert Sommer suggested the name for
the band. True or not, Mountain was adopted, their first album called
Mountain Climbing was not released until months after the festival, and
Woodstock was only their fourth time playing together. Shortly after
the festival, the keyboard player was dismissed and N. D. Smart was
replaced by a friend of Leslie's from Canada named Laurence "Corky"
Laing, thus comprising the trio of musicians best remembered to this
day as Mountain.

Their set list at Woodstock included the following: "Blood of the Sun," "Stormy Monday," "Long Red," "For Yasgur's Farm" (then un-titled), "You and Me," "Theme from an Imaginary Western," "Waiting to Take You Away," "Dreams of Milk and Honey," "Blind Man," "Blue Suede Shoes," and "Southbound Train."

"For Yasgur's Farm," obviously a reflection of their experiences at Bethel, was reworked and retitled for their debut album. Though it didn't approach the anthemic level of Joni Mitchell's song, or even Melanie's "Lay Down (Candles in the Rain)," it became a staple of the group's live performances and garnered significant airplay on the nation's FM progressive-rock radio stations. Asked about the song by *ZigZag* magazine in 1971, Pappalardi replied:

Felix Pappalardi: It was written over a long period of time . . . We played Woodstock and because of the emotional impact it had on us, we sort of changed the words around to fit that occasion.

Here's a sample:

Happy dreams and somehow through the day
We haven't come so far to lose our way

Many Woodstock memories are totally intertwined with the five senses. One of Leslie West's most vivid recollections involved his late at night/early in the morning sense of smell.

Leslie West: We were on Saturday night right when the lights came on for the first time. 'Cause Friday night it rained and they just had acous-tic acts. Saturday night it was beautiful. I mean, because Jimi was the headliner, really—nobody really was, but he was the top name. We got a great time period. In fact, they made me hide until it got dark because it was a matter of like, "Well, who's ready?" "Who will get on?" 'Cause it was chaos in the beginning. We flew up in our own helicopter. We were smart. We rented our own. Unfortunately, because I was much heavier at the time, the helicopter pilot did not want to fly one trip. So he took three guys and two. And I remember this distinctly, Bud Praeger's wife, Gloria, gave him six chickens—barbecued chickens, and he didn't want to take them. He said, "They have food there, they have everything—they have for the entertainers—they have bagels." Well, that was gone in the first hour. Janis Joplin ate everything. And all of a sudden, about two or three in the morning, after Sly and the Family Stone were on, I think, we were starved. We were sitting behind the stage—there was nothing, and Bud whips out these chickens. And there were people coming up and over 'cause it smelled pretty damn good at that time. And Gloria, if you're listening, thank God for you, we fed forty-eight people, I think, that night.

By 1972, done in by intragroup squabbling, Mountain had broken up. There were subsequent reunions and breakups through the years and, in fact, there is an incarnation of Mountain featuring West and Laing that still plays together occasionally in the twenty-first century. But a different kind of rock tragedy—one *not* related to drugs, alcohol, automobile or airplane crashes, suicides, or fatal illnesses—put an end to any real possibility of the three original Mountaineers to ever play together again.

On April 17, 1983, Felix Pappalardi's wife, songwriting partner, and visual design director Gail Collins-Pappalardi shot her husband to death in their New York City apartment. She was convicted of criminally negligent homicide and sentenced to sixteen months to four years in prison after which she withdrew from public life and hasn't been heard from much since. Pappalardi is buried in Woodlawn Cemetery with other music greats in the borough of his birth, the Bronx.

In 2007, Mountain was part of a tour called HippieFest, and one of the stops was the new performing arts center on the site of the original Woodstock festival. Leslie told *Modern Guitars Magazine:*

Leslie West: We played on that tour . . . and we played up in Bethel Woods at the new amphitheater up there, and it's right next to the original site. I went and saw the monument with all our names on it. It was a good feeling, and I'm sorry Felix wasn't around to go back to it.

Asked if Woodstock was everything he had envisioned beforehand, Leslie replied·with his usual candor and bluntness.

Leslie West: I had no vision of it. I had absolutely no idea what this was. I don't think anybody had a vision, come to think of it. They were going up there to get high and hear a lot of music.

JANIS JOPLIN

Joan Auperlee: Backstage a helicopter landed. Out walked Janis Joplin and a girlfriend. I ran over to the garbage cans, grabbed an ice cold bottle of champagne, and offered it to Janis . . . she smiled sweetly and said, "No thanks, I'm off that stuff!!"

She may have been off champagne, but she had plenty of substitutes. Janis was at the epicenter of a pentangle where five very powerful late-'60s forces converged: booze, drugs, music, sex, and talent. She stood toe-to-toe in those areas with any man in music, and it was, of course, the overwhelming interaction of these very forces that killed her. Good people knew it. Good people tried to stop her. She knew it herself. Whether she could or would or even wanted to stop it herself is a matter of sheer conjecture at this point, but the basic facts are these. Janis Joplin ate up and spit out every single stereotype for women in rock 'n' roll. She matched and even surpassed the hard drinking, hard drugging, hard rocking exploits of her male counterparts.

Myra Friedman: I remember one time, Janis wanted to go hear Elvis in Las Vegas, and I asked Albert [Grossman] if I could go and he said no. The sad thing about that is she never even heard Elvis. She locked herself in her hotel room and stayed there. People didn't know about the heroin. It was a different time. They certainly knew that she was drinking on the stage. They thought that it was cute. And if you didn't understand that she was seriously alcoholic, I guess you would think that it was cute.

A favorite of both crowds and musicians, Janis was shuffled around just like all the other performers. When she finally made it to the stage at Woodstock, she addressed the ocean of fans.

Janis Joplin: How are you all . . . I mean . . . how are you out there? Are you okay? [Cheers] You're not, uh . . . you're staying stoned and you've got enough water? And you've got a place to sleep and every-thing? [Pause] What does that mean? Because, you know, because we oughta—all of us, you know—I don't mean to be preachy, but we oughta remember, and that means the promoters too, that music's for grooving, man. The music is not for putting yourself through bad changes, you know. I mean, you don't have to go take anybody's shit, man, just to like music. You know what I mean? You don't. So if you're getting more shit than you deserve, you know what to do about it, man. You know, it's just music. Music's supposed to be different than that . . . [Here's] a song called "Try (Just a Little Bit Harder)." You better, baby. You know you gotta!

With that, whatever insecurities, personal squabbles, drinking, or drug abuse that was plaguing her at the time disappeared as she launched into one of her signature primal scream/songs. In addition to "Try," the set was peppered with well-known, road-tested material such as "Ball and Chain" and "Piece of My Heart" as well as her remarkable reinventions of George Gershwin's "Summertime" and the Bee Gees' "To Love Somebody." She could actually make the Bee Gees sound as if they had balls! Janis was, after all, unlike any performer before or after her.

Myra Friedman: Janis had a very, very interesting sound. You could hear it right away. Her voice was a fraction sharp as in C sharp versus B flat. There was that quality, and that's the sound difference that makes all these other rock singers not sound like her. But you know, it is an amazing thing. There are very few performers—rock singers—who can let it out. Janis understood what she was saying. I've heard singers where they're just words that are there, they're not really investing in the meaning to the word. She cared about the lyric. A lot of singers—they're just sounds that are coming out. "Try (A Little Bit Harder)" . . . She really meant it!

Where did her talent come from?

Myra Friedman: I would say it was a God-given talent. Her mother was very smart; the father was very bright. I think more than anything, she had God-given talent and fearlessness. I don't know where that came from because that's certainly not from her mother. Her mother was more like my mother in the sense of "Would you please be like everybody else." And Janis never was, except as a little girl.

Ellen Sander: She was very gritty, very passionate, very intense, dramatic. She had this way of singing where she did something unique with her voice. She could sing two notes at once. She could sing harmony with herself. And the first time I heard it was the opening night at the Fillmore East, and I thought, This is impossible, but there was nobody else singing. And then of course I heard it again and again and again, and I recently confirmed it with somebody who worked with her very closely. She just had this unique thing with her voice. It was a very unusual and very compelling vocal style.

Janis was exploring territory that no woman rock performer had ever explored before her. Roles for women in rock 'n' roll were pretty well defined in the music's first decade. There were pop princesses such as Connie Francis and Lesley Gore. There were sex bombs epitomized by Jo Ann Campbell. There were precocious young belters such as Brenda Lee and Little Eva Boyd. And there were motion picture and television stars who carried their mass media fame onto the Top 40 charts: Shelley Fabares, Annette Funicello, Patty Duke, and Connie Stevens. Then too, on a planet all their own (probably Venus), there were the legendary "girl groups" such as the Chiffons, the Crystals, the Ronettes, the Shangri-Las, et al. Janis looked toward unexpected places for her inspiration. Unexpected, especially for a white woman.

Myra Friedman: Bessie Smith, Etta James, Otis Redding—these were people that she learned from and really admired. By the way, I never heard her one time mention James Brown. And I don't blame her, because I didn't like him that much either. Otis Redding—that is who Janis really loved. She loved a lot of the moves, the general fearlessness of being completely uninhibited in terms of emotion.

Michael Wadleigh: I have had the great privilege to have filmed so many great people. Two of my favorites were Aretha Franklin and Tina Turner. I happened to be at the Fillmore when both of them had specifically come out to hear Janis Joplin. I was standing with them. Let me tell you, both of those women were drop-jawed. Of course, Aretha Franklin was one of the greatest blues singers ever. They just couldn't get over what they heard out of her. The inventiveness that she puts into her screams, in a song like "Summertime." Her unexpected phrasing. Her actor's performance as an interpreter of those songs is phenomenal. She proves that white people can sing the blues.

As the '60s began to burn, baby, burn, the archetypes became even more sharply defined: the folk Madonnas, the sex symbols, the earth mothers, the flower children, and the blues belters. Though Woodstock, much like rock 'n' roll itself, was mostly a cauldron of testosterone, a few of those archetypes were represented front and center: the folk Madonna was Joan Baez; the sex symbol was Grace Slick; the flower child was Melanie; and way over there, all by herself, carving out a new template for women in rock—was Janis Joplin.

As always, the audience at Woodstock ate it up. But audience approval was nothing new to Janis. The "little girl" never went away. Buried deep inside of her, that vulnerability undermined every relationship and accomplishment in her all too brief life. Whatever she tried to deaden the pain with—alcohol; drugs; unattainable, insatiable levels of love from individuals and mass audiences alike—was always undone by the paralyzing childish inability to be mollified, coddled, or reassured about her value as a person or a performer. Many folks behind the scenes knew that while the audience cheered, all was not right with Little Girl Blue. Her handler and biographer Myra Friedman accompanied Janis backstage.

Myra Friedman: Backstage she had tremendous anxiety. I remember being worried about her because she looked so damned anxious. And she griped, "What did they do this to me for?" She wasn't happy about when she was playing. You know, she could get very testy.

Myra knew Janis on a personal level that many others didn't.

Myra Friedman: To me, she trusted me. I knew that, not from day one, it took a little while. She liked me right away. I was supposed to be the intermediary between her and [manager] Albert Grossman. She was very warm, very funny, outrageous sometimes. I was backstage at the Singer Bowl—this was before Woodstock—when Janis was on the bill with Hendrix, and I remember that the two of them downed a quart of Southern Comfort! Anybody oughta know that this is not good for your health. They were friendly, and she had great regard for him as a musician.

The foundation she had in place to support all of this high-stakes swagger didn't just have cracks, it had fissures. Unresolved childhood conflicts, bohemian leanings completely at odds with those of her conservative Port Arthur, Texas, peers and authority figures, prevented her from being completely comfortable in her own skin. She once famously proclaimed on national television that she ". . . was laughed out of class, laughed out of school, and laughed out of town."

Michael Wadleigh: She was a very sad person, of course. I met her a few times. She was always drunk. It was terrible. She was a classic ugly duckling. She was completely unappreciated. She was fat and unpopular. She was brutalized as a kid, and a lot of that rejection came through her songs.

Her safe place was the arts: painting, poetry, folk music, and the blues. These passions fueled a rebellious streak in her teens, and she left home at seventeen in the early '60s to sing in the music clubs of Austin and Houston. When she felt ready for a bigger stage, Janis headed to the fertile, growing music scene evolving up in San Francisco. After enjoying some success there, she returned to Austin in 1966 at the invitation of a local country and western band. However, Janis had made a real impression in the Bay Area and was lured back by famed San Francisco impresario Chet Helms to become lead vocalist for an up until then all-instrumental band named Big Brother and the Holding Company. The matchup was electric and electrifying—primarily because of the dynamism that Janis brought to the group. The girl from Port Arthur had found her new port of call and her new calling—"old

SATURDAY

school" blues belter in the "brand-new school" rock revolution. Janis clearly just wanted to be "one of the boys," but right from the beginning critics, advisers, friends, and fans alike raised questions about whether the band was worthy of her talents.

Stan Schnier: If she had lived, I don't think anybody would have given a rat's ass about who her band was. It was about live energy, and the live energy of that show was incredible. I think that Big Brother and the Holding Company, had they stayed together, they would have risen to the occasion. They were pretty good musicians, they just weren't great, you know? But they would've figured it out, I'm sure.

Others thought that it never really mattered who her band was.

Ellen Sander: Everybody has always kind of made these comments about Janis Joplin's band, whether it's Big Brother or the Full Tilt Boogie Band or the studio band or whatever. In my opinion, you never noticed the band! She was so out front and center that the band, you know, was just backup and honestly, it was just very hard to have any thoughts about the band because she was so riveting.

Initially, Janis ignored the rumblings and dug in her heels to make the band the launchpad to stardom for all of them. By 1967, the group's and particularly Janis's reputation for doing roof-raising concerts (even if they were outdoors!) earned Big Brother an invitation to the Monterey International Pop Festival. You would have to flip a coin to decide whether it was Jimi Hendrix, Otis Redding, or Janis Joplin who stole the show. But she certainly stood out from her competition. With Jimi and Otis, it was business as usual: sexy, charismatic men singing sexy, charismatic songs. But Janis used the occasion to proclaim to the world that a woman was claiming star billing in the rock 'n' roll pantheon. Her explosion could only be paralleled perhaps by Elvis's appearance on the scene in 1956.

Nick Gravenites: She's doing the hardest thing you can do—carrying a whole band on her shoulders, all the personalities, plus doing her own thing. But it's worth it. The benefits are mystical; it's a compulsion, nothing to do with reason, logic. See, first and foremost, Janis is a blues singer. Think what that means, really think. The tradition of hardship, tragedy, early death. Like Bessie Smith. Robert Johnson died at twenty-one. A blues singer isn't a performer, doesn't need an audience. Can sing to the ocean, the moon. Even when there are ten thousand people out there, there still might be no audience. But the blues sustain you. Blues are a faith in beauty and peace, coupled with extreme worldly knowledge; the ultimate decision is always positive.

Bob Santelli: If I'm not mistaken, she played the Atlantic City Pop Festival as well. I know I had seen her that summer and had been blown away by the big blues band and how she could capture, this white kid, the sense of deep dark blues in a way that I had never heard or could even imagine.

Just watch Janis's career-defining performance at Monterey to remind yourself what a force of nature she was. Just take a look at another formidable female vocalist in the audience at the conclusion of Janis's set—Mama Cass Elliot—disbelievingly mouthing the word "Wow!" caught on film. The song "Ball and Chain" by Big Mama Thornton became one of her signature concert pieces.

Michael Wadleigh: Who will ever hear a song like "Ball and Chain" again? It was a black song, and she took it and she wiped Big Mama Thornton's ass.

Janis once spoke to journalist Richard Goldstein about it:

Janis Joplin: "Ball and Chain" is the hardest thing I do. I have to really get inside my head every time I sing it. Because it's about feeling things. That means I can never sing it without really trying. See, there's this big hole in the song that's mine, and I've got to fill it with something. So I do! And it really tires me out. But it's so groovy when you know the audience really wants you. I mean, whatever you give them, they'll believe in. And they yell back at you, call your name, and—like that.

The impact of her star turn at Monterey was palpable. Bob Dylan's manager Albert Grossman came calling. Columbia Records president Clive Davis, who was at the festival, offered up the big record contract. He recalled the day in his autobiography:

Clive Davis: She was electrifying [at Monterey]. She strutted up and down the stage banging a tambourine, and as the audience got turned on, she got <u>more</u> turned on, almost childlike in her exhilaration. For me it was spine-tingling . . . awesome . . . hypnotic. My eyes riveted wherever she went. She was choked up at one point, laughing at another. She just couldn't contain herself, and you didn't know how to take it all. It was ebullience thrust at you in the most basic, primitive ways . . . trembling . . . shaking . . . almost a violent tremor when she got extremely <u>into</u> what she was doing. She seemed bursting with emotion; and it was so pure. I knew immediately that I had to go after her.

From that Saturday afternoon in June 1967 to her final day in the world in October 1970, Janis's personal and professional life careened wildly in and out of control. High highs. Low lows. More of the latter than the former. One-night stands with men. One-night stands with women. And one-night stands at every major concert venue and festival across the country and around the world.

One of those gigs took her to Woodstock in August of '69. Big Brother had been jettisoned by then, and the new, short-lived substitute Kozmic Blues Band never quite jelled either, but Janis's star continued to ascend.

One of her pre-superstardom relationships was with fellow Woodstock icon Joe McDonald, who even wrote a song about her called "Janis." It went:

> Into my life on waves of electrical sound
> And flashing light she came,
> Into my life with the twist of a dial
> The wave of her hand—the warmth of her smile.
> And even though I know that you and I
> Could never find the kind of love we wanted together,
> Alone I find myself missing you and I, you and I.

They had broken up even before their joint appearance at Monterey in '67, but they crisscrossed around one another and met up again many times on the rock circuit, including at Woodstock.

When interviewed for this book, Joe added an afterthought about her new group and about how she had changed from their dating days.

Joe McDonald: Yeah, I didn't like her new band. And her attitude was putting me off. Her new persona of being a <u>big star</u> was hard for me to take. Her band—it was okay. But Big Brother was— I loved her with Big Brother.

Joe wasn't alone in his assessment.

Mike Jahn: When Janis signed with Columbia, she came to New York and I met her at a party someplace. She came over and started talking to me. I'm a magnet for women with issues. I had one of those hideous drinks with her, Southern Comfort and Coke. And I asked her about the new band. She told me about them and I asked, "What are you going to call them?" She said, "I was thinking of Janis and the Jackoffs, but they didn't like that too much." The first time I saw her play with the new band was at Woodstock, and I didn't like them that much. They were kind of mediocre. And the following morning, I went back to the hotel where some of the performers were staying. Janis was there, she had just gotten up. She was wearing a housecoat with flowers on it. She didn't look very good. She came over and asked me, "How did you like my new band?" And I said to her, "I think you could do better." She said, "Well, that just shows how much some people know," and turned and stalked off. I felt bad about that, but it was the truth. And six months later she fired them and went out and got Full Tilt Boogie and they were much better. I gave them a glowing review.

The descent that led to her death at twenty-seven was well underway during those three days of peace and music in Bethel. The clock was clearly ticking on the 414 days that she had left to live.

John Morris: She was wasted. And that is the worst performance I ever saw her do. She was gone. So it was like, "Oh shit. Here we go." And I'd done her first concert in New York at the old Anderson Theater and I'd watched her like a terrified little girl because the opening act was some guy named B.B. King who was playing to a white audience downtown for the first time in his life. And he must have played for two hours because he couldn't get off the stage—encore after encore after encore. And she was shivering in the dressing room. She was scared to death. And she said, "I can't follow that. He's just too good. I can't do it." I said, "Sure you can. You can go out there and do it. They want to see you.

They came to see you. They got a special treat with him." I don't think I even knew B.B. well enough to know how great he was. Well, we got some Southern Comfort. And she drank that. And I said, "Look, let me give you a suggestion. Open with 'Ball and Chain.' Just go out there and bash them in the head." And she went out there on the stage and when the curtain went up, she literally charged the audience. And just got 'em. And they roared so much at her, that they physically moved her back ten feet. And that was all she needed. And she did a great performance. But she was not so great at Woodstock. She was sloppy. It was sloppy. The audience didn't react badly, but I would say questioningly. I've never heard anyone say that that's one of the greatest performances she ever did.

Despite her superstardom, her performance did not make the first cut of the *Woodstock* film.

Dale Bell: There were some instances where we had edited material that we did not feel that strongly that we should include because it was indeed embarrassing to the performers. I'm going to say that those two sections were Janis Joplin and Jerry Garcia and the Dead. Their performances were not up to snuff. Or perhaps there was too much snuff. I don't know which one.

Despite this, there were still those who excused her bad behavior and ranked her performance as one of the high points of the festival.

Joshua White: If I had to pick someone who I think was able to truly be perfect for Woodstock in terms of her ability to take the focus of hundreds of thousands of people it would be Janis. Grace [Slick] less because she was still part of a group, she still sang in close harmony with other people, she still was political and felt she had to make statements. Janis, she didn't give a shit, she just sang.

Ellen Sander: Well, I don't think there are more superlatives you can add to Janis Joplin's performances. I can't say she outdid herself there, because she outdid herself everywhere. I mean, she was one performer that always gave one hundred ten percent, and she was fantastic. And she <u>looked</u> fantastic, she looked great.

After Woodstock, her personal problems deepened as the powers that be pushed her career in a different direction.

Tom Law: I knew her from Haight-Ashbury. Just before she died, Albert had her up on my farm in New Mexico. He asked me if I could go on the road with her; he thought maybe I could handle her. But I had three kids and a farm and I couldn't do it. But she hung out for a couple of days. She was pretty whacked out. I didn't know she was an addict, and a month later, she was dead. Had I gone on the road with her, who knows?

Stan Schnier: That little period after Woodstock, so much stuff happened very quickly. Because Woodstock was Janis Joplin appearing live without Big Brother. I think there was this convergence going on where suddenly everybody saw the dollar signs and the music went from being this kind of grassrootsy, small scene, and suddenly there were these big guys like Albert Grossman and record companies and people in suits showing up and manipulating artists; telling Janis Joplin she should have a better band, and taking the Jimi Hendrix Experience and firing Noel and Mitch—it all happened at the same time. That all happened around Woodstock. The other thing that happened right after Woodstock was that Joe and the Fish broke up. And I met them right after Woodstock, and I got hired and went off. I had quit my job at the Fillmore, and went off with Joe and the band to Europe, and that's when I did stuff with Led Zeppelin. But it was that period between summer of '69 and '71: that's when Janis died, Hendrix died, Jim Morrison died. The music biz became huge in just a couple of years. It's like Woodstock wasn't enough, it was the Isle of Wight, and so on . . . festivals, festivals, festivals, you know?

The bigger stages, the bigger audiences, the bigger spotlights just seemed to amplify Janis's terminal sadness. To explain the emptiness in her soul, she delighted in telling the story of an opera singer who invited a man that wanted to marry her up onstage after a particularly triumphant performance to see what it was like to receive that kind of acclaim. "Do you think you could give me that?" the opera singer asked her suitor. Janis punctuated the story by proclaiming, "I know no guy ever made me feel as good as an audience." Writer Michael Lydon explained the Joplin duality this way in his great rock read *Rock Folk:*

Janis is a rock 'n' roll woman, perhaps the greatest that ever lived. There have been great women singers of rock 'n' roll, but only a few have dared take full place in the essentially masculine world of rock stardom. Diana Ross, Martha Reeves of the Vandellas, Grace Slick, Tracy Nelson, and even Aretha Franklin are in the end female singers in the long "chantoosie" tradition; they can sing tough if they want to, but they never risk losing their essential femininity on or off stage. But Janis and a few of her sisters express their woman-ness with a raunchy boldness that is magnificently sexy though not one bit ladylike. Janis is a girl who has always wanted to be one of the guys, though she has always known she is a woman, and a tender one, inside. She has a masculine scorn for the politely devious wiles of acceptable femininity, yet losing a good man can break her heart. The ambiguity of brashness and soft-ness is at the heart of her appeal; onstage, second to second, she is one and then the other, so you first glory in her strength and then want to reach out and soothe her sorrow.

Let's give the last word about Janis to a woman. One of the best writers about rock 'n' roll and women's issues that ever was, Ellen Willis in her essay about Janis in *The Rolling Stone Illustrated History of Rock & Roll*:

Joplin's revolt against conventional femininity was brave and imagina-tive, but it also dovetailed with a stereotype—the ballsy, one-of-the-guys chick who is a needy, vulnerable cream puff underneath—cherished by her legions of hip male fans. It may be that she could have pushed be-yond it and taken the audience with her; that was one of the possibili-ties that made her death an artistic as well as human calamity. There is, for instance, the question of her bisexuality. . . . A public acknowledg-ment of bisexual proclivities would not necessarily have contradicted her image; it could easily have been passed off as more pull-out-the-stops hedonism or another manifestation of her all-encompassing need for love. On the other hand, she could have used it to say something new about women and liberation. What makes me wonder is something I always noticed and liked about Janis: unlike most female performers whose act is intensely erotic, she never made me feel as if I were crash-ing an orgy that consisted of her and the men in the audience. When she got it on at a concert, she got it on with everybody.

GRATEFUL DEAD

Jerry Garcia: Woodstock was a bummer for us. It was terrible to play at.

What's to say about the Grateful Dead at Woodstock? Well, we can start with John Fogerty's observation that they "gave a sleepy performance," or his annoyance that they put the crowd to sleep before Creedence was set to take the stage. Fogerty wasn't the only one critical of their performance.

Leslie West: They wanted a do-over. They didn't like their sound or something. Everybody was moaning and screaming, "You're not going on again. It's lucky enough everybody got on once!"

Joshua White: And the Dead were the Dead. The Dead were perfect because they were beloved. Everybody loved them, myself included. Some people loved them a little too much, and they were at their very best when they weren't the headliners.

Billy Altman: In their history, they had several misses at a lot of these very big festivals. At Woodstock, they did not play a particularly memorable show, which is something that you would think that they would do great. The Dead were always a crapshoot in terms of their sets. They could play great or they could be hit or miss. There was so much improvisation. On an "on night" you wouldn't know where they were going. Much like watching a jazz band where they did so much improvisation once they hit their rhythm and they were doing great you would get swept along with it. I saw any number of shows where that happened. Everyone would get caught up in the moment in the best sense of being an improvisational group.

What Billy Altman says is exactly right. As famous a live band as the Grateful Dead are now, in the earlier part of their career, one of the things they were famous for was blowing two major gigs—Monterey Pop and Woodstock. At Woodstock, you could blame the weather. The rain was short-circuiting the electrical cables all over the stage—shocking anyone plugged into the current (electric guitars, mics, film cameras, et cetera). Or you could blame the drugs. Or maybe it was just one of those days. The band blamed a combination of all these factors.

Jerry Garcia: We were playing at nighttime in the dark; and we were looking out, in the dark, to what we knew to be four hundred thousand people. But you couldn't see anybody. You could only see little fires and stuff out there on the hillside, and these incredible bright spotlights shining in your eyes.

Phil Lesh: Back down in the mud, the electrical ground had failed completely, producing in the sound system [and all the band gear and monitors] a sixty-cycle hum the size of New Hampshire. Compared to the background hum you'll hear in any electrified edifice, this was a saber-toothed crotch cricket of a hum; almost obliterating any signal passed into the system. A steel pole fifty feet long was sunk, seeking dry ground. Not a chance.

Jerry Garcia: The stage was all wet. There were electric shocks from your instruments.

Phil Lesh: At the front of the stage, there had been lights set to illuminate the audience; these had gone off and would not return. We went on in a howling wind, the screen flapping behind us and blue balls of lightning scurrying across the stage. The simple act of plugging in one's instrument became fraught with peril; we were all still playing high-impedance instruments, so the differential in electrical potential was large enough to make any shocks potentially lethal. Bob steps up to test his mic—and a big blue spark blows him back to the amp line flat on his ass. He bounces back up, his eyes bulging, yelling, "I didn't even touch it!" Yipes. I manage to plug in my bass without losing any demons, and out of the hum comes a sharp burst of static: then "Roger, Charlie Tango, [static] I'm landing now"—the command radio signals from the chopper fleet are homing on my pickups and playing through my speakers. Double yipes.

Jerry Garcia: People were freaking out here and there and crowding on the stage. People behind the amplifiers were hollering that the stage was about to collapse. All that kind of stuff. It was like a really bad psychic place to be when you're trying to play music. We didn't enjoy playing there, but it was definitely far-out.

Mike Jahn: I had a typical '60s conversation with Jerry Garcia at Woodstock. We were sitting on the side of the stage, drinking our beers. And I said to him, "Hey, man." And he said to me, "Hey, man," and that was the end of it. That was a typical '60s conversation.

John Morris: It was not a great set. Well, I did them nineteen times, and their act didn't translate that well to the setting.

Jim Marion: The Grateful Dead were a big disappointment. They subsequently claimed this was their worst gig ever, and they certainly would get no argument from this listener, who was fortunate to see them a dozen other times when they had the magic. Even from afar, it was obvious they were having serious technical problems.

Considering how much the Dead bombed, the fact that they were there was a huge feather in the promoters' cap. As detailed in the Santana chapter, the promoters had to appeal to the all-powerful Bill Graham in order to secure the Dead in the first place.

And although their performance was weak, they cannot be discounted. They were and still are a huge cultural icon of the Woodstock generation. From Dancing Bear stickers to Ben and Jerry's famous Cherry Garcia ice cream flavor, the Dead became a brand that stood for hippies, jammin', and sharing a big fattie among friends. The Dead were followed by their fans, the Dead Heads, nearly everywhere they went.

Bob Santelli: They made their name as this jam band that could play to large amounts of crowds for long periods of time, which they obviously did later on in their career.

John Morris: The band had always been a commune group, but they were also at that point getting more important. The Grateful Dead did not gain anything particularly career-wise from being at Woodstock. It was San Francisco, and it was the road shows, and it was the people following them, and all the rest of it that made the Grateful Dead. Woodstock is a comma in the paragraph about the Grateful Dead.

Bob Santelli: Their performance at Woodstock could've been much, much better. I was never a big Dead fan, and so I could never quite get it. Even at Watkins Glen when they had a whole lot more time because there were only three bands playing. I kinda missed it, so I'm probably not the one to talk to about the Grateful Dead. I remember being at Monmouth University and I was the entertainment editor and I had done a review of one of the Grateful Dead albums, and it was my first instance as a journalist of getting hate mail, and I mean serious hate mail because I had said things that discredited the Grateful Dead. I felt that way beforehand, but when I actually put it in print and then when I got this barrage of letters, I thought maybe there are things about the Dead that I am not capable of absorbing. So I'm probably not the guy to talk to because I didn't think much of them at any of the festivals or any of the other concerts I've been to. Yet I know hundreds of thousands of people would think I was crazy.

One such person is our other resident Woodstock rock critic.

Billy Altman: I saw the Grateful Dead a lot. In fact, I saw them in June of '69 at the Fillmore and they were just absolutely spectacular and then played their encore in Central Park the next day. They played the late show and had finished around five in the morning and Bill Graham came out and said that he couldn't let the club stay open any longer without getting in trouble but told the crowd that he would get a permit so they could play their encore for them in Central Park at two o'clock. He also told them not to tell anybody because if too many people show up, they won't be able to do it. They actually played in the band shell, and when they started playing, there were probably a thousand people there and by the time they finished there were probably two thousand people there.

If you watched the Dead in the spirit of the Dead, you may have not even noticed that there were complications.

Ellen Sander: I remember everybody enjoying their set very much. First of all, the Dead bring with them a great deal of charisma and community spirit and legend, so I remember it being a good performance. It may well have been plagued by technical problems, but I don't think anybody noticed. People were so thrilled that they were there. It seemed to be that this kind of event kind of personified their spirit. So I think they were thoroughly enjoyed even though they may feel it was not their best set or there was technical problems. Then again, I know I was beyond it, it almost didn't matter at this point everything was so whipped up.

By the time of Woodstock, the Dead had been playing together for four years already. The band was an outgrowth of Ron "Pigpen" McKernan's blues band in San Francisco. Though overshadowed by the ultimate fame of Garcia, Pigpen was really the heart of the Dead.

Jerry Garcia: He was the star of the Grateful Dead when we started—definitely the star of the band. He was the guy that carried the weight. He was the guy with the most talent, I think, really, in the band, the most natural talent. He had a fabulous voice—he could really sing good and played good harmonica—and had a real good understanding of the blues. I mean, a really good understanding of the blues.

Bob Weir: Plus that, he was a maniac—he could rave for hours on end.

Jerry Garcia: Yeah, he was a great guy, a real pixie.

Bob Weir: One time from onstage, we did an extended version of "Love Light" or one of those songs we did an extended version of—and he sold the guy the Brooklyn Bridge.

Jerry Garcia: Yeah, right. He had a fabulous extemporaneous mind—he came up with some of the most amazing stuff.

Unfortunately, Pigpen met an untimely end.

Bob Weir: He drank himself to death.

Jerry Garcia: Yeah, he was a stage fright guy case. I think he was a fragile guy. He was much more fragile and sensitive than the rest of us. The rest of us went through the traumas and rigors and calluses that you get taking psychedelics. Pigpen was too fragile for this world, really, man. It was hard on him to be a performer—it really was. It used to be tough for us to get him to do his tunes. We'd have to really kick his ass to get him to do his tunes. It was one of those things.

Bob Weir: Alright, Pigpen, now we're gonna do "Midnight Hour."

Jerry Garcia: Yeah, we pushed him. I don't know. I've never really felt too bad about Pigpen dying. I felt like maybe that this world wasn't really good enough for him in a certain way.

The bond the Dead members have with each other is just as spiritual as the most idealistic Dead Heads would want it to be.

Bob Weir: One time, we got him up on a Ouija board.

Jerry Garcia: Yeah, we picked him up one time. We were too spooked to find out, though. It put us on such a weird trip that we didn't bother going through with it. It really happened fast. There was a Ouija board and all of a sudden, we say, "Hey, let's see if we can get Pigpen." And we put our hands on it and immediately there he was.

Bob Weir: He was undeniable.

Jerry Garcia: Immediately, first thing.

Bob Weir: Alright, if you are really Pigpen, what's your middle name? And, he spelled out a middle name that only Pigpen would have said—and spelled it only the way Pigpen would have done. "My God, this is Pigpen."

Jerry Garcia: It was freaky, man. We folded that thing up and split!

Though, sadly, Jerry has passed since that last interview, I was lucky enough to have Bobby return for a solo visit to my show. The conversation inevitably gravitated to a discussion about life without Jerry and about how he still feels his presence when he's performing:

Bob Weir: After a long time, friends just rub off on each other. I can explain it most particularly in the music while we're playing. I can more or less hear him still around the edges. I know where he's going with it, with the flux of the music, and I can try to go in a complementary, contrapuntal place. I know where he's going, and I kinda know when he's going to get there. And I can be there with a complement and a surprise or something like that. Just like it always was. And it's like that with the rest of life for me, too. He's just there. I can hear him laughing. I can hear him being caustic, whatever. "Go there! Go there! Don't go there, that sucks!" I miss the yuks. We laughed our way back and forth across America and around the world. His one big quote was "Music is something we do, but comedy is really our thing!" We had some fun.

With Jerry's death on August 9, 1995, an end parenthesis was put around the legendary career of the Grateful Dead. But, as one of their great performances proclaimed, The Music Never Stopped. Nor will it, as long as there are ears on this planet that can hear it. The Dead are now the stuff of legends. Just like Woodstock. And even though they may have hated their own performance at the event, they certainly came to understand the greater significance of it all.

Jerry Garcia: It was like I knew I was at a place where history was being made. You could tell. You could be there and say, "This is history. This is a historical moment." It was obvious that it was. There was a sense . . . when you were there, there was a sense of timelessness about it. You knew that nothing so big and so strong could be anything but important, and important enough to mark somewhere. I was confident that it was history. That was my feeling, really. See, at the time, man, it was like all this stuff that we'd seen coming. We'd seen it coming. And it's just like scratching an itch. 'Cause it's just "Ah, here it is." And then it's on to the next one.

I suppose we could leave the Grateful Dead's Woodstock saga right there, but as I was putting these words together, I knew there was something else Jerry once said about peace and about love and about music that really nailed still another fresh way of thinking about the Woodstock Music and Art Fair and what it meant, what it means, and it will continue to mean as we move forward into the future. Then it came to me. In one of the best books ever written about rock 'n' roll, Michael Lydon's 1971 tome *Rock Folk*, he quotes Jerry:

> We are trying to make things groovier for everybody so more people can feel better more often, to advance the trip, to get higher, however you want to say it, but we're musicians, and there's just no way to put that idea, 'save the world,' into music; you can only <u>be</u> that idea, or at least make manifest that idea as it appears to you, and hope maybe others follow. . . . My way is music. Music is me being me and trying to get higher. I've been into music so long that I'm dripping with it. I can't do anything else. Music is a yoga, something you really do when you're doing it. Thinking about what it means comes after the fact and isn't very interesting. Truth is something you stumble into when you think you're going someplace else, like those moments when you're playing and the whole room becomes one being; precious moments, man. But you can't <u>look</u> for them and they can't be repeated. Being alive means to continue to change, never to be where I was before. Music is the timeless experience of constant change.

CREEDENCE CLEARWATER REVIVAL

They were an overnight sensation that took ten years to be proclaimed one. When they hit their stride, they put hit after hit on the Top 40 AM radio surveys without sacrificing an iota of their FM hipness and credibility. They were also the last of the "two-sided hit wonders" and musicians who other musicians truly respected.

Leslie West: I remember hanging backstage. Creedence Clearwater Revival went on and they did one hit after another. I couldn't believe how many hit singles they had!

John Sebastian: My favorite performance was Creedence Clearwater. I guess John Fogerty didn't think their performance was up to par, but as an audience member, I was just totally twisted. I thought, Wow! What a great four-piece band!

Bob Santelli: Creedence were another band that was kind of lost in terms of Woodstock and inexplicably so. I haven't seen their performance in a while, but I don't remember it being especially bad or especially good. I certainly love that band, and at the time, I was a huge fan. In fact, the band that I played in was a Creedence tribute band, if you will. But it's funny you bring them up because I hadn't even thought of their performance at Woodstock in so many years.

Bob Weir: *He wasn't bending over backwards to make hit singles. I mean, he was just making the music he made best.*

Jerry Garcia: *They really made the hit singles, God, they certainly did.*

In the days when a hit single was distributed on 45s, record companies routinely put a throwaway, filler song on the B side and put all of its promotional muscle into driving the A side to national hit-record status. This set in motion a number of aberrational occurrences. Sometimes, a disc jockey or a fan would flip the single over and find it more compelling than the A side. "Be-Bop-a-Lula" by Gene Vincent and the Blue Caps was an early example of this phenomenon. Often, if the act were popular enough, artists such as Elvis or the Beatles would generate interest in both sides of the single just because it was new material from a megastar. On some rare occasions, both sides of a new single would get radio airplay and simultaneously race up the charts.

Creedence achieved this status consistently—"Green River" b/w "Commotion," "Down on the Corner" b/w "Fortunate Son," "Travelin' Band" b/w "Who'll Stop the Rain," and so on. While compiling an impressive list of Top 10 hit singles from the fall of 1968 to the spring of 1972, not one of their singles ever made it all the way up to the coveted Number One position. Six of them—"Proud Mary," "Bad Moon Rising," "Green River," "Travelin' Band," "Who'll Stop the Rain," and "Lookin' Out My Back Door"—all made it to Number Two but were prevented from going the distance by slightly bigger hits those weeks.

Jerry Garcia: *John Fogerty is one of those guys that had a real, definite kinda concept of what music should sound like. You know what I mean? And that band functioned very nicely in terms of conveying that concept. He and his brother were both kinda like two of a kind in terms of their taste and music—in what they liked to listen to—what they'd been influenced by. You know who reminds me of them now but on a whole other level is Dire Straits because there is also a pair of brothers in there playing lead guitar and rhythm guitar.*

Creedence was indeed built around two brothers from Berkeley, California, named Tom and John Fogerty. They teamed up with classmates from El Cerrito Junior High School, Doug "Cosmo" Clifford on bass and Stu Cook on drums, and began performing locally in 1959 as the Blue Velvets. They changed their name to Tommy Fogerty and the Golliwogs, then just the Golliwogs, and in 1964 signed a recording contract with Fantasy Records out of San Francisco. There were some regional successes, but big-time stardom eluded them until another name change in 1967 to Creedence Clearwater Revival.

It was an unusual name even by late-'60s standards. What did it mean? Not much, really. *Creedence* came from the name of a friend of a friend of Tom Fogerty's named Creedence Nuball. *Clearwater* was a word that John Fogerty picked out from a locally advertised beer commercial. And *Revival* was a nod to the fact that they were once again reinventing themselves and experiencing a rebirth. An eponymous debut album as *Creedence* in 1968 yielded a couple of chart successes—Dale Hawkins's "Susie Q" and Screamin' Jay Hawkins's "I Put a Spell on You." But CCR was no mere cover band. Fogerty's exuberant reworking of classic rockabilly sounds and styles struck an immediate chord with record buyers, radio stations, and concertgoers.

You can imagine how badly the Woodstock promoters wanted CCR to appear on the bill. When they became the first actual big-name attraction to agree to appear, it was the first notch in the Woodstock belt.

The deal was sealed in the second week of April. Creedence was willing to sign on the dotted line for a guarantee of $10,000 for an hour set. That was at least $2,500 more than they had ever gotten up to that point for a full two-hour concert, but Lang and company were in no position to quibble. Nailing down an act like Creedence could open the floodgates for other name attractions to appear.

While most musicians stayed out of negotiations, Fogerty participated in the conversation.

Michael Lang: They had no idea where they were going to play until we figured it out. It's mostly a business of agents and managers at that point. The bands weren't really involved. Except for John Fogerty who called us up and said, "I'm not playing in any cow field." I booked the first three bands by overpaying them because I had no standing in the music business. So I overpaid them. I think the amount was probably somewhere around $10,000 for Janis or the Airplane, which frankly a year later was nothing once everyone figured out that these people could bring people to a show. I think once word went out in the industry that this was real and happening, bands really wanted to play the event. We were booking to represent bands of that era and generation.

They were booked for an appearance on Saturday, and while an act of their stature should have probably gone on during prime-time concert hours, Creedence got rearranged, pushed back, and juggled around just like everybody else, and so didn't come onstage until after the hour-long, problem-plagued Grateful Dead set.

Unfortunately, some of the technical problems that plagued the Dead continued with Creedence, particularly the sound of the guitars and bass, for at least half of their set. Still, they roared through a mighty impressive list of hit singles and album cuts including "Born on the Bayou," "Green River," "Ninety-nine-and-a-Half (Won't Do)," "Commotion," "Bootleg," "Bad Moon Rising," "Proud Mary," "I Put a Spell on You," "Night Time Is the Right Time," "Keep on Chooglin'," and "Susie Q." The whole set (probably illegally) is posted on many sites on the World Wide Web.

Billy Altman: The thing about Creedence live is that they really played like their records. They were a tremendously tight band. When you saw them, they were almost like a jukebox kind of a band, and I don't mean that in a bad sense. They weren't that charismatic of a band. Fogerty was a great singer, but it was the kind of band that you listened to. You weren't going to see anything spectacular happen onstage. So that might be why people don't have specifically gigantic memories of them as a live band.

Ellen Sander: Oh, Creedence is always so reliable. They have that wonderful sound and everybody knows their songs, they were easy songs to know, to remember, to sing; and the audience was fully with them, too.

While some audience members loved their set, Fogerty, a true perfectionist, was not satisfied with the band's performance either.

John Fogerty: You just need to control—there's that word! I like to make sure all the details are taken care of. And you try to eliminate all the things that are gonna go wrong, 'cause they will! I'm talking about your own equipment, your guitars, your amps, your drum equipment—your own health. There's so many things to think about. And you just try to take care of all the details, so the audience gets your very best. That's my driver. That's the thing that makes me go.

Despite their status in the industry at the time, Creedence was excluded from the film.

Michael Wadleigh: They were a super group. I think they were the all-time great American rock 'n' roll group. They had such a unique sound and clever lyrics that Fogerty wrote. He has a great voice, that nice screaming, raspy voice. Again, it was a situation where we just didn't have the room.

Fogerty claimed that he refused the inclusion.

John Fogerty: We didn't do very well at Woodstock because of the time segment and also because we followed the Grateful Dead, therefore everybody was asleep. It seemed like we didn't go on until two a.m. The Dead went on and pulled their usual shenanigans. Even though in my mind we made the leap into superstardom that weekend, you'd never know it from the footage. All that does is show us in a poor light at a time when we were the number-one band in the world. Why should we show ourselves that way? So I prevailed.

It is said that John came up with the idea for another iconic CCR hit at Woodstock: "Who'll Stop the Rain," which mixed images of what he observed at the festival with dark, brooding reflections about American involvement in Southeast Asia. The song raced up the pop charts in the winter of 1970. Today, John cryptically introduces it in his solo concerts saying, "I went to Woodstock, then hitchhiked my way home, then wrote this song."

Creedence was off to another golden goose year in 1970, but Fogerty's perfectionism and inclination to control the group's affairs ignited internal dissension not only with his nonrelated band mates but also with his own brother. Tom left the group in early 1971, and they continued on as a trio, enjoying recording successes and sold-out concerts. It was at one of these that I first crossed paths with John. On July 17, 1971, I emceed a sold-out show starring Creedence at

Forest Hills Tennis Stadium in Queens, New York. Decades later, John recalled the evening vividly.

John Fogerty: I actually remember that show very well. Everything went wonderfully well. We had a good night musically, and it was a huge crowd, so it was a lot of fun. And, not a bad opening act either—Mr. Bo Diddley!

Unfortunately, those good nights became fewer and farther in between. Tensions continued to grow and fester. Creedence disbanded in October of 1972. Fogerty was so embittered by the experience and by the draconian ways of the record business that he began a pattern of stop/ starting his hoped-for solo career over the next couple of decades, sometimes disappearing from public view for long periods. Tom Fogerty tried for a solo career, but illness derailed it and he died on September 6, 1990, from respiratory illness brought on by tuberculosis. Clifford and Cook tried various configurations but ended up in recent years on the oldies circuit performing as Creedence Clearwater Revisited.

John Fogerty remains one of the happiest, healthiest, most tireless, and most charismatic of all the actively performing Woodstock alumni. In parting, I asked him if he was chasing the clock, trying to make up for lost time, and he answered simply:

John Fogerty: I would say I ain't got any time to screw around here [laughs]. I'm very aware of that almost every day. Because I lost a lot of time for a number of reasons, I don't really have a lot of time to mess around. I better mostly do very high quality stuff. I better not make too many mistakes. That's certainly my driving motto these days.

CREEDENCE CLEARWATER REVIVAL

SLY STONE

Jim Marion: I had seen pretty much every band on the bill at Woodstock. I recall at one point after Janis's set on Saturday night thinking to myself, Why am I sitting in this muddy stench, feeling like crap, and listening to bands I usually love sounding horrible? I'm not sure I had the answer at the time. Still, just when we were at the bottom, salvation came in the form of Sly and the Family Stone.

I had really lost track of time, and all I knew was that it had been dark a long time. They got people on their feet, no small accomplishment considering how physically wasted a lot of us were. A lot of the performances at Woodstock are far better represented in the movie than they were for some of us in the crowd seeing and hearing it live, but watching the movie only confirmed the impression we had at the time that Sly's performance was pretty special, especially since we assumed that he had played on Friday night as originally scheduled and we weren't going to see him.

Only the rare individual can command the attention of thousands of people like some sort of god. This exclusive group includes world leaders, religious figures, and last but not least, pop icons. This power can be a responsibility and it has certainly been known to take a toll on the individuals who've "got it."

Bono has it. Bruce Springsteen has it. Tina Turner has it. People arrive at their concerts with expectations. They want to be entertained, uplifted, to escape, to be moved, or to simply rock out. It takes a truly

164

talented, determined, focused, and powerful personality to fulfill any one of those goals, let alone all of them simultaneously.

Bruce Springsteen's analysis of Bono at U2's induction into the Rock and Roll Hall of Fame summed up "that kind" of performer. He described Bono as "shaman, shyster, one of the greatest and most endearingly naked messianic complexes in rock and roll. It takes one to know one."

When these messiahs succeed, both performer and audience share a transcendent experience. The crowd of individuals turns into a single, pulsing unit that responds to every note, lick, lyric, and gesture. At Woodstock, where a high percentage of the audience was on some form of mind-altering substance, that sensation of being one organism was particularly heightened. It was ecstatic. For many, it was a religious experience.

> **Arthur Levy:** There's no separating the acid experience at Woodstock from the events of the weekend. It was an integral part of what happened there. It revolved around the usage of acid by the audience as well as the performers. Acid pushed one to have heightened perceptions about your experiences. I remember a high level of hallucinatory interpretation that my friends and I attached to the music. You were attaching a very symbolic meaning to everything that they were playing. It wasn't just music. It was the revolution. It was God. It was perception. It made everything bigger, more important, more cataclysmic than it was. And maybe it was. Here we are forty years later talking about it, so obviously it was big.

Some artists choose to pursue becoming this kind of performer. Others just have it thrust upon them. Both types comingled at Woodstock. But no artist that weekend fulfilled the role of "high" priest better than Sylvester Stewart fronting his band Sly and the Family Stone. It was the most joyful noise of the entire festival, and it was made by just seven musicians: Greg Errico on drums, Larry Graham on bass and vocals, Jerry Martini on saxophone, Cynthia Robinson on trumpet, Freddie (Stewart) Stone on guitar and vocals, Rosie (Stewart) Stone on piano, and Sly Stone (Sylvester Stewart) on guitar, keyboards, and vocals.

Sly Stewart started singing gospel music in his native Dallas, Texas, at the age of four in 1948. Soulful music was dripping from his pores. In the '50s, the Stewart family, including Sly and his siblings Fred and

Rose moved to San Francisco. It was there that the family began to soak up the wide, divergent musical influences that this new home base had to offer. Sly's interest in music was formalized at Vallejo Junior College, where he studied music theory and composition while learning to play guitar, keyboards, and trumpet simultaneously. He played in several short-lived bands in the Bay Area including one with his brother Fred called the Stewart Brothers, and later one with Cynthia Robinson called the Stoners.

Immersing himself in all aspects of the music business, he wrote, played, sang, and produced songs for himself and a host of other artists, and even did a short stint as a disc jockey on a local soul music radio station with the call letters KSOL. He spoke to a local television reporter in the early '70s about his time as a DJ:

> **Sly Stone:** I used to sing all the time anyway. I brought a piano. I had a piano live in there. There were some times when, there were some commercials—I made them up myself. I played the piano, and I sang the commercials, and then, some songs that I liked, I'd cut in on the part, turn the record down, then turn the record back up, you know?

When asked if he would trade the pressures of being a superstar for the simpler life of a DJ, he responded:

> **Sly Stone:** I think if I were doing anything else, I'd be bored. So I just take it all in stride. I have to do what I do anyway, 'cause that's what I want to do so much. So it's like I'm trapped doing what I want to do anyway. A lot of people get to be made happy by what I want to do. It seems to turn a lot of people on, and that is a lot of fun. I think it has to do with songs that involve everybody and a message that involves everybody. Everybody wants to be happy. The songs that we do are songs that I feel, you know, should make everybody happy, and I think that's basically it. I like to do positive things. I don't like to bring anybody down. What you put into it is what you get out of it.

That was clearly the attitude of the group that gave him free rein to incorporate all of his many influences and talents—Sly and the Family Stone. His hits weren't just passively enjoyable, they were declarative commands to his audience and to the world: "Dance to the Music," "Stand," "Sing a Simple Song." He had absorbed every song, every style, every riff he had ever heard and forged and reconfigured them into something unique and completely his own. These were the sounds that comprised the "stew" in Stewart, and he made the most of them. Critic and author Dave Marsh described it this way in his essay about Sly and Company:

> Sly Stone was, for a while anyway, one of the greatest musical adventurers rock has ever known. Almost single-handedly he effected a revolution in soul music, one whose consequences reverberate everywhere today. With his band, Sly ended the domination of the sweet soul sound practiced by the Stax, Motown, and Muscle Shoals rhythm sections. Eighteen months after his first hit in 1968, "Dance to the Music," everyone was following his lead. And the great bulk of the disco and funk rock of today simply works off variations of Sly and the Family Stone's innovations. No one has gone past them.

> **Joshua White:** They were just amazing at that point; they had a drive and energy and were a tight band. They rose to the occasion and Sly sat there and his sisters and the other members of the band just played and were just amazing. "Everyday People" and "Dance to the Music," and "I Want to Take You Higher," and "Stand," were anthems—they played anthems. I don't know anyone—myself included—who didn't stand when they said "Stand." They just pulled you into it and were just amazing.

There was, however, a corresponding dark side. Sly voraciously consumed drugs, but then, as usually happens, drugs just as voraciously consumed Sly. The abuses, the addiction, rendered him oblivious to and incapable of fulfilling his responsibilities to his fans, his record company, his friends, his band, and, ultimately, himself. In the end, this behavior cost him his career.

> **Mike Jahn:** Sly himself was a miserable human being, a complete asshole. I almost got into a fistfight with him a year later. I was interviewing him at the New York Hilton. And Sly's publicist was some young guy who gave the impression that this was his first gig, his first big client—talk about jumping into the deep end, you get assigned to Sly Stone. And Sly is dressed like Sly. He's shirtless with sheepskin boots, tight pants, a huge Afro, of course. He's out of his mind on something, and he starts ragging on this publicist, this kid who is wearing a three-

piece suit. "You're such a square. You need to lighten up." And I was enraged. I quoted "Everyday People" back to him. "What happened to different strokes for different folks, Sly?" And he got mad and his bodyguard got agitated. I got up and walked to the door, and he told me, "If you touch that door, I'm gonna tackle you." And I said something helpful like "You and what army?" He came charging at me, and the bouncer caught him and got between him. Things calmed down and he took me to his personal room. It's just the two of us and we're sitting at a glass coffee table and he reached into one of his boots and pulls out about ten-thousand-dollars' worth of coke and laid it on the table. It was like the scene in Scarface—a mountain of coke. I finally just turned and walked out and told him, "Sly, I'm here to interview you. I don't want your coke." I never reported about it because this was in the pre-Watergate days when a gentleman reporter didn't write about these things. Reporters knew about Kennedy and Marilyn Monroe and that Lyndon Johnson would have meetings with his aides while he was in the can, but nobody wrote about it.

Stan Schnier: Sly was notorious for not showing up. So there we are one night in Providence, Rhode Island. I was working with Larry Coryell. We got there on time, we set up, we did our soundcheck, marked everything with tape, and got out of the way so Sly can do their soundcheck. Three o'clock, four o'clock, five, six, seven, eight o'clock. Nothing. I'll never forget it. And in those days, there were no cell phones. How do you contact somebody? We were calling the booking agency in New York, and they said, "We'll find their road manager." How do you find the road manager if they're on I-95 somewhere? And the show was supposed to start, the doors are supposed to open at eight. They open the doors. We're supposed to go on at 8:40. We didn't go on at 8:40. But by nine o'clock the kids were starting to get really antsy and restless and there were a lot of inner-city kids in Providence to see Sly. This was like in the early '70s, so there's like a certain kind of violent vibe kind of going on, stuff starts to get thrown around, one thing leads to another, and we gotta go on. Now the state police are there, and I'm in the back of the venue with the head of the state police and the dean of the school telling me, "We have a situation here." I'm only twenty-two years old, what do I know? I'll never forget it. And basically, what we ended up doing was playing three sets. Sly eventually showed up, but that was at 9:30 and he was totally wasted and he played like crap. I mean, he just couldn't go on. Apparently, at that point that was like the beginning of the end for him, and then he went into not showing up at all.

Comeback attempts over the years have fallen short, but for the reasons already stated, his place in music history seems assured. And that includes, of course, that magic, middle-of-the-night apparition at the Woodstock Music and Art Fair.

The bad-boy behavior was not completely in check. While most of the other artists rolled with the punches of the ever-shifting performance schedule, Sly chose to exhibit those unattractive "diva" tendencies and initially refused to come out of his trailer to go on at the appointed time, thus keeping the already exhausted crowd waiting.

John Morris: We'd done him at the Fillmore. I'd seen him in California—a real prima donna act. "I'm not going on, I'm not ready. I'm not going on, I'm not ready." And he did it for about forty-five minutes at Woodstock. So I went into the trailer where he was, and I did the best imitation of Bill Graham that I ever did. I banged on the door, I swung the door open, I walked straight over to him, I don't know if I laid hands on him, but I got right in his face and I said, "You are fuckin' going on this fuckin' minute and play, or I'm gonna feed you to the crowd and they'll eat you like piranhas!" And I just terrified this guy who was just in another space anyhow. "You are going onstage not in five minutes, not in ten, <u>now</u>!" I did everything physically short of dragging him out the door and shoving him onstage. "It's my music, man—" he started to say. "Shut the fuck up and follow me." And we went on the stage and he did one of the great performances of all time, enhanced by some of the greatest photography of all time.

The members of the Family Stone remember the night vividly.

Larry Graham: Woodstock was a big concert that we were going to play that had a lot of artists. I had no idea that it was going to be as big as it was. Getting to the concert, I realized that there were a lot of people, but still not how many until we played.

Jerry Martini: We thought that it was going to be a regular festival. We had no idea that it was going to be that big.

Greg Errico: We were scared. I've heard the other acts that were on it say the same thing; you look out there, butterflies. Before you even looked at the audience, you could feel the energy there, and you knew it was intense.

Jerry Martini: We were staying at a little motel. We didn't play till the second night. We went over there and walked around in the mud. They didn't fly us in helicopters; they were being used for Medivac. They drove us in through the maze in a couple of limousines and treated us like royalty. We were supposed to start at ten o'clock. We sat around in tents and didn't go on until three-thirty in the morning.

Greg Errico: We were supposed to go on at eight o'clock. We were in the trailer, our adrenaline up, ready to go. Mike Lang kept coming in. Things were running behind, he said, hang in there. Two hours went by. We didn't go on till three-thirty. We were physically tired, just from all the adrenaline going through your body, peaking and coming down again, getting fired up to go on, for six or seven hours.

Jerry Martini: Everybody was asleep in their sleeping bags. We were a little bit bummed, but people got up out of their sleeping bags. Everything was so late, we got onstage and just kicked ass.

Greg Errico: We went on, and you could feel the weight of it. It was heavy. This was the second day, the middle. People were sleeping, it was the middle of the night. It had just rained. Just the experience of getting there for the audience was a major no-one-had-planned thing. They had already been there for twenty-four, maybe thirty-six hours, hearing music, having to find food, standing in line to go to the bathroom. They were spent. It was nighttime. You had been waiting to do your thing for hours now. They were in their sleeping bags, tired, burnt out, hungry, who knows what, asleep. And you went on the stage to make these people get up and going. You could feel it. We started out and did the best we could. You could feel it drag and then, all of a sudden, the third song, I think, you started seeing heads bop up, people starting responding a little bit. Sly could feel it. He had it down by this time. He was great at working an audience in any situation, any diverse situation. He started talking to them. You could feel everybody start to listen to the music, wake up, get up, start dancing. Halfway through the show, the place was rocking. Really incredible experience.

Larry Graham: Our songs would segue one into the other, and many times there wasn't a place where you could get a big audience response. When we did stop playing, there was this tremendous roar unlike anything we had ever heard. It was dark and you couldn't see all those people, but to hear that was like, wow. To go back out and play the encore after hearing that, it made us rise to a level we had never been musically. There was so much energy, everybody reached deep down inside and pulled out some stuff we didn't know was there. From that point on, once you tap into a certain zone, you know you can go back there because you have now tasted that. The audience might not be as big as Woodstock, but to play anything after that, you know you have capabilities beyond. So that took our concerts up to a whole 'nother giant notch, to where the concerts became an experience, for the audience and for us. We started playing in this new zone we had never played in before and it was some of the heaviest stuff I had ever been involved in. That is what I felt Woodstock did for us.

Their performance, immortalized by the film, made one of the longest-lasting impressions on those that were fortunate enough to experience it.

Michael Wadleigh: Sly Stone got the biggest audience reaction of any group. Sly is legendary for being able to do that. If you want to choose a band, and an individual who fronted a band, for getting an audience going, well, he is the King of Funk. He is just unbelievable in his ability. You can't tell in the movie. When he says, "I wanna take you higher," the audience was so revved up. When Sly says, "Dance to the music," you can't not dance to the music. Really, I still go to a lot of rock 'n' roll concerts, and I tell you, for an ability to get you going, that group was just stunning. Sly in particular, but also his brothers and sisters, their extended mates, all the people that made up that band. When he set up a beat, I think it connects with people's heartbeats and neural synapses going off, stomachs growling. I've had the great fortune of filming a lot of great people. James Brown and Sly are similar in that when they play people can't help from moving. Sly's two songs that we used, "Dance to the Music" and "I Want to Take You Higher," we had to use them. We couldn't have not used them. It was impossible. He was just so good.

Mike Jahn: It was nighttime, it wasn't raining. He sounded great. And the crowd just got so into it, more than for anybody else I saw.

Bob Santelli: Sly had everything going for him. For starters, he was playing at night. And the kind of music he performed was funk-driven soul with horns and incredible funky beat, thanks to Larry Graham and a rhythm section that was just about as flawless at that time as you could get. It captured the essence of the festival at night and clearly. It was almost as if Sly and the Family Stone had taken each and every one of those people at Woodstock by the hand and said, follow me, and they did not only willingly but enthusiastically. The music was beyond powerful. It reached every one of those kids on that hill and into the campsite. You could not escape it. I remember talking to friends who had gone and come back and said, "Man, it was lots of mud and it was lots of rain, and we didn't eat for two days, but it was worth it because if you could have seen Sly and the Family Stone, you would've understood why."

Ellen Sander: That was amazing, that was the start of the crescendo. He had on this white outfit with fringe on it, and so every time he moved there'd be these long fringes flapping around and they were all incredible. That band, you were aware of the band because they were all such great singers and musicians.

John Morris: I was staggered! Blown away! In a series of amazingly effective performances, it was staggering. What I would say is that it was way above their position and stature. That's pompous, but it was way above their position and stature in the business.

Ellen Sander: It was Sly who made it the start of a crescendo. He is a very savvy performer; he knows how to build and build and build. And that's what he did. Every subsequent couplet he sang was more intense, louder, clearer, more to the audience. There are times when singers kind of sing to themselves, they have their eyes closed and they have an internal dialogue going, and there are times when their eyes are wide open and they're just out, everything out.

That was Sly. When ill or physically out of sorts, some performers can compartmentalize those feelings and overcome almost any obstacle when pushed onstage in the spotlight in front of a live audience. That certainly turned out to be the case with Sly at Woodstock. Whether it was sheer adrenaline (mixed, perhaps, with some other herbal or synthetic stimulants), Sly conquered Woodstock like the Greatest Generation conquered Normandy. No quarter. No prisoners. He wanted that sleepy crowd to respond. He wanted them to participate. He wanted them to sing along, and he wasn't about to take no for an answer.

If the music woke you up from a deep sleep in the cow pasture, you would have been perfectly justified thinking that you were in heaven, or at least in church with the hippest preacher in the pulpit who could speak in tongues, and a choir capable of a heavenly harmonic convergence! The medley that Sly put together of "Dance to the Music," "Music Lover," and "I Want to Take You Higher" propelled the festival to one of its highest, hardest, hippest, holiest historic moments. Drawing from equal parts of Bible-thumping preacher and silver-tongued snake-oil salesman, Sly addressed, cajoled, and exhorted the revelers:

> What we would like to do is sing a song together. Now, you see what usually happens is you get a group of people that might sing, and for some reasons that are not unknowed [sic] anymore, they won't do it. Most of us need approval. Most of us need to get approval from our neighbors before we can actually let it all hang down, you dig. What is happening here is we're gonna try and do a singalong. But a lot of people don't like to do it because they feel that it might be "old-fashioned." But you must dig that it is not a fashion in the first place. It is a feeling . . . and if it was good in the past, it's _still_ good. We would like to sing a song called "Higher," and if we can get everybody to join in, we'd appreciate it. Everybody please do what you can for me.

Then in the best tradition of call-and-response at a church service, Sly screams out, "I wanna take you higher" and right on cue the audience screams back, "HIGHER!" It was one of the defining moments of the whole festival.

> **Mike Jahn:** I walked around the rim of the natural amphitheater during "I Want to Take You Higher." People had sparklers, and when he sang the word "higher," they lifted their sparklers up in the air.

Ellen Sander: The pinnacle of that was the song "I Want to Take You Higher," and I can remember that very clearly, and the whole audience echoing "higher, higher, higher," and he was just triumphant; he was just incredible.

Bob Santelli: Everyone remembers the call and response that Sly initiates in the song "I Want to Take You Higher" where Sly says, "Higher," and the crowd says "Higher." That's exactly what the crowd was doing physically, emotionally, and spiritually. They were going higher.

The sermon continued:

Get up off your feet and say "Higher" and throw the peace sign up. It'll do you no harm. Still again some people feel that they shouldn't, because there are situations where you need approval to get in on something that could do you some good. Wanna take you higher—HIGHER!—So if you throw the peace sign up and say "Higher," get everybody to do it . . . There's a whole lotta people here and a whole lotta people might not want to do it, because they feel that they can somehow get around it and feel that there are enough people to make up for it and on and on, et cetera, et cetera. We're gonna try "Higher" again and if we can get everybody to join in, we'd appreciate it. It can do you no harm. Wanna take you higher—HIGHER! Way up on the hill, Wanna take you higher—HIGHER!—Wanna take you higher—HIGHER!— Wanna take you higher—HIGHER!

It just simply couldn't get any higher than that.

THE WHO

As removed from politics as Woodstock wanted to be, there was no denying or ignoring the tumultuous atmosphere of the '60s that surrounded the festival. It permeated the event in so many ways that we've already seen with Country Joe, Joan Baez, and John Fogerty—and in many other ways as well.

Michael Wadleigh: People like Ginsberg and others said that what happened in the '60s was long overdue. It had been building up in the US and around the world. This sort of movement away from commercialization and toward essential values. Growing your hair long and expressing your own personality in a nonconformist and exploratory fashion was part of that.

The chasm between parents and their children drove young people toward one another. It united them in a way that only the sense of impending danger can.

Ellen Sander: It was a counterbalance of trauma and celebration . . . and I don't think anybody will ever know the answer to the mystery of why didn't Woodstock descend into chaos and violence—because all the elements for that were there, but instead it was a very peaceful thing. And people there at the time, we felt that it was kind of a destiny, that that would kind of be the path of the future—of peaceful cooperation, of a spirit of community, of tribalism, those things . . . it didn't quite go the way they expected [laugh] but at least for that weekend, we had it. And there was a feeling of being in control of it, there was a feeling that what happened at Woodstock was the result of the collective mind-set of everybody.

Capitalizing on the presence of all the idealistic, eager-to-change-the-world minds, was the movement, which is really just rough nomenclature for groups of people who organized social and political protest. The promoters felt it was necessary to include the movement in their plans for the festival. At the time, if you weren't playing with and for the movement, then you were playing against them. And there could be nothing worse for the promoters than the movement portraying Three Days of Peace and Music as an overly commercialized, capitalistic, soul-sucking venture.

Stan Goldstein: My recollection is that I was in the New York offices one day when I was shuttling back and forth between New York City and Wallkill. A call came in from Paul Krassner and it came to me. Paul denies this. Whether it originated from Paul or not, we got a call from people representing the movement. The movement was a conglomeration of activists of all kinds who traveled in similar circles with sometimes-similar aims. They were politically active, civil rights active, antiwar active, and all of these people were involved with one another. Mostly on the left. They were loosely aligned in this thing called "the movement." Everyone had everyone else's name in their Rolodex. A call was received by Woodstock. Abbie Hoffman later described it as "requesting," we heard it as "demanding," a meeting.

And what happened at this meeting?

Stan Goldstein: There were several meetings and Abbie was not the only one, nor was he necessarily the leader, although, like Wavy Gravy in the Hog Farm, he was granted the title of leader because he was the person who spoke. Abbie and others were the vocal representatives of the movement and presented a series of demands. Give us a printing press and some money so that we can—and no charge for us to have a concession area where we could set up—from which we can extend our message at the festival.

Perhaps the most famous member of the movement who was present at Woodstock was Abbie Hoffman.

Paul Krassner: He was relatively short and stocky. Even though he told me he never brushed his teeth, he had a great smile. His hair, dark black, curly, long, and Medusa-like. If you were stoned, it would have looked like there were snakes twisting around him.

Ellen Sander: Well, he had a lot of big hair, he was very skinny, he had broad shoulders, he had a big smile, very kind of flashing eyes. He was very attractive, he was witty, he had a kind of crackly voice.

Krassner, a journalist, humorist and political activist, formed a close bond with Abbie.

Paul Krassner: On the Lower East Side of New York there was a group called the Community Breast where we tried to figure out ideas that would nurture various groups in the community. And Abbie was at those meetings, but we never really talked. It was at a pre-demonstration rally, in protest of a military parade on Fifth Avenue in New York. We were all gathered in the park before going to Fifth. That's where we first talked. And after the protest, we had some soup and our friendship began. So that was in 1967.

Ellen Sander: He was very interesting, I thought he was joking most of the time, but . . . when we got back to New York, we started going to some Yippie events, and there was one at Grand Central Station where people . . . there was an antiwar demonstration, unsanctioned, unpermitted, at Grand Central Station. And the police came out and people did get hurt. Somebody got pushed through a plate glass window and lost the use of their hands or something like that. I mean, that was the end of it for me. I said this is not really where I'm going, anyway.

In 1968, Abbie had envisioned the Democratic National Convention as something similar to what Woodstock turned out to be.

Paul Krassner: At Woodstock people could camp overnight and there was no violence. And the convention was officially labeled by a government report as a police riot. One thing that they had in common was police surveillance. At the press tent, some guy pointed out to me this photographer who he said was part of the CID, the Criminal Intelligence Division of the army . . . they just knew that virtually none of the four hundred, five hundred thousand or whatever it was, virtually none of them would be interested in fighting in the Vietnam War. And of course, it goes without saying that in '68 there was more than police surveillance. So it was a connection in their minds between the counterculture and the antiwar people.

But 1969 was a new year. And Abbie, the fighter he was, persisted to get his message across. The movement was housed in its own tent, known as Movement City, where they made pamphlets and did their best to reach people.

Paul Krassner: I was staying in what was called "Movement City," which was a huge tent. And while they were cranking out mimeograph machines, remember those? They get your hands all messy? That's before the internet—just churning out leaflets telling people the event should be free, which was perhaps unnecessary since a lot of those people were busy pushing down the fence and getting in free yesterday. There were the movement leaders and also the people who considered themselves part of it. They were there. They weren't movement celebrities. They were just people who had a common sense of responsibility. There were volunteers in there who were against the war and participated in demonstrations. But I don't know if any of the leaders were there except Gravy who had a pig that the Yippies were going to run for president the previous year. Even though Wavy was essentially a clown, he was a committed clown. And there were those that thought he should be committed.

While most participants, both in the audience and on the stage, were basically on board with the movement and its various messages, one of the unfortunate most publicized political events at Woodstock occurred onstage between Abbie Hoffman and Pete Townshend.

Ellen Sander: The time was irrelevant, everybody was quite wide awake and there was a break. You know, the Who have a great deal of equipment. I do remember there being a kind of longer break than usual as their equipment was being set up, and Abbie Hoffman had somehow gotten on the stage, or close to it, and he called me over and he expressed some . . . antagonism about the festival; he felt like the music scene was stealing the thunder from the political movement that he was trying to foment. He made a number of bitter comments, like he said, "This isn't such a big deal because the Beatles aren't here and Dylan isn't going to be here," and I said, "Don't kid yourself. This is the most amazing thing that's ever happened and this is going to be what's remembered." He didn't like hearing any of that. He was not in a very happy mood. He was in a very unhappy mood. He was not enjoying himself.

Paul Krassner: Abbie Hoffman, who was tripping on LSD at the time, went onstage while the Who were performing. And between numbers, he grabbed the mic, the message he wanted to get across was that the politics behind the event was that John Sinclair, the manager of the Motor City Five, was in jail for ten years for having two joints. So he was making the connection between music, marijuana, and political repression.

Pete Townshend: I was nervous because we didn't go there by helicopter. We went by road. We got as far as the car could go in the mud and it got stuck. It became the hundred and ninety-fifth limo to get stuck. We got out and landed in the mud and that was it. There was nowhere to go. There were no dressing rooms because they had all been turned into hospitals. There was nowhere to eat. Somebody came out of the canteen, which was where we had been naturally gravitating toward in order to sit down and eat because we were told that we wouldn't be on for fifteen hours.

It was well after midnight when the Who took the stage. Townshend was already a bit grumpy. Meanwhile, festival organizer Michael Lang invited Abbie Hoffman to sit on the stage next to him to watch the set. Hoffman had been working as a volunteer in one of the medical tents, consuming large amounts of LSD to keep himself awake. Lang thought it would be beneficial for him to take a break, chill, and enjoy some great music.

Abbie Hoffman: That was a big crackdown year, 1969. Nixon was already into Operation Intercept and everything, and there was a big war and one of the twelve major wars on drugs in this century was happening then. There was a symbol of the Youth International Party, John Sinclair, because he was a leader of the White Panther Party—they were Yippie affiliates in Ann Arbor—and he was given ten years in jail for either passing a marijuana cigarette in a circle to a narc, or selling him two—I'm not exactly sure about that. Anyway, the sentence was way outrageous. It was obvious they were going after him because he was a political leader as well. So, "Free John Sinclair" was, for the counterculture, the same as "Free Huey Newton" was for the black power movement.

Pete Townshend: As we were going toward the canteen, somebody came out saying that the tea and coffee had got acid in them and all the water was polluted with acid. I spent a bit of time on the stage, but everybody was very freaked. I would find a nice place to sit and listen to somebody like Jefferson Airplane and then some lunatic would come up to me like Abbie Hoffman or some stagehand and go, "Ahhhhhhh! Aaaaaaaah! Buuuuuuuupw."

Abbie Hoffman: So we're sitting around the stage. A huge stage—wow!—I don't think there's ever been a bigger stage in the world. Kind of Indian fashion—our legs crossed—and being in the movie, having a good time. It was the most relaxed state I'd been in days. And I said, "Well, when are you going to announce this?" And they said, "We're thinking of having a press conference when it's over." And I said, "<u>Over</u>! No! You don't understand. I like you guys, but you've got to announce it now. There's five hundred thousand people. The world should hear it now. Just tell them." "Well, we don't want to interrupt the music," and all of this. And they're just hemming and hawing.

Joe McDonald: I knew Abbie and I knew Jerry [Rubin] because I moved in circles where there were radicals. I knew that it was not uncommon for the pontificators, politicians, underground politicians to get up and try and make a speech. I knew he had been making a scene around there. He was stoned. Someone said he had taken acid and he was stoned, and I can believe that because it was crazy what he did. I was watching and all of a sudden, there was a pause because they didn't introduce their songs. Which was something that bands would do. Then—boom—Abbie walks up to the microphone and starts giving this talk, which I knew about. I remember thinking at the time that the audience was not going to be able to process this.

Abbie Hoffman: So I got up and said, "If you're not going to announce it, I'm going to announce it." And I walked up to the microphone and I started to give a quick rap, which I'm good at. If you've given political raps at musical concerts, you know you've got to be quick; you've got to be visual. You've got to ask one thing and get the hell out of there as quick as you can. So I said something to the effect of "Four hundred thousand of our brothers and sisters for no more than we're doing on this hill. It's only fair that we help out. We are the Woodstock Nation. We are one." Something like that. And the mic got cut off. They cut the mic, which was an insult. Because this announcement was just as important as all the other announcements they were making.

Joe McDonald: The Who was well into their set, and all of a sudden, this guy shows up and starts talking politics and anti-marijuana laws. I don't think Townshend was even aware that he was there. He just kind of looked up and "Who the hell's this guy?" A stranger shows up and starts talking in your microphone. It's your turf, but it wasn't a hostile takeover.

Abbie Hoffman: It could have been the Who doing a song, then readjusting their instruments. It could have been before the Who came on, or during their set. But they weren't playing. I didn't run up and grab the mic out of Peter Townshend's hands, that's for sure. There was a pause, and I got up to make my announcement. So they cut off the mic and I exploded. I said, "What the fuck did they do that for?" and I kicked the mic. And as I turned around to walk back, I remember, Townshend was turning around and we bumped—that was it, we bumped.

Henry Diltz: I remember standing on the stage. I think the Who were about to go on. It was one of those times when the stage was quite crowded. I'd be on one side of the stage looking across at Chip Monck and all these faces of people out on the fringes of the stage, which was just this big open platform. And Abbie Hoffman suddenly ran out and grabbed the microphone and said, "Remember John Sinclair and the guys in prison for smoking pot," or something like that. And he was haranguing the crowd, and he wasn't supposed to be doing that.

Joe McDonald: Peter walked over and bonked Abbie in the head with his guitar. Abbie's response was so funny because he just looked at Peter and then jumped into the press pit and went through the crowd and kept going.

Henry Diltz: [Hoffman] grabbed the mic and suddenly Peter Townshend was standing there with his guitar and I saw him raise it up, kind of holding it over his shoulder, and walk up behind and just go boink right in the back of the neck. It was almost like a bayonet thrust. He had it shoulder height with the body of the guitar next to his head and his hand outstretched holding the pegs of the guitar. And he just thrust it, you know—one quick little jab right in the back of Abbie Hoffman— who fell down, I remember. It looked like a fatal blow. He was really pissed at this guy taking over the microphone when they were about to go on. And I thought, Whoa! It was like an electrifying moment that kind of just passed.

Abbie's behavior did not leave a good impression with many of the festival participants.

Michael Wadleigh: I was disappointed. Certainly, it was not the organizers who had no politics and didn't want people speaking from the stage. That is just not correct. There were plenty of venues.

But what about Pete Townshend? Boinking Abbie in the head in the midst of three days of peace, love, and music? Was he sending some sort of political message? No. He was simply a passionate and sometimes violent performer.

Michael Wadleigh: Pete Townshend booted me off the stage. He physically inserted his boot into my rear end, so to speak. But he apologized. It broke his concentration that I was constantly getting up there and getting close to people. Pete apologized by saying "I'm out of control." I've filmed a lot of different rock 'n' rollers over the years, and I think people don't realize that these are performers. They do various things to themselves to get into it and put on a great performance. They lose themselves. Pete has told me a number of times that he is very high-strung. He is not laid-back. He's really concentrating and into it and trying to put on the best show he can. My take on it, both with

Abbie and myself, is that Pete's point is "This is my show, and I do what I have to do to get into things." I don't take it seriously at all that he kicked Abbie off the stage. Jesus Christ, those stages were up there for four fucking days. Abbie could have done his thing another time. There were plenty of opportunities for people to speak, especially for someone like Abbie. To try and do it in the middle of somebody's set—if it had been a different musician who was wound up a different way, then that musician may have said, yeah cool. But again, Pete Townshend is not that kind of person. Abbie was so ripped that he never even came back. I never got anything from him that was worth including in the movie. One could say that that was Abbie's fault. He wrote his book, he had his say anyway.

What did Wadleigh think about the Who as performers?

Mike Wadleigh: It may look easy when Townshend does those windmills and hits the strings on his guitar, but it's not. He has to take aim. He's really playing. If he misses, then the music doesn't go on. He's the only guitarist. You really have only three people who are playing: one guitarist, one drummer, and one bassist. Roger Daltrey sang. If he misses his guitar and fucks up that way, you're going to notice, it won't be there. He's not just standing there. They are a choreographed group. They're leaping all the time and falling to their knees and Roger's just singing, Entwistle is standing there, Moon is all over his drums, and in a way, Townshend is doing way more physically than anyone else, in terms of playing his instrument and doing gymnastics.

And with that focus and passion came the occasional violent moment. One particular scene from the Fillmore comes to mind.

Jim Marion: I had been to another Who show earlier in the year, with Sweetwater and It's a Beautiful Day, where the building next to the Fillmore East had caught fire and a fireman had tried to interrupt the Who to tell people to evacuate. Townshend didn't take kindly to that interruption either, and he had kicked the man into the front row. Eventually, we had to evacuate the building and the show was canceled (the silver lining was that we got free seats to see the Who when they came back shortly thereafter and played with Chuck Berry and Albert King).

Stan Schnier: The Fillmore caught on fire one night, and the Who were onstage. There was a little grocery store on the corner attached to the building; it was like an apartment building, an old tenement building, and they had a fire in there. So the fire department comes and they're trying to contain the fire. At a certain point the fire chief said, "We've got to evacuate this theater." There were maybe twenty-five hundred kids in there. And the firemen came to the stage door—they didn't ask, they just came in and they walked out onstage in the middle of the set. And Townshend smacked this guy in the mouth. I swear to God. "Get the fuck off the stage!" And they arrested him, and they put him in jail down in the sixth precinct or whatever it was. Bill Graham went down and Pete was in jail until three, four, five in the morning. He told him, "You don't punch the fire chief in the mouth!" And Townshend's attitude was "Hey, we're playing rock 'n' roll, mate! Who the fuck are you?!"

Mike Jahn remembers that incident a little differently.

Mike Jahn: I was there that night. He threw the fireman off the stage. I was friends with this folkie named [Steve Barron]. And he was a Jerry Jeff Walker type. And he was friends with Pete from somewhere. I was friends with Pete from San Francisco. We had split a six-pack at some sleazy hotel in the Tenderloin. Steve calls and says, "Pete's here. He's hiding from the cops. He threw a fire marshal off the stage and the cops are looking for him." I said, "Just keep him there until the lawyers can sort it out." Pete's lawyer sorted it out and that was the end of that. Back then, the Times didn't really care what rock stars did in their spare time as long as they didn't kill anybody. Today I could sell the story for fifty thousand dollars to US magazine.

From the start, booking the Woodstock Festival was always a matter of quantity and quality. There could be disagreements and esoteric altercations about the latter, but the former was strictly statistical. Creedence Clearwater Revival had the biggest hit singles of 1969? Book them! Janis Joplin was selling out concerts and knocking out audiences all over the world? Book her!

The litmus test for picking acts to play at Woodstock started with three basic questions: Who was selling lots of records? Who was attracting sold-out crowds at all of their concert appearances? Who was getting heavy airplay and lots of rotation on the nation's hip FM rock radio stations? It didn't take long for the promoters to figure out that the answers to those three questions were very simple. The Who was selling lots of records. The Who was attracting sold-out crowds at all of their concert appearances. And the Who was getting heavy airplay and lots of rotation on the nation's hip FM rock radio stations.

Book them!

Only it wasn't that easy. The Who was an international sensation in 1969. The key word being: *Tommy*. Though groups such as the Kinks and the Pretty Things had experimented with long-form rock 'n' roll recordings, *Tommy* was the first rock opera to gain any sort of recognition. Peter Dennis Blandford Townshend delivered this musical experience with more passion, class, panache, and authority than any of his predecessors.

The Who was not a big part of the original, mid-'60s British Invasion, at least not in the States. In 1964, 1965, and 1966, the biggest English hit makers burning up the US charts were the Beatles, the Dave Clark Five, the Rolling Stones, the Animals, the Kinks, and even Herman's Hermits. The Who made no appearance.

Billy Altman: They were not a giant national band. They had played two years earlier at Monterey and nothing had much happened. At the time of Woodstock, Tommy had just come out, and they had had some hits, "Pinball [Wizard]" was the first single. And over the course of the summer, Tommy became a big deal. Woodstock helped make them a band in terms of popularity.

I received a promotional copy of the Who's first American 45 rpm single on Decca Records in January of 1965. It was called "I Can't Explain" and (for reasons that "I can't explain" even up to this very day), it didn't make a dent on the Top 40 charts. It was a terrific record, and remains a huge part of the Who legacy. (They even performed it as one of the warm-up songs at Woodstock before launching into *Tommy* in its entirety at the festival.)

That all changed in the spring of 1967 when their single "Happy Jack" climbed onto the American Top 40. That was followed in the fall by one of the most powerful and dynamic records ever released at any time by any group called "I Can See for Miles." It has the distinction of being the Who's only US Top 10 single. A few of their other post-Woodstock releases ("Join Together," "Squeeze Box," "Who Are You") flirted with the Top 10, but never quite got there. But with the Who, singles were just simply not the name of the game. It was the albums from first track to last such as *The Who Sell Out, Tommy, Who's Next,* and *Quadrophenia,* as well as sold-out concert tours all over the world that solidified their image as the hippest, hardest-rocking quartet in the world.

Groups with staying power evolve and go through changes as time marches on. Just think about the Beatles. The Fab Four went from lovable mop tops to wildly creative, experimental progressive rockers in a remarkably short period of time. The Who went through definable changes of their own, but nobody ever mistook them for lovable mop tops. They were more like prepunk punks, part of the English Mod movement described by Dave Marsh as "violent displays of unbridled joy from young, newly affluent, pre-fabricated hoodlums. Outrage for its own sake; consumption without guilt." The Who certainly manifested this in their swaggering, arrogant early anthems such as "My Generation" and "The Kids Are Alright." But the line "hope I die before I get old"? I wonder how quickly Townshend realized what an albatross that would be to carry around for the rest of his life. How soon did he get that journalists, fans, and wags would use it like a taxi meter to count down the days of his life? The meter ran out for Keith Moon on September 7, 1978. And for John Entwistle on June 27, 2002. Drugs were involved in both fatalities.

Hubris aside, it became apparent very quickly that the Who had so much more to offer than just bombast and posturing. As early as the *A Quick One* album in the UK (called *Happy Jack* in the US to capitalize on the hit single), Townshend was dealing with the paradox of long-form songs in a primarily short-form medium. But that was just the tip of the iceberg of Who contradictions. Were they cerebral or visceral? Both. Were they pretentious or profound? Both. And finally, how did the anger and violence that the group seethed with garner such warmth and acclaim from the hippie-dippy, peace-and-love generation? I can't answer that last one, but it found its deepest, richest, most inexplicable alchemy on their visit to the Woodstock Music and Art Fair.

John Morris: Michael and I did the booking. And Michael booked a lot of people that he wanted to have and a lot of people he wanted to do favors for. A lot of the people I brought in I brought in because either I had done them at the Fillmore, or I'd seen them, or their managers were really good friends. Frank Barsalona and I wore Peter Townshend down at about three o'clock in the morning after having had a spaghetti dinner in Frank's apartment. He said, "Alright! Alright! I'll do the goddamn thing! Let me go to bed!"

The Who were the last act of that evening, and there was another problem with the Who that unless they got paid in cash, they weren't going on. They stayed in their dressing room and John Wolf, who was known as Wiggy, because he was bald-headed from scarlet fever when he was a kid, just said, "We're not going on unless we get paid in cash."

Why?

John Morris: Well, you gotta remember that Peter didn't want to do it in the first place. And they were a major, major, major band. And they saw the chaos. We flew 90 percent of the people. They had to get loaded into a helicopter from the place where they were staying at and come back, and they'd been hearing from the artists who came in, "It's amazing! It's wild! It's out of control." Well, it wasn't out of control. So their attitude was we don't want to be here. And we're gonna make sure we get paid. They'd been around enough to sniff that there was the possibility that the money wouldn't happen . . . John and Joel were presented with the problem and John and Joel knew the guy who was the head of the local bank. They went to the bank, opened it, and got the money. I don't remember if it was a cashier's check or cash. But it was one or the other. It was in the vault. The bank manager opened the vault, got them in there, got them the instrument that they needed and I don't remember if it was a check or cash. I sort of thought it was cash, but it may not have been. We're talking about probably one o'clock in the morning, so the guy was in bed. I know that's what happened . . . They wanted to play, but you gotta remember—English rock 'n' roll—all of those guys had been burned and stiffed and fucked around, and they just weren't gonna have it happen on this one.

Our superfan in the trenches, Joan Auperlee, had this mind-boggling encounter in the midst of all this:

Joan Auperlee: The Who were supposed to perform that night. As my friend Tommy and I were walking backstage, we noticed a Jeep parked near the stairs. Pete Townshend, Keith Moon, and John Entwistle were in the Jeep. They seemed to be arguing about something. Tommy urged me to go say hello because I was such a big fan. I approached, and they were nice to me and asked me if I wanted to sit with them. I did and Tommy stood nearby. We talked a bit, but they were distracted and were trying to decide if they should play because they wanted to have money up front and it was a free concert at that point. That night I sat on the stage for the Who and Sly and the Family Stone. I caught one of Keith Moon's drumsticks and promptly dropped it between the wooden slats on the stage. It was a great night with high energy all around.

"High energy" doesn't begin to describe Roger Daltrey's recollections about the festival. I asked him about his dearest held memories on one of his visits to my radio program.

Roger Daltrey: The sun coming up to "See Me, Feel Me" was the top. I mean, that was an amazing experience. As soon as the—the words "see me" came out of my mouth from the end of <u>Tommy</u>, this huge, red, August sun popped its head out of the horizon, over the crowd. And, that light show you can't beat!

What other impressions did he have from the performance and the festival in general?

Roger Daltrey: The smoke, just the whole event was something very, very special. And the other thing I remember most, was that I dreamt the whole thing three weeks before it happened. And I thought I was in Vietnam, because I had this dream about helicopters and towers and fires and smoke. When I got to Woodstock, it was Woodstock. That was extraordinary. I don't really quite know how to come to grips with it, because to me the success of Woodstock and the importance of Woodstock was that it was a triumph for humanity. The audience was the star of Woodstock. We were the catalyst that brought them there, but this was the first time that this young generation had got together in such numbers, and these people, unlike us—we were English—American youngsters at that time were under incredible pressure from the Vietnam War and it made people in power take notice. That was the importance for me at Woodstock.

The audience was simply blown away.

Bob Santelli: If you had to rate the top five performances at Woodstock, I would put the Who in there as well. I had seen the Who; they played Asbury Park at the Convention Hall, oddly enough. What made the Who set so legendary is how it was captured in the film. If you recall the slow motion with Pete Townshend and the windmills and the fringe jacket and the flowing hair of Roger Daltrey; it was perfect cinema. I think the Who in the <u>Woodstock</u> film was better presented than any of the other acts. It really gave the impetus for critics and historians to consider their performance one of the greatest at Woodstock. I remember owning the video of the <u>Woodstock</u> movie and going back and playing the Who performance for my young kids and saying, "Here's a good example of rock 'n' roll," and "Here's a good example of how it could turn a possibly ordinary moment into an extraordinary one. This is a band that can do that." My kids were looking and watching, and the oldest one is thinking, "Oh my God, this is pretty cool, Dad." I'd always hoped to be able to take them to see the Who. To more or less carry on from showing them the Woodstock footage, but never had the opportunity to do so, unfortunately.

What was so special about the Who as performers?

Billy Altman: It was a remarkable experience to see them do an entire double album in order. They were really at the height of their powers, and I had been a Who fan for a long time. They were such an interesting group in terms of everybody's contributions. Seeing them was always really an exciting experience. A great band on record but much better live. They had a lot of dynamics going just in terms of the four of them. They really understood what each of them contributed to the band. They all were the stereotype of each of their instruments. John was really the rock solid bass player who really centered the entire band. Keith Moon was this wild drummer who could fill in these great solos with double drums and could do anything—a tremendously exciting drummer. Townshend was the thinker of the band and the songwriter and a tremendously exciting live performer as a guitar player. And Daltrey was a prototypical lead singer. A really good-looking guy, he could throw the microphone and the mic cord around. They did everything that you would expect everybody on their instruments to do. It was textbook.

Pete Townshend's memories of the festival have changed over the years. Several years ago, he said:

> **Pete Townshend:** Woodstock was horrible. Woodstock was only horrible because it went so wrong. It could have been extraordinary. I suppose with the carefully edited view that the public got through Michael Wadleigh's film, it was a great event. But for those involved in it, it was a terrible shambles. Full of the most naïve, childlike people. We have a word for them in England. Twits.

But of all people, Pete Townshend is entitled to a bit of revisionist history. When he went back to perform as a solo artist at the Thirtieth Anniversary Concert, he spoke these words to the crowd before performing "Behind Blue Eyes":

> **Pete Townshend:** I'm gonna mention somebody I kinda wished I'd met after what happened up here on the stage that day it happened, but we never met. We never talked about it. We never met. We never touched. We never spoke. We never kissed. He never wrote. He never rang . . . and I was his mother! This is Abbie Hoffman, and I'd like to play this song. You know, he was sincere about what he was trying to do up here way back then, and, uh, some of the songs I've picked to play tonight are about the way things have changed in the thirty years since the last gathering here, and some people want all of that stuff back, and I don't want it back. I think that what happened after the Woodstock concert was kind of miraculous and everybody moved on, and America is a better country because of it. And that's how I feel, and I'm from another country, so you can take that or leave it. And there's lots of things wrong with lots of places in the world, but what happened at that concert was something that took a long time to land with me, you know, and I think maybe even last year if they'd asked me to play here, I probably would have said no, you know, I probably shouldn't really be there. So I'm really glad to be here today, and I dedicate this to the Chicago revolutionaries who likely got a lot of things wrong, but their hearts were in the right place.

JEFFERSON AIRPLANE

Hungry and fatigued, half a million kids were still sitting in the mud on Sunday morning. By this point, the concessions stands had already run out of food. Roy Landis, a kid from New Jersey who had made his way up to the festival, recalls the scene.

Roy Landis: The first day it was possible to buy food. But that ran out very quickly. They dropped in some food. I managed to find some people who had some food. Of course, I brought a lot of pot with me, which became more valuable than currency. I was able to get food; sometimes people would give you food. You could trade for food. No one went hungry. I didn't see anyone in serious trouble. There was enough food to go around. The whole thing was so much bigger than anyone anticipated that there was no distribution network or anything like that. They had set up some stands to sell food, but that was exhausted by the middle of the afternoon on Friday. You couldn't buy any food from the concessions. There wasn't any more to be had. One morning I remember having cereal and milk out of a hat that I had been wearing on my head. There was cereal and milk but no bowls. I thought it would be a better idea than not eating at all. That hat wasn't that valuable by any means.

But the festival organizers weren't leaving everyone high and dry. From the beginning, they had a plan to manage the crowd in the least authoritarian way possible.

Stan Goldstein: The idea was that we would somehow need to feed the crowd. We also needed help with security. We needed an unusual cop because we were doing an unusual thing in an unusual way. We knew that with having so many people gathered together in unfamiliar sur-roundings that the situation <u>could be</u> volatile. We could have a mass of people moving in one direction all at the same time. People could get hurt. I interviewed dozens of cops, presented them with that scenario, and said if suddenly, masses of people could begin to move, how do we stop the herd? We know that tear gas doesn't work, Jeeps with barbed wire don't work, snarling dogs don't work, how do we stop this crowd from getting hurt? The typical cop's response was to just fumble and stumble all over themselves. Wes Pomeroy was the guy who said that the only way you could stop those things is by creating an atmosphere in which that won't happen. I conceptualized a commune. If we could find a commune that embodied all of these capacities and could live up to our highest ideals for that, that's what we would wish for. I set out to find such a group.

Enter the Hog Farm.

Tom Law: The Hog Farm was living in LA on an actual hog farm. In exchange for rent, they took care of the hogs. But it was kind of a dead-end street. They were doing shows in LA, experiential light shows, psychedelic circus stuff. My friend and I decided they had to get out of LA because we knew they were getting tired of it. We wound up orchestrating that. My brother's an actor and Otto Prem-inger was a friend of ours. Like a lot of people we knew, he would come up and stay with us at this castle we had. One time we were smoking some dope and he told us about a movie he was working on called <u>Skidoo</u> with Jackie Gleason, Carol Channing, Groucho Marx, Mickey Rooney, Peter Lawford, Burgess Meredith, all these famous people. Eric Preminger and I hired the Hog Farm to be the hippies in the movie. He wasn't known as Eric Preminger back then because it was a secret that he was the son of Otto Preminger and Gypsy Rose Lee. But now he's copped to it and he's Eric Preminger. It has to be the most repressed movie of all time. You can't get it. It's the ultimate cult film. I'm in it. And that's where the Hog Farm got the money to get out of LA. And after that, we went to the Southwest and did street shows all over the Southwest, which were a blast. I was the front man.

How did Stan find the Hog Farm?

Stan Goldstein: A friend of mine suggested that I talk to Howard Smith who wrote a column for the <u>Village Voice</u> called "Scenes." There was nothing going on in the culture that Howard didn't know about. He was an information facilitator particularly as it related to undercurrents and underground. I told him I was looking for a group like the Hog Farm. He said, "Lucky you. The Hog Farm happens to be here. And I can put you in touch with Hugh Romney." We got in touch with one another and before I was allowed to meet with the Hog Farm, I had to meet with Wavy at a friend's loft downtown on Canal Street.

Wavy Gravy was still known by his given name of Hugh Romney at the time of the Woodstock Festival. He began his career as a stand-up comedian in Greenwich Village.

Tom Law: He is a real good storyteller. And he would tell stories about jazz musicians. I think he could evoke a soulful jazz experience in words. His act also contained a lot of obscure but powerful messages about becoming more conscious. That's what he was about. He had a lot of jokes, but they weren't ha-ha jokes. He had a thing called Hugh, TT and the Moon, which was him, Hugh Romney, Tiny Tim, and the Moondog. They did a lot of shows together, very much on the edge of bohemian reality. Really pushing the edges of consciousness but not in a very graphic way at all. I think he had a sympathy and an empathy for the drug experience, and that's where most art comes from. Most art comes from alcohol and drugs, let's face it. Very few people will not admit to that unless they're nuts or don't know.

Wavy Gravy: Stan says to us "How'd you like to do this festival in New York State?" And we said, "We'll be in New Mexico," because that's where we were all going, we had put a hold on some land near Black Mesa. Stan didn't even blink and he said, "That's alright. We'll fly you in an Astrojet." And we just figured he was one toke over the line and thought nothing of it.

But Stan and the Woodstock organizers were dead serious.

Tom Law: Stan Goldstein came out to Aspen Meadows to where we had what we called the Great Bus Race. My bus against Ken Kesey's. I wasn't officially part of the Hog Farm, but I hung out there a lot.

Wavy Gravy: There we were high in the hills up above Santa Fe during the summer solstice, which was a very, very big deal for people in New Mexico. We brought the buses up there. Ken Kesey came up in this white Cadillac convertible with his tennis racket on the back shelf, and lots of beer. They had just invented screw-on tops and we didn't know that, so we thought the beer was safe. But the beer was electric so there we were out of our skulls and we actually had an electric bus race, which was filmed by John Philip Law. Not to be believed without being seen. Suddenly there's Goldstein with this aluminum rock 'n' roll attaché case. And indeed we had our own American Airlines Astrojet. Far fuckin' out. So what we did was take the best of our folks and the best of every commune in New Mexico. So it was indeed eighty-five of us, not all Hog Farmers, and fifteen Native Americans.

Lisa Law: We were at the summer solstice celebration in New Mexico at Aspen Meadows when Stan Goldstein came and asked us to come to Woodstock to help with the free food booths, the trails, the campgrounds. So we agreed. They sent us there on an American Airlines jumbo jet. So we arrived and they decided that we were the head of security, we were the security people.

Wavy Gravy: When we arrived at Kennedy, we were surrounded by the world press. There was an unbelievable amount of cameras and reporters, and this reporter said, "Hog Farm, you guys are doing the security?" I said, "Oh my God, they made us the cops?" And then I asked the guy, "Well, do you feel secure?" and the guy said, "Yeah." And I said, "See it's working already." He got really pissed and said, "Come on, what are you gonna use for crowd control?" and I said, "Cream pies and a seltzer bottle!" and they all wrote it down, I swear to God, I felt the power of manipulating the media.

What happened next?

Despite all the great musicians who performed, the real stars—the reason we're still talking about Woodstock forty years after the fact—was the audience itself. Reports vary on how many people actually showed up, but in the end, the whole world went to Woodstock.

At 5:07 p.m. on Friday, August 15, 1969, Richie Havens took the stage at the Woodstock Music and Art Fair. He was originally booked to play fifth, but fate had other ideas and Richie turned out to be the opening "act"-cident at the festival.

Arlo Guthrie was the quintessential hippie and the Woodstock performer who in many ways most resembled the audience. He is pictured here in a still from Arthur Penn's <u>Alice's Restaurant</u>, the film inspired by Guthrie's epic song.

Folk madonna Joan Baez brought poetry, politics, and her soothing, beautiful voice to Woodstock. She was the last act on Friday, and as John Morris said, "She was the lullaby so that they could make it through that night."

Country Joe McDonald was another one of the people pressed into service. Originally booked to play with his band, the Fish, on Sunday, Joe did a solo acoustic set on Friday afternoon and galvanized the crowd with his pro-soldier, anti-Vietnam "Fish cheer."

LEFT: Joe Cocker's mesmerizing performance of Lennon and McCartney's "With a Little Help from My Friends" remains a favorite of many festival attendees. His complete reinvention of the song was a perfect metaphor for the subtext of the entire weekend.

BELOW: Crosby, Stills and Nash didn't go to Woodstock for a concert, they went for a coronation—their own! Their second live performance together established them as the group to watch in the early days of the coming new decade.

Santana was the ultimate wild card at Woodstoc Their debut album was still a month away from release and they weren't at all well known on the East Coast. Nevertheless, their performance, particularly "Soul Sacrifice," as captured in the Woodstock movie, catapulted them into international superstardom.

By late Saturday night, the audience was getting weary. But salvation came in the form of Sly and the Family Stone. Sly Stone conquered Woodstock like the Greatest Generation conquered Normandy. No quarter. No prisoners. He wanted that sleepy crowd to respond. He wanted them to participate. He wanted them to sing along, and he wasn't about to take no for an answer.

WARNER BROS/PHOTOFEST ©WARNER BROS

WARNER BROS/PHOTOFEST ©WARNER BROS

LEFT: Alvin Lee and Ten Years After played an energetic set, but the pièce de résistance was the set closer, "I'm Going Home." The song was always a highlight, but the Woodstock performance raised the level of excitement and enthusiasm and pure joy to completely unimaginable proportions.

RIGHT: 1969 was the year of the Who. Pete Townshend's rock opera, <u>Tommy</u>, captured the imagination of music fans everywhere. And their appearance at the festival, represented here by the iconic image of Roger Daltrey's flying fringe and swinging microphone, brought them to a new level of success in America.

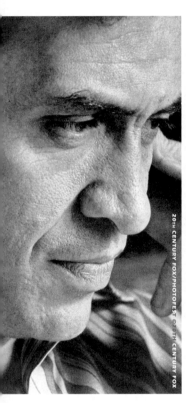

20TH CENTURY FOX/PHOTOFEST ©20TH CENTURY FOX

ANNE WELDON

WARNER BROS/PHOTOFEST ©WARNER BROS

LEFT: Impressario Bill Graham wasn't officially involved at Woodstock but did help in securing spots on the bill for Santana and the Grateful Dead. Just his name gave credibility to the neophyte Woodstock promoters.

MIDDLE: John Morris is one of the unsung heroes of Woodstock. His actions bring to mind Kipling's line, "If you can keep your head while all about you are losing theirs . . . you'll be a Man, my son."

RIGHT: Flying by the seat of his pants, director Michael Wadleigh still managed to film and create arguably the best music documentary of all time. His efforts earned him an Academy Award in 1970.

LEFT: Janis Joplin ate up and spit out every single stereotype for women in rock and roll. She matched and even surpassed the hard-drinking, hard-drugging, hard-rocking exploits of her male counterparts.

BELOW RIGHT: Since the Grateful Dead wasn't included in the movie, Jerry Garcia's only appearance is the one pictured here, where he holds up a joint and proclaims, "Marijuana, exhibit A." As Henry Gross observed, "There were fifty million pounds of marijuana consumed at Woodstock and not one reported case of glaucoma."

BELOW: In a weekend of "Oh my God!" moments, at a festival of "Can you believe this?" performances, Jimi Hendrix's version of "The Star-Spangled Banner" was then and is now one of the most talked about events in Woodstock history, in music history, even in American history.

WARNER BROS/PHOTOFEST ©WARNER BROS

PHOTOFEST

A view from the garden.

Wavy Gravy: We were loaded onto buses and brought to the site where we rendezvoused with our folks that had done the land clearing. The only money that we would take is the money that we got for the land clearing, which was like six or seven thou. We took no other money because if we were doing security we did not want to be under the pay of the festival so they couldn't say we were being duped or co-opted or anything like that. I started the Please Force with Tom Law and the password was "I forgot." Which is a great password if you're ever looking for one.

Tom Law: We were there to set up the grounds and the vibe. My particular role was as head of security. Wavy was also. He played it from his end, and I did nuts and bolts of it. Wes Pomeroy was the chief of police. He was in charge of the New York cops. I grew up in a family where my father was a detective for the LA sheriff's department. I grew up around cops and I had no problem talking to them. So I became sort of a front man for the Hog Farm. I was a little bit older than most of them, as was Wavy, and we realized that these cops were a lot of sweet young people who were looking for what's real. Wes and I had a talk. I said to him, "I have a walkie-talkie. You can call me if you need anything. Other than that, don't do anything. Just relax, have a good time. If a situation comes up, don't get your guys involved. Give me a call and give us the first chance of working things out." I was worried that if he showed a repressive face, we could have a real problem. He shook my hand and said, "I agree with you 100 percent."

Lisa Law: We were the heads at that point, with the help of Wavy Gravy and the entire Hog Farm. Without the Hog Farm, Woodstock wouldn't have been what it is. When I got there, Johanara and the Hog Farm was working on the free food and feeding everybody that was coming in. They were coming in from all over to help, setting up booths and camps, and I volunteered to drive into New York with Peter White Rabbit and get the food. We bought 1,500 pounds of rolled oats, 1,500 pounds of bulgur wheat, soy sauce, apricots, almonds, wheat germ, and pots and pans and 160,000 paper plates and knives and spoons, and we ended up feeding somewhere around 160,000 people. Once the kitchen got going, we could stand back and the volunteers took over. We worked in the trip tents. I ended up with my daughter Pilar; she was two. I ended up shooting a motion picture of it documenting the event. I think Wood-stock was one of the most important events of my life.

Both Tom Law and Wavy Gravy became famous as a result of their appearances in the *Woodstock* movie. Law famously leads the Hog Farmers through a series of yogic kundalini breathing exercises.

Tom Law: I was teaching yoga. I was getting all the Hog Farmers up in the morning and leading them through breathing exercises to get them going. We had a huge amount of work to do. I'd blow a conch in the morning and we'd do these exercises, have breakfast, and get to work. How did I get to the stage? There was a lot of down time. So I got up there and did a little rapping. I talked to people about the benefits of learning how to breathe. I just got up onstage and did it.

Law's appearance in the *Woodstock* movie was a seminal moment for yoga in America. How did he get into it?

Tom Law: I discovered yoga in LA. I was with a friend of mine named Leigh French, who played a character named Goldie Keefe on the Smothers Brothers' show, who was a send-up of the drug culture. She and her husband at the time found this yogi teaching at the East West Cultural Center. This is the guy who became Yogi Bhajan. And pretty soon, there were all these young people, hippies, learning from him. It became a mega-business. The whole idea of yoga is to balance yourself out and be a mensch. People think of it as a way to exercise and that's part of it, but it's much more than that. It's about calming your mind down so you can see what's going on. Good drugs can do that, too. Yogi Bhajan got so much action after the movie came out because of my involvement. A lot of people were curious about Kundalini yoga. He and his delegation came up to my medieval farm in their limos. They come in and we all sit down. He leans over to me and says, "One hundred thousand dollars. One year. You go and speak at colleges all over America." I said, "Thanks very much, yogi, but no thanks." I wasn't into it in the same way he was. I'm not a religious guy; I'm a spiritual guy. I believe in freedom of religion and freedom from religion equally.

Years later, Law had an amusing encounter with another celebrity yogi.

Tom Law: I was over at Sting's house on Central Park West. We were sitting on the couch and he said to me, "Were you really the guy teaching yoga at Woodstock?"

I said, "Yeah, man."

I guess he saw the movie and somehow it got to him. He said, "You changed my life."

"Anything to be of help, Sting."

Wavy's popularity took off like a rocket because of his appearance in the film. In his most famous moment, on Sunday morning, he stood on the stage, spoke into the mic, and said: "What I have in mind is breakfast in bed for four hundred thousand."

Wavy Gravy: And that's when we introduced hippies to granola. We had the Hog Farmers go out into the audience with Dixie cups full of granola and give it to hippies in their sleeping bags. And they looked at it and said, "What is this shit, gravel?" But obviously, they liked it because granola is the staple of conscious people on the planet now.

Any way you look at it, the Hog Farm's involvement at Woodstock was a resounding success.

Stan Goldstein: I believe that the Hog Farm was the beating heart of the festival. The Hog Farm set the example for all of what followed in terms of sharing and caring about the person next to you and down the line and being involved, whether for a minute or for hours, and in the formation of a community that truly took shape and formed for a couple of days.

Tom Law: Having the Hog Farm at Woodstock was a good move. The music at Woodstock was great. But looking back, I give a lot of the credit to us for how the people behaved and how they were taken care of. It sounds egocentric, but I think it's right. What would Woodstock have been like without the Hog Farm? I don't know, man.

Even backstage, there was some improvisation surrounding food. Joshua White, who'd come up to do his light show as a hallucinatory visual accompaniment to the acts, brought his girlfriend at the time, P. J. Soles (who would later be a favorite cult actress for her roles in *Carrie* and *Rock 'n' Roll High School*) to hang out and host what they referred to as the Pamela Dinner Show. From the trailer they had behind the stage, Pamela threw together tons of sandwiches, cookies, and other snacks for the performers and Woodstock staff.

> **P. J. Soles:** It was scary. There was obviously a lot of pot smoking. And yet, I wore the hippie braids, and I had a headband, and I had a suede fringe thing, but I felt like a hippie pretender because it was just not in my realm of experience—I was eighteen and had barely spent any time in the United States at that point. I was thinking, I'm so glad I'm behind the stage making sandwiches!

What other memories does she have from backstage?

> **P. J. Soles:** I remember walking around, and everyone who passed was a performer. I was playing it cool because I didn't want to bother them. I knew from being an actress myself in high school, you just need your time to concentrate. I had made a lot of chocolate chip cookies and I went around offering, and Jack Casady from Jefferson Airplane took one. I remember he asked me, "Is there anything in them?" and I said, "No. They're made with love. They're pure." At that time, I used whole-wheat flour. I used butter. I used very pure ingredients. I was very conscious of making pure organic kind of foods. He sat there and he ate one and then he ate another one and we had a brief conversation. I saw him years later and asked him, "Do you remember I passed the cookies to you at Woodstock and we talked?" And he said, "Yes! Those were the best chocolate chip cookies I've ever had in my life!"

Joan Auperlee, the superfan, remembers the Airplane's presence backstage:

> **Joan Auperlee:** They had a long table at the back with small round tables set up. There was fruit and lots to drink. Soft drinks, wine, and champagne were loaded into large ice-filled garbage cans to keep them icy cold. There was fruit juice and a punch bowl. I remember at one point that the Jefferson Airplane was being scolded for putting something psychedelic into the punch bowl. At that point, I noticed that my beaded bag was missing . . . looked for it to no avail . . . but I needn't worry . . . drugs of every type were being handed out freely.

As with every other act, Jefferson Airplane's set had been moved around quite a bit. They were supposed to play at 9:00 p.m. on Saturday night, but didn't go on until the following morning at dawn.

There has never been a consensus about what the first rock 'n' roll record was. Scholars, journalists, and fans have made compelling cases for a wide variety of possibilities. There are similar arguments about the actual birthplace of rock 'n' roll, though Chicago, Cleveland, Los Angeles, Memphis, New Orleans, and New York always get mentioned. But there is little argument about the epicenter of the rise of progressive rock in the mid- to late '60s, and that is simply the City of San Francisco. Whether natives such as Jerry Garcia and Paul Kantner, or émigrés such as Janis Joplin or Carlos Santana, San Francisco was the nexus of a certain kind of rock that flourished starting in 1965 and redefined attitude, hipness, and musicianship for the next decade. Throw in the city's legendary FM stations—KMPX and KSAN—the concert promotion explosions at Winterland and the Fillmore, and the founding of one of the most serious and successful magazines about rock 'n' roll ever published—*Rolling Stone*—and you've got all the ingredients for the San Francisco recipe for rock 'n' roll greatness.

Jann Wenner: In 1967, the greatest rock 'n' roll city in America was San Francisco. And the most exciting and successful rock 'n' roll band in San Francisco and the country was Jefferson Airplane. With their electrifying live shows and two great anthems of that euphoric summer, "Somebody to Love" and "White Rabbit," Marty Balin, Grace Slick, Paul Kantner, Jorma Kaukonen, Jack Casady, and Spencer Dryden—the classic Airplane lineup—were both architects and messengers of the psychedelic age, a liberation of mind and body that profoundly changed American art, politics, and spirituality. It was a renaissance that could only have been born in San Francisco, and the Airplane, more than any other band in town, spread the good news nationwide.

Michael Wadleigh: Just look at any history of music, and the Airplane are such an important group due to their innovations and also because they had a lead woman singer. Here you have a bunch of guys, very, very good musicians, and a woman lead singer who completely contributed to everything. The Airplane were the perfect missionaries. Casady's opening bass lick in "White Rabbit," Kaukonen's searing guitar solo in "Somebody to Love," and the heartbreaking voices of Balin, Slick, and Kantner evoked everything that was magical about San Francisco: the poster art and light shows; the hallucinatory joy of a night on the Fillmore dance floor; the spirit of camaraderie and radiant change. In their musical influences and personal histories, the band members also embodied the roots and contradictions of their birthplace. Balin was the working-class romantic with the heartbreaking voice; Kantner was a refugee of Jesuit schooling, rescued by folk music and Beat culture; Kaukonen and Casady came from serious educations in blues and R&B. And Slick was an icon of cool and fight, a product of prep school and upper-class privilege who brought style, biting wit, and incomparable singing to the revolution.

In a very short time, Jefferson Airplane found itself at the top of the heap—the titular heads of the San Francisco musical revolution. They did this the old-fashioned, Elvis Presley kind of way—a generous record deal with a *big* American record company. The same one as Elvis, in fact—RCA Victor Records. A solidly successful debut album, *Jefferson Airplane Takes Off!*, was followed by an even more successful one, *Surrealistic Pillow,* with two huge Top 40 hits—"Somebody to Love" and "White Rabbit"—that put the sex, drugs, and rock 'n' roll of the counterculture on everybody's AM radio in 1967, while finding a warm welcome and a permanent hangar on the nation's progressive-rock FM stations.

It always amused me when the Airplane et al. were referred to as "underground" bands or "underground" music. They were all very aboveground, very visible trees in the international rock 'n' roll forest. During the Monterey International Pop Festival, East Coast titans such as Simon and Garfunkel and the Blues Project made the trek west to break bread with their California counterparts. So it made perfect sense that a contingent from the West Coast should come east to repay the favor at Woodstock. They comprised some of the biggest and most revered acts at the festival—the Grateful Dead, Janis Joplin, Creedence Clearwater Revival, the surprise of Santana, and the solid-as-a-rock dependability of Jefferson Airplane. Their originality was admired by all their contemporaries.

Michael Wadleigh: I remember being with the Grateful Dead before the festival, all of a sudden there was a gigantic commotion and in came Jorma with the latest Jefferson Airplane album. Back then, you'd slam the disc down and listen to it. You wanted originality. They wanted to hear what another band was coming out with. Originality was the name of the game. Imitation is now the name of the game. You hear a new sound and then you run it into the ground.

The fact that Airplane had a unique lead, Grace Slick, was significant as well.

Michael Wadleigh: Of course, she has a great voice, is a great interpreter of lyrics, is a great blues singer. Very different from Janis Joplin. We're not dealing with suffering here. Grace Slick is a gorgeous woman, of course—much more in keeping with the more disciplined blues singers. Very capable, great kind of bend toward the minor notes and looks beautiful, whereas with Janis Joplin you could never claim she was more than dumpy and homely or whatever. Of course, Gracie grew up with all the advantages. She was never an ugly duckling. That comes out in her personality.

Despite the fact that they were tired, frontwoman Grace Slick rose to the occasion when she took to the stage and greeted the crowd with these famous words:

Grace Slick: Alright, friends, you have seen the heavy groups. Now you will see morning maniac music. Believe me. Yeah! It's a new day . . . yeah . . . the regular group . . . and Nicky Hopkins . . . good morning, people!

Actually, the story of Jefferson Airplane at Woodstock in 1969 is also the story of canceled flights, stranded passengers, idled pilots, and endless take-off delays! They may have been tired, annoyed by their appearance being pushed back or the chosen time for their set, but they delivered a tried and true set of sure things: "Somebody to Love," "The Other Side of This Life," "Plastic Fantastic Lover," "Volunteers," "Won't You Try/Saturday Afternoon," "Eskimo Blue Day," "Uncle Sam's Blues," and of course, "White Rabbit." The set played well for the fans, but not for the group. They allowed audio recordings from their performance to be used on the albums but not in the film, until Michael Wadleigh edited a piece of their set into his twenty-fifth anniversary director's cut edition of the movie.

Ellen Sander: Well, now they were a little rusty, I would say, but they were certainly well received. They were, you know, one of the messengers of the movement and she, of course . . . I described her before as a queen, she was a goddess, really, and she was . . . wonderful and they were wonderful. But when I complimented her on the set—I got a ride back to New York with them—and [when] I complimented her on the set, she said, "Goddamnit, this band, we never rehearse, you know, we never get together, we just come out and play and everything is so unmanageable," and, you know, she wasn't happy with their performance at all.

Bob Santelli: Airplane had two problems. One, they had to follow the Who, and two, everybody was absolutely exhausted. Not just because of the Who's performance, which was part of it, but because of the hour. People had been up twenty-eight, thirty, thirty-five hours at that point and to hear yet another band coming on at that hour . . . I think the Jefferson Airplane set was a little underrated. You know, when Grace Slick announced that "This was morning maniac music," and they break into "Volunteers," and to me "Volunteers" is one of the greatest songs of the late 1960s. It had definite political implications. It's a powerful song and for me that song saved their set. And for those who were able to wake up or did wake up and listen to that song and connected to it. But for a vast majority of people, they just didn't have the physical stamina to react to them anymore.

And what did he attribute that to?

Bob Santelli: Playing festivals back then was very difficult for the band because there was just no sense of organization. Everything was being done at the moment, on the spot, and the bands had to wait. And again with all of the other opportunities to do other things backstage, it's not surprising that some of these groups went on and felt directionless or off their game and didn't give the kind of performance that they should have. I think those bands at Woodstock that happened to would have given anything to take those performances back knowing what ultimately Woodstock would come to mean.

Like some other big names that we've heard from already, the Airplane's appearance was threatened by more than the elements. *New York Times* columnist Thomas Friedman likes to point out that "The only thing bigger than Mother Nature is Father Greed." Sure enough, old man money muscled his way right into the last-minute Airplane negotiations for their appearance.

Grace Slick: I'd been blissfully unaware of the extent of the financial fuckups going on around the Monterey Pop Festival, but it seemed that Airplane, Big Brother, and a couple of other bands had to hire attorneys to find out what happened to the profits. The lawyers for the promoters said the revenue had been directed toward "charitable purposes," but what about television syndication? No money was ever distributed to any of the bands and donations to charities were unrecorded, if they had occurred at all. We didn't want a repeat performance of that one, so our manager, who'd learned the hard way, was determined to do it differently this time.

Bill Thompson: In 1968 when I came in as temporary manager, there was a date booked in Salt Lake City, maybe the first show that I was acting manager at. The guy gave me a check and it bounced. I had it shoved up my ass by the band members, people grumbling about, "We need a real manager. What are you, stupid? You take a check?" Usually you say money order or cashier's check or cash. So I was very leery of not getting money; that was my job. The Airplane was the headliner at Woodstock on Saturday night. We were one of the biggest acts there at that time. So I went to [festival coproducers] Michael Lang and Artie Kornfeld, and I said, "Where's the money?" And finally, what I did was I got some of the other managers together and I said, "Look, these guys are gonna fucking burn us unless we get this. This is bullshit. Look at all this money. They're making a movie, and the whole thing." So we all went on Saturday afternoon and demanded we get the money. Saturdays, in '69, used to be like Sundays are now with banks. They weren't open. Somehow, Michael Lang got this guy to go in the bank on Saturday and open up the vault and we all got paid. That was our big bluff.

The bluff worked. The Airplane took off. And here is the final roll call of the original group members' recollections of and reactions to the event.

Marty Balin: I remember a gigantic stage and a sea of people that just went way over the mountains, and I remember just roaming around for days through the crowds and taking helicopter rides back and forth and playing cards because it was raining a lot. And I remember being drunk four or five times, and sobering up and waiting to go on, seeing all these great acts.

Jack Casady: The first day we were trying to get to the stage, which was a hard experience at that point. We rented a station wagon, we all piled in the station wagon, we went down a little quarter of the road—I believe it's a little horse track or something—to get into the middle of the field, and there were cars parked to both sides. The path opened for our station wagon, it was exactly one inch less than our station wagon, which we—we mashed the accelerator and we went "Yahoo!" and we went down about a good four hundred cars one inch less than the width of our car and we got to the stage, more or less, then we were trapped there for three days.

Grace Slick remembers arriving at the site a little differently.

Grace Slick: There was no more road access to the concert site because of the relentless rain, so a helicopter flew us from the hotel to the platform. We soared down over a field of muddy but smiling faces a little before 9:00 p.m. That was when we were supposed to perform, and I felt magic in the blue-black night as we got out of the helicopter and placed our feet on the stage. But due to transportation and scheduling fuckups, we didn't go on until sunrise.

In her book, *Somebody to Love,* she described the wait.

Grace Slick: Seated for nine hours in a darkness broken only by the towering white beams of spotlights that flowed downward from the sky, I was part of a congregation of musicians from the tribes of a temporarily undivided state. No bathrooms—my body, seemingly obeying a higher order, shut down and I had no need. No chairs—we gathered on the floor of the gigantic stage to watch and be watched without the heavy cover of imperatives. After arranging ourselves in an arc around center stage, engaged in nondenominational rite, food seemed to come from nowhere. We partook from each other's stash of fruit, cheese, wine, marijuana, coke, acid, water, and conversation.

Marty Balin: I remember, finally, we were flipping coins with everybody to see who got to go on next. We won the toss at the end of the whole concert, so we went on just as dawn was coming up. I don't think we were too good that day, but I remember everybody was asleep and laying in the mud and it was kind of an odd scene. The dawn was coming up and the sun, and it was just like—ugh!—you know. It was morning already and we had missed the night, but I didn't really care about that. It had been an experience up to that moment all the time.

Spencer Dryden: That was acid-taking days. We had all timed it to go on at midnight. Now it's five, six in the morning, the sun's just coming up. We had peaked already. Paul had said, "Well, if we can't go on at midnight, we want to go on as the sun comes up." Well, unfortunately, the Who were playing and they were in the middle of their set when the sun came up and they didn't care a whit whether the sun was coming up or not. So we went on and people were falling asleep, and we're trying to stir everybody up. I don't remember it as being one of our best shows. I do remember Nicky Hopkins being there, which was nice, because he helped glue the band together. But enough music is enough music, I don't care if God's playing. I thought we played badly; it was real creaky and out of tune. The band was spread out a little too much. Plus, watching cameramen falling asleep and people in the front going in their sleeping bags in a pile of mud was difficult. It was daylight and all the gloss and the sheen had been taken off the picture. I still enjoyed being there. It was great. We'd all made a lot of friends and it was like a big party.

Paul Kantner: It was a little harsher than normal but fun, interesting. I like dealing with the unexpected, particularly if you deal with it semisuccessfully. We didn't necessarily deal with being onstage semisuccessfully. We were pretty ragged.

Jack Casady's sarcastic response backs up this idea.

Jack Casady: I will never forget going on at sunrise either. We were in great shape, we looked really fine—we had been up I don't know how many days, sun streaking into your eyeballs—Paul was trying to tune his twelve-string guitar. It was really glorious.

Jorma Kaukonen: My wife was there, but I had this girlfriend who had also shown up at the show, so I was really concerned with keeping the two of them as far apart as possible. My ex-wife used to claim that one of the reasons I played so long was that I was afraid to face her when I came offstage. And there could have been some truth to this. I could hardly wait to get onstage at this particular venue. I didn't have any grand epiphanies or moments of extreme clarity, but I do remember thinking, This truly is unbelievable.

Grace Slick: It was unique in that there were a half million people not stabbing each other to death at a concert, and that hadn't been done before. That was its main claim to fame. You could hear all those musicians at one time or another, it's just that they were all in one place at the same time. And it was a statement of look at us, we're twenty-five and we're all together and things ought to change.

On the way back to New York however, Grace Slick put the weekend into perspective.

Ellen Sander: I remember I was driving back in the car with them and we hit the city and she said, "We're just going to go right to The Dick Cavett Show, why don't you come along? It's going to be great, a lot of people are going to be there." And I said, "I have been up for forty-eight hours; I have been boozing and using and everything . . ." you know, for so long, I'm just wiped. She said, "Oh, try it every day of the week!" She laughed at me. Because I was kind of falling apart and I needed to crash. Of course, I could've kicked myself for missing The Dick Cavett Show.

Jim Marion: The last band we saw was Jefferson Airplane, early Sunday morning, and, as they tended to occasionally be, I thought the Airplane were pretty loose and sloppy. We decided to head back to the tent. I can even remember the song being performed, since we started singing "Saturday Afternoon" in an altered form, "Won't you tryyyyyy, to get the hell out of here" as we snaked our way back toward the rear of the crowd.

Surprisingly, when we eventually made it back to the partially erected, mud-stained tent, our other friend was still in it, asleep. All the food and beer was gone, four days' worth in about thirty-six hours. The car was still parked across the street, and we were torn about our next move. Missing Hendrix, the Jeff Beck Group (who didn't show anyway), the Band (and possibly Dylan), and particularly Crosby, Stills, Nash and Young, was a very major disappointment, but we were unanimous in our feeling that we had basically had enough. I'd have to say, as we piled our muddy gear into the back of the car, that my initial overall impression of Woodstock was one of disappointment. We'd come for the music, and it hadn't met our expectations. We'd expected an organized, well-produced show, and got anything but (Bill Graham had really spoiled us with the Fillmore). I think all of us felt that way as we departed (incidentally, even at noon on Sunday, there was a line of cars and someone was ecstatic at getting our parking space as we pulled out). Even departing, traffic was jammed, and three of us sat on the tailgate as we moved slowly away. One of my friends pulled out his tickets, tore them up, threw them off the back, commenting, "These were totally worthless." I would have done the same, but I couldn't find my tickets. I found them later and still have them. I probably slept a good bit of the way home, but we got home in a flash compared to the trip in. When we arrived at my house, we dumped the tent, sleeping bag, and my other gear in a big muddy pile on our front lawn and I sat down on top of it. I remember my mother coming out of the front door, taking one look at the carnage, and saying "Good Lord! What happened to you?" She still talks about that moment forty years later.

Other concertgoers were not so easily deterred.

Joan Auperlee: After the Airplane set, we walked back to the car and there were still people everywhere, sleeping on the ground, in pitched tents, under cars, et cetera. I don't remember seeing any police, and drugs were being smoked openly and shared by all. It was very peaceful and surreal. Sleep did not come, and I remember going to a large puddle and shaving our legs and brushing our teeth with water from a canteen. Walking back to the car, there were people sharing food with strangers. Someone had a large watermelon, which was being carved and handed to anyone that wanted some. We went back to the car, put on clean shirts, and went to an outdoor bathroom which had about four toilets and sinks, located back at the festival site. It was heaven— we washed up and were ready for another day.

Sunday

JOE COCKER

Bob Santelli: Joe Cocker was not well known to a lot of people, and his performance at Woodstock was not only galvanizing, but legendary.

British rock of the late '60s was very different from British rock of the early and mid-'60s. The acts from across the pond that were invited to perform at Woodstock prove the point dramatically. The dissonant poetry of Mike Heron and Robin Williamson of the Incredible String Band was a far cry from the folk-rock and pop of Peter and Gordon and Chad and Jeremy. Keef Hartley was Ringo Starr's replacement as the drummer in Rory Storm and the Hurricanes, but by the late '60s he had put together a tasty amalgam of blues, jazz, and rock that was compared favorably to Blood, Sweat and Tears but never came close to the latter's resounding commercial success. The Who were poised to take British rock out of the '60s and bring it roaring into the next decade. Alvin Lee and Ten Years After electrified audiences with their amazing blues rock. But the relatively unknown Brit who stole the show from his more illustrious countrymen was a former gas fitter from Sheffield, England, by the name of Joe Cocker.

Fronting a group called the Grease Band with stellar keyboard player Chris Stainton, Cocker stood out as a singular presence on the Woodstock stage. His long, stringy hair was part of it. So was his psychedelic, tie-dyed tee-shirt that gave John Sebastian a run for his money. Then there were those blue and red shoes emblazoned with shiny, five-point stars, which were certainly Woodstock's most famous footwear next to

Richie Havens's sandals and Stephen Stills's mud-splattered boots which he displayed so proudly to a national television audience on *The Dick Cavett Show* the Monday after the festival.

But more than any of this—more than the band, the music, the voice, the songs, the hair, the shirt, the shoes—there were the stage movements: the body language, the finger ballet, the facial tics, the convulsions. I think it's fair to say that American audiences had never seen anything like it.

> **Dale Bell:** Joe Cocker must have had about four heart attacks when he sang "A Little Help from My Friends."

Sure, Elvis Presley's hip swiveling and Jerry Lee Lewis's piano humping had caused a stir in the '50s. Then James Brown's explosive choreography and Mick Jagger's preening helped to define stage presence in the '60s. But Joe Cocker? Joe Cocker was something else again. At a time when you thought you had seen every possible performance move, along came Joe with an arsenal of jerks and twists and thrusts that no one had seen before.

> **Ellen Sander:** He was very ragged and gruff and gritty. He was gritty, I think that would be the word for it. And he had a lot of power in his voice. But he was one of those singers that, you know, kind of had this internal dialogue going: he closed his eyes a lot, he was intense. And he had this beautiful, raspy, gritty voice, and an incredible choice of material always.

I asked him about his unique performing style on one of his visits to my radio program.

> **Joe Cocker:** I never quite know until I get out there just what I—I don't think I'm as frenetic as I used to be, but I can't wait to get out there and lose a few pounds. That's the only way I can lose weight—performing. But, you know, the thing with the old spastic motions that they used to talk about, I got very self-conscious about that for a while. I don't think I am quite as awkward as I used to be. I still do a bit of it—what do they call it? Air guitar or something? [Laughter] I see other people do it too . . . the way I used to move about was a bit different!

A bit different? That could be the musical understatement of the century! If imitation is the sincerest form of flattery, how did he feel about the late John Belushi's spot-on impression?

Joe Cocker: I wasn't that familiar with him when I did the show. And I'd never seen him do "A Little Help," you know? I mean with the beer, and laying on his back—'til later on. So it was like—he just did a strange—he was a lovable kind of guy. I don't see how anyone could be offended by being impersonated. And he also did a very good version. I was telling my friend that he played me a tape of "With a Little Help from My Friends" that time, and I was convinced he'd gotten an old vocal of mine from somewhere, so he was—I know he told me he practiced for ages on it. We did "Feelin' Alright" together, but I never heard the other one. I had friends who were really offended by it. When I saw it, I just laughed my head off!

John Morris recalled for us how Joe came to be booked at Woodstock.

John Morris: I'd seen him in England. We'd done him at Fillmore East. He was just amazing. He was a talent and energy that was incomparable. Then Michael heard him and went, "Oh, yeah!" So that was it. We booked him. Michael became his manager for years.

Michael Lang: We were engaging acts no one had heard before based on our own personal taste. Joe Cocker for example, sent a tape to Artie Kornfeld, who sent it to us. John [Morris] and I listened to it and were completely blown away by it.

In 1969, Joe was nearing the end of a grueling, summertime US tour, but there was one last career-altering stop to make.

Joe Cocker: We had done a very hectic tour, and it was the last gig on the tour. But it was just a very strange feeling hearing all this downwind about this, you know, because we played some pretty big places that year—Atlanta Race Stadium—that was seventy thousand. So when we got there, it was quite mind-blowing to see—to fly over, in a helicopter, such a mass of people. We knew it was no—I mean, that was the—still is the big—you know, because people have asked me to reflect on it,

*and it's just that initial jolt of seeing—like Zulu dawn, or something—
just coming over the edge and seeing all these people.*

Joe was scheduled to open the show at two o'clock on Sunday afternoon just a few hours after the Jefferson Airplane's sunrise "morning
maniac music." The sunshine that accompanied them turned out to
be a tantalizing tease. By the time the Grease Band took the stage to
warm up the crowd for Joe with a couple of instrumentals, some of the
most threatening storm clouds of the entire weekend began to accumu-
late overhead.

Cocker came on for the third number and launched into Bob Dylan's
"Dear Landlord." Two other Dylan songs would appear later on in the
set: "Just Like a Woman" and "I Shall Be Released." It was all part of
the road-tested, tried-and-true Cocker formula that worked for him like
a charm. Take the song poems of the world's greatest rock writers such
as Bob Dylan, Leonard Cohen, and John Lennon and Paul McCartney,
and transform them into soaring, searing, screaming, blues-drenched
rave-ups that became uniquely his own.

Another such gem was written by the very successful songwrit-
ing team of Nick Ashford and Valerie Simpson called "Let's Go Get
Stoned." (He would follow it with another Ashford-Simpson classic,
"I Don't Need No Doctor.") But the real nod here was performing
"Stoned" as an homage to his idol and inspiration who had made it
famous, Ray Charles.

Joe Cocker: [Ray] was more than an inspiration, really. I did a TV thing
with him. I finally got to—we did a duet on "You Are So Beautiful." It was
an NBC show about his life, I think. So that was quite a thrill. He was
a mentor, more because I just found that his vocal style and his whole
approach—because he was one of the pioneers of soul music, right?

Michael Wadleigh: If you want an example of a great, white rock 'n' roll
blues singer, can't do better than Joe Cocker. Ray Charles told me that
"this man can certainly sing as well as I can."

Joe Cocker: I'm gonna say that he definitely is a genius, yeah . . . I'm trying to think the first time we met—oh yes—it was backstage and he was
in his underpants in the dressing room, and, I don't know, I was just like
a schoolboy, very shy, you know.

There were a couple of showstoppers in Joe's set, but the undisputed, nonstop, steamrolling pièce de résistance was the set closer—as unique a cover of a John Lennon–Paul McCartney song as has ever been done: "With a Little Help from My Friends."

Michael Wadleigh: It comes down to the phrasing, his interpretation of "A Little Help from My Friends," it just blows the Beatles away. Their version becomes irrelevant. He understood what that song is about. He screams it out. He's a goddamn actor. He acted that song so superbly. He gets lost in the lyrics. He has a profound understanding of what the lyrics mean and he gets completely carried away. I'm told by people that they play that song over and over and over again as a stand-alone experience because he's just so interesting to watch. Playing his air guitar, he's pigeon-toed, nearly falling over, staggering everywhere, sweat just flying off of him . . . it's a phenomenally genuine performance. Why do you need a set? You look at people now who need all these accoutrements to ensure that they're noticed by people. But a performance like that? What do you need? You just need him. He does it all. He's into it. He's a good example of why '60s music and the '60s have lasted and will last presumably forever. They're truly emotional, moving, fundamental performances and writings. The lyrics "Do you need anybody? / I just need somebody to love" it's just great writing.

Joe Cocker: That was mine, really. I just sort of dreamed it up on the toilet one day. Just the idea of doing. I don't know why I chose that song—I just wanted to take some well-known tune and three, four-it, you know. And I tried it with a song called "Bye, Bye Blackbird" before. That worked pretty well. And it just—it turned into more of an anthem in the end. It was just a simple idea, by the time we added all of the girls. I still do it onstage and it still gets quite a good reception.*

Joe Cocker: In America, it was not that big a hit. It was in the Top 200, but it certainly got us, you know, a contracted tour with Dee Anthony, Premiere Talent in New York. We got a great thrill from that when we played it that time [at Woodstock]. It was like a marvelous sense of

---

*Author's note: Cocker placed eleven hit singles on the American Top 40 charts including the number one single "Up Where We Belong"—a duet with Jennifer Warnes from the soundtrack of the motion picture *An Officer and a Gentleman*. But "With a Little Help from My Friends" never appeared on the US charts as a single.

communication. It took, it was the last number of the set, I remember, but I felt that we had finally gotten through to someone, eventually.

Cocker's mesmerizing performance remains a favorite of many festival attendees. I spoke recently to one of them about it. Chip Rachlin was a relative newcomer to big-time rock 'n' roll in 1969 who has spun his experiences into a very successful four-decade career as an agent, manager, promoter, and entrepreneur. At the time, Chip was friendly with a woman named Chris Cavallo who worked for Chip Monck. Chris was unable to get "free" tickets to the event, but she was able to secure a couple of backstage passes. That pass gave Chip a matchless vantage point from which to view the Cocker performance.

Chip Rachlin: Clouds had come up over the horizon, and it was obvious that rain was on the way. Joe Cocker was onstage. Now almost nobody in the crowd had heard of this wild man. His spastic body movements and screaming vocals would eventually prove intoxicating, but right now, it was a bit shocking to the predominantly suburban crowd. Those first few drops of rain fell, and I took refuge underneath the stage. It was a great place to hear the show and stay dry, but the view was pretty limited.

Joe finished that closing song and walked off the stage in triumph. In the grandest show business of any kind of tradition, he may have figuratively stopped the show, but Mother Nature had other ideas about what could bring the proceedings to a halt. The ensuing rainstorm—the worst of the weekend—stopped the show and shut down the whole operation for a maddening, anxiety-producing couple of hours. It was the storm before the calm.

MAX YASGUR

Warning before you read this! You might want to hold your head together with both your hands so it doesn't explode as you hear the incredibly different recollections about how destiny brought Max Yasgur and Woodstock Ventures together. Four weeks before the first day of the festival, the original Wallkill location fell through.

Michael Lang: I think panic best describes the mood. We lost the site on a Friday. Elliot called over the weekend. We put word out over the air, and three days later, we had another site. We lost a few steps along the way—four or five months at the original site. We got the crews up to Bethel, John and Joel went up and put together a deal together with Max Yasgur, whose farm we were using. And we continued to roll. It was an insane effort to get everything up. And as history will tell you, the gates were one of the last things on our list and they never did quite make it up.

Elliot Tiber: If it wasn't for me, you wouldn't be here . . . I had the permit for a festival for ten years in stinking Nazi-controlled Bethel–White Lake. They were being thrown out of Wallkill for good reasons: hippies, homosexuals, lesbians—that's what the papers said. I was broke and the bank was taking away my stinking theater, and I called Mike, I didn't know him, and he said "What do you want?" and I said, "I have a permit." Within ten minutes a helicopter came, followed by a dozen limousines with Stan Goldstein. And he said, "Show them what you got," and I showed him the permit—I had done it on my typewriter, I was the president of the chamber of commerce, nobody else wanted to do it.

Sam Yasgur: Michael Lang and Johnny Roberts came to the house, and they were looking to rent a field for three days. No one anticipated it would be what it was. And it was a simple, straight deal: "Can you rent us a field for three days?" That's how it started . . . as a straight business deal. The summer of '69 was a very wet summer. We couldn't get hay in the barn. This was a hayfield. When you have that many cattle, and you've gotta put up enough hay to get 'em through the winter, and you can't make it yourself, the prospect of having to buy that amount of hay was daunting, to say the least. Johnny Roberts and Mike Lang came on, I think it was a Sunday afternoon, and said they'd like to rent a field for three days. This field would be appropriate because it has a bowl-shaped topography. And that's all it was, "for a few days."

Joel Rosenman: From a financial standpoint, back in New York, it was pretty much a deathblow to any hopes of having a profitable festival. It's because we expended so much of our resources in building this first site, when we were booted, we had little but credit to build the next site on. Essentially, the effort had to be overtime, triple time. Everybody worked round the clock. All shipments had to be rushed shipments. Everything was done at the most expensive pace possible. So by the time we got to the day the festival was supposed to begin, what we had been able to prepare for that time period beforehand, which I believe was around five weeks, did not include things such as ticket booths, and really the fences looked more like an afterthought, or a gesture, not a real fence. As it was commented from the stage, it was a free festival, except somebody had to be paying for it, which we were. All of that was the result of the reversal of the zoning board in Wallkill, New York. I think because some of the children of the members of the zoning board had commented at dinner a few times that this amazing thing was going to descend on Wallkill, New York. And it didn't resemble the several thousand people, and classical and folk music and crafts that we had applied for. When we tried to argue this with a fancy New York lawyer, they said, "You're outta here, and if you want to sue us, we'll see you in court sometime in the next several years." We fell back from Wallkill, and Max Yasgur appeared. It was pretty much a miracle.

Mel Lawrence: Now comes the Rashomon part . . . I was deeply involved in this aspect. I was in charge of building the first site. We'd gotten all the poison ivy off the site; that was a major part. And were, through many trials and tribulations, kicked off the site. Elliot did call. Stan and I went up to look at the site that Elliot proposed. It was a perfect bowl. And like a perfect bowl at the bottom, it was filled with water. Stan was standing up to his knees in water. Elliot said, "It can be drained." We said, "What happens if it rains?" We left. We went back to Wallkill. I remember telling Michael, "Wow, that didn't work out." Then we were approached by some Hasidic guys in Bethel. They said, "We've got a guy here. His name is Max Yasgur, he's a farmer," and Michael and I, and I believe Stan, went up to meet Max Yasgur. And he took us out to his farm. It was a flat field. You wouldn't believe it, it was so flat. "We said, no, people are going to come and they won't be able to see from the back." And he said, "I have other fields," so we get in the car, we start driving, and we get to the top of what is now the historic bowl, the historic place. And Michael and I look out. There it is. It was Michael and I and Max.

Michael Lang: It was not Max. It was Mel, and we had left Elliot Tiber's place, totally disillusioned. And Elliot said, "I have this friend he's a real estate agent . . ."

Elliot Tiber: Max was my neighbor, he gave us milk.

Michael Lang: No, no, no, we didn't know anything about Max. We went with the realtor. We went looking around. We were traveling the back roads and we came up to the top of the bowl, and Mel and I looked at each other and said, "This is it." And we said, "Whose is this?" And the guy said, "Max Yasgur, he lives down the road." So he went and got Max. Max came to meet us at the field.

Mel Lawrence: Let me pick up here. I didn't remember the first part. But there we were at the top of the bowl, with a lake at the bottom.

Elliot Tiber: It didn't happen that way either. There was no lake. You were all on drugs. I was the only one there that didn't do drugs.

Mel Lawrence: So there we were with Max. Michael and I looked at each other and said, "This is it, this is perfect." Michael and Max walked over to the side, said a few words, shook hands, Max shook my hand. He only had three fingers. That was it; we knew that was the spot.

Trish Agree: I remember getting the call from Elliot. This guy says, "Oh, I have a beautiful piece of land." So you and I drove up there.

Elliot Tiber: Flew helicopter.

Trish Agree: No, we drove. We saw the swamp. We saw this sign and it said "Happy Avenue," and we said, "That's where we're going," and it drove us right to the bowl.

Bill Hanley: Max Yasgur was a really fine gentleman. I met him at the house with Michael. Michael had brought up a limousine, and we all jumped in the limousine, and that was the first field we got to, and I said, "I think this is the best place, Michael." And we just stayed right there; we never went and looked at another field. It just seemed to have all the prerequisites for a nice area for one hundred thousand people to see.

The opportunity to make a little "hay" proved irresistible. But it soon became much larger in scope than anyone, including Max, could have imagined. A slight variation on the story from the late John Roberts:

John Roberts: Max came into our life—Monday or Tuesday following the July 4 weekend. He had been reading about this—he had been following it. He had a farm up in Bethel—six hundred acres—beautiful farm. He said, "I've got a place for you guys, if you want to pay my price." He said, "I think you've been mistreated, you know, I think this is all nonsense—this generational war that's going on here; and I can make it right." He said, "But I am a businessman, and it will cost you. But I'll go to bat for you." And he did. Max basically added a zero to our rent. Instead of seventy-five hundred, we paid Max seventy-five thousand. But I am not sure he didn't suffer at least seventy-five thousand dollars' worth of ill will and financial hits to his dairy, as a result of his support of our efforts.

Max had no problem being stereotyped as a country bumpkin, especially when it gave him an advantage in his negotiations with city slickers of every conceivable type. But John was right about one thing in particular. Once the Woodstock juggernaut got rolling, Max got way more than he bargained for.

Sam Yasgur: Then things changed, and they changed fairly dramatically because some of the neighbors had a very negative reaction to what were then called "hippies" coming to western Sullivan County. And that bothered Dad. I can remember him saying to one of them, "Look, the reason you don't want them here is because you don't like what they look like. And I don't particularly like what they look like either. But that's not the point. They may be protesting the war, but thousands of American soldiers have died so they can do exactly what they're doing. That's what the essence of the country is all about." And, from that point on, he became a champion.

John Morris confirms this notion.

John Morris: I think he had a major desire to do something that would help the new generation and help that progress. I think Max got . . . seventy-five thousand, which is a bunch of money, but not compared to what we were talking about. His major concern was that the place be restored to the shape it was in before the festival began so that he could continue to run his cow farm. I mean, Max wasn't saying to himself, "Oh boy, we're gonna do the biggest thing in the world and then I won't be doing farming anymore." Well, he was gonna do farming, and he did do farming . . . They were America. They were middle America. He wasn't a multimillionaire farmer. This wasn't John Lennon's cows. He ran dairy cattle, and he made milk and he sold it. And he'd been there for twenty or more years. That's what he understood. That's what he wanted to do. But he just suddenly went, "These kids need a chance. If it makes sense, I'm gonna give it to 'em." I guess we made sense . . . before Max spoke to the crowd after Cocker [and the] rain, I asked him to do it, and . . . he said, "No! I don't speak in public. I don't do that." I said, "You don't understand. You understand an awful lot, but what you don't understand is that you are a culture hero now. You have done something really great for an entire generation of people. And they would like to know you, and they deserve to know you." And he went and gave that speech, which if you listen to it, it'll make you cry.

But whatever the version, there is no doubt that without the kindness of the dairy farmer Max Yasgur, there would be no Woodstock. There are a number of laymen who get an asterisk in rock 'n' roll history. For example, "Officer Obie" of "Alice's Restaurant" fame is one of them. Arlo Guthrie (and director Arthur Penn) went so far as to have the actual person—William Obanhein—play himself in the motion picture version of the song. Maharishi Mahesh Yogi, the Beatles' erstwhile spiritual guru and the subject of Lennon and McCartney's "Sexy Sadie" is another classic example. But, arguably, no civilian in this realm is regarded with more affection or high regard than the aging, balding dairy farmer in upstate New York who allowed his land to be used for the Woodstock Music and Art Fair in August of 1969.

He was a slight man, missing a couple of fingers on his right hand, due to a farming accident. He also had heart problems that plagued him most of his adult life and ultimately ended it in 1973. But during and after the Woodstock Festival of 1969, the words you might use to describe the organ beating behind his breast might be "lion-hearted," "heart of gold," or even "home is where the heart is." The staff was well aware of his medical issues and were wary of straining him out too much, which was impossible considering that his field was about to be trampled by half a million kids.

Chris Langhart: Max and I could discuss all the mechanical things that were associated with the dairy. I had installed air-conditioning at the Fillmore and other places, and it was equivalent to milk-cooling equipment. So we could talk about water and ice cream making and equipment involved in freezing the stuff and cooling. I realized that he had put all those slate walls that existed at the edge of the farm here, and then he'd tell me that after he'd gotten it all done it was so smooth that he could ride his bicycle along the top. We had wonderful moments together. But he was having trouble breathing all the way through; that was the nature of aged infirmities. When I organized his favorite contractor to dig a diagonal hole from that water tank setup down the road, across the intersection, and down to the wells where I needed to have more pipes, I was told—but I didn't see him at that point, I was so busy—I was told that they put him back on his oxygen tank because he was afraid that something horrible would happen to the field and there would be horrible results. There wasn't. But there was no way to tell. He was worried that the farm would be permanently damaged by this. He had only agreed to a temporary thing there. We got on famously.

Here was a man who had devoted his life to farming, and like most middle-aged Americans of his time, knew or understood little about this generation of young people eager to stretch their wings and have their voices heard. The experience Max had at Woodstock altered both Max's and his wife Miriam's perspective on these outsider kids.

Sam Yasgur: If you think about it, in August of '69, Dad was forty-nine years old. He was a Republican; he was, in many respects, except socially, a conservative. He had nothing in common with them. And he was establishment. And the crowd who occupied this field on that day were very anti-establishment.

Michael Wadleigh: As he said, the more of the young people he saw, that he met, the more Joan Baezes and John Robertses, who had gone to Princeton, the more articulate rebels. The more reactors against America that he was exposed to . . . He told me that by the end he thought it was a free speech issue. That by the end he just felt he had to give us his farm because it wasn't right that America stood for free speech. He became convinced that it wasn't just a moneymaking deal. That it had real artistic and social constructs that were a fundamental part of it. Someone should provide that opportunity. That idea, I hate what you stand for, but I'll die for your right to stand for it. As you know, Max turned against the war and appeared on <u>The Dick Cavett Show</u>.

In a radio interview a week after the festival, Miriam Yasgur, Max's wife, articulated how the festival had changed their opinion.

Miriam Yasgur: The people who have not been in—in close contact with this view it as something that other than it is. I want to make it very plain that every young person: tired, hungry, muddy, thirsty, disheveled, that we dealt with, was so polite that all of us were overwhelmed. I've never seen so much patience in so many people. There was not one incident, not only of crime, but of even rudeness, pushing, or shoving that has been brought to our attention or to the attention of any of the sheriffs or troopers who were in and out of this office . . . wouldn't you assume that in a group of—of even ten thousand people, there would be at least one argument? As far as the youngsters proving that they could get together peacefully and listen to music, they proved this . . . I'll tell you what I took out of this. I took out of this the—the realization that I've been bigoted. I haven't approached youngsters because I didn't like the way they dressed and I didn't speak with them. And I discovered a whole generation of very nice kids.

Emboldened by this demonstration of the "new," Max addressed the crowd in a way that brought many in the live audience and the film audience to tears.

Max Yasgur: I'm a farmer. I don't know—I don't know how to speak to twenty people at one time, let alone a crowd like this. But I think you people have proven something to the world. Not only to the town of Bethel or Sullivan County, or New York State. You've proven something to the world. This is the largest group of people ever assembled in one place. We have had no idea that there would be this size group, and because of that, you had quite a few inconveniences as far as water and food and so forth. Your producers have done a mammoth job to see that you're taken care of. They'd enjoy a vote of thanks.

But above that, the important thing that you've proven to the world is that a half a million kids, an' I call yuh kids because I have children that are older than you are. A half a million young people can get together and have three days of fun and music and have nothing but fun and music. An' God bless yuh for it!

His appearance in the film was iconic. His words proved to America and the world, that even a farmer, if he opened his mind wide enough could understand and sympathize with the message of the revolution.

Sam Yasgur: When he would come into the city to visit me, because I was living in Manhattan at the time, I, a prosecutor, uh, the kids would see him walking on the street, and they would yell, "There's Max!" and a crowd would form . . . I still have a bumper sticker that became very popular after the festival. It said "Max Yasgur for President." I think kids circulated it and they had it on all the beat-up Volkswagens.

COUNTRY JOE AND THE FISH

After Country Joe began his solo career on Friday—highlighted by "The Fish Cheer"—he took the stage again on Sunday, this time with the rest of the band. They were in the difficult position of having to follow Joe Cocker after his star-making performance. While the sun had been shining through Cocker's set, the weather shifted dramatically the moment he stepped off the stage. There ensued a two-hour, raging, soaking thunderstorm that took a messy, sloppy, grimy quagmire and made it worse.

Phil Lesh: Rainwater had collected in a shallow depression near the right side of the stage, near the path from the stage itself to the lines of Portosan toilets that were so essential to the collective experience. The sheer volume of traffic forced pedestrians into the pool of water, and as the rain stopped and more people passed, it turned into a pool of mud. I don't know who it was that first threw propriety to the winds and lunged headlong into the center, emerging coated with mud from head to toe—perhaps figuring that it was better to be muddy than merely wet. At one point during Sly Stone's set, I did see dozens of very stoned people dancing furiously, with mud flying off in all directions.

Joan Auperlee: When the rain came on Sunday, the backstage area was in a panic. It got very dark and windy, and they were afraid the towers would blow or somebody onstage would get electrocuted. I was backstage with Bert Sommer at this point. There were tents and mobile trailers everywhere. When the rain really started to come down, Bert and I ducked into the closest tent. Inside were about eight people sitting on the floor staring at someone playing acoustic guitar. It was Jerry Garcia sitting on a stool. Jerry was talking and laughing with everyone. We all had a great time.

Marty Brooks: When the rains came on Sunday and didn't seem like they were ending soon, we split the concert grounds and went back to the car. While the movie may have left the impression that most people were willing to sit in rain and mud, I wasn't among them. When the rains persisted, we drove off of the grounds and into town to try and get something to eat and to call home. The rumors were that the concert was going to be canceled. We drove to Route 17, but then a miracle happened: the rain stopped and I turned to my girlfriend and said, "I want to go back."

With the wisdom of hindsight, if mud had been the only problem on Sunday, it would have been no problem at all. Just as Governor Rockefeller's threat to send in the National Guard almost converted the Woodstock dream into a nightmare on Saturday, there was another hidden danger on Sunday that, in retrospect, could have been the tipping point between Woodstock becoming a cultural landmark versus a true, tragic, unprecedented national disaster:

John Roberts: I guess [that would be] the electrocution story, which was that when the very heavy rains came on Sunday, we got a call from John Morris who said, "We're a little worried here. We buried the power cables running to the stage under the crowd areas." We buried them pretty deeply, but with the rain and the masses of people there, they were worried that the dirt was wearing away, and there might be some erosion. What they wanted to do was shunt the power from those cables to the side and bring the power in some other way. And I said, "Well, what's the practical effect?" He said, "We'll have to stop the show for a little while, but if we don't and those cables wear through and fray and all those people are wet and packed together—we could have the largest mass electrocution in the history of the world." So I said, "Well, the answer is pretty obvious. Let's stop the show for a while and do what we have to do to make sure that it's safe." And that was a pretty nerve-wracking hour. I think that was the single, scariest moment for me."

John Morris: During the storm, there's a scene, actually, you could see me near as close to a nervous breakdown as I have ever been in my life. I got very concerned about the light towers. And they were swaying back and forth. And there were tall spots on the top of them, big ones. So what I did was take the mic and talk to the people. Tried to calm the people and keep it as calm as possible. During that period of time, somebody came up to me and told me that my wife had fallen and broken her ankle, that my dog was lost, and that Joan Baez had had a miscarriage. The only one of those things that was true is that my wife had broken her ankle, but I didn't know that then. I was onstage with a mic that was shocking me in the hand trying to get people to take it easy and stay off the towers. The only other person onstage was Michael Wadleigh down on one knee with a camera pointed in my face. And he recorded it and it's in the film. And Michael and I have a strange bond because of that moment because he knew that I was on the edge. But I told them to stay off of those towers and they did.

At various points during the festival, Morris looked for support from an unlikely source.

John Morris: My dad was the chief of staff of something called the 301st Logistical Command, which was an army logistics unit. I called him two or three times during the festival to ask his advice. At one point I called up to ask, "Can you get up here? I need your help." And the advice he said to me was, "You don't need my help. I've seen you on television. I've heard about it on the radio. You guys are doing okay."

Many years removed from the actual events, John Roberts was able to speak very calmly and somewhat dispassionately about the crisis, but eyewitnesses to the incident use words such as despair, exasperation, frustration, and panic to describe the scene. In his book *Barefoot in Babylon*, Robert Spitz quotes John Roberts around the tenth anniversary of the festival saying,

I think I had very clearly decided at that time, as a concept, that if thousands of people were electrocuted, I was going to find a reasonably swift and painless way to take care of myself. It wasn't a suicide pact of any kind, but it was something that I knew I would never be able to live with.

Fortunately, it didn't come to that.

> **Wavy Gravy:** There's a little bit of heaven in every disaster area. I think
> that's true. In Mississippi, if people are filling sandbags together, there's
> no rich, no poor, no black, no white. We were all police at Woodstock.
> Everybody helped everybody else out. It was the mud that congealed
> us together. If it hadn't been declared a disaster with the whole world
> looking at us, it would have just been a great rock concert.

That is the backdrop against which Country Joe and the Fish prepared
to walk out onto the rain-soaked stage. Some of the less hearty souls in
the audience were washed away by the rainstorm and began the long
journey back to wherever they came from, but hundreds of thousands
of dauntless, unfazed revelers remained, at least because several huge
headlining rock 'n' roll stars were still waiting in the wings to perform,
including the Band; Blood, Sweat and Tears; Crosby, Stills, Nash and
Young; Jimi Hendrix; and Ten Years After. But the assignment of getting things back on track musically fell to Country Joe and the Fish.
They welcomed the challenge. After all, they were quite used to over-
coming obstacles and getting the job done. We sketched Joe McDonald's career path and politics for you earlier. His insatiable appetite for
exploring diverse kinds of music led him to participate in a variety of
performing combinations. One of these was a group called the Instant
Action Jug Band, whose name kind of tells you what they did—political
statements wrapped up in a framework of traditional acoustic instrumentation. One of the members was a guitar player from Brooklyn,
New York, named Barry Melton, who formed an instant bond and
friendship with Joe. An early version of "I-Feel-Like-I'm-Fixin'-to-Die
Rag" made an appearance on an extended-play recording in 1965 distributed through an underground publication called *Rag Baby*.

Some sources claim their set began with something called "Barry's
Caviar Dream," though Country Joe himself has no memory of that.
He's not the only one.

> **Barry Melton:** Oh God, I don't know exactly what that was, but our set
> opens up with me holding up a large green cigarette!

Barry Melton has enjoyed one of the most interesting post-Woodstock
career transformations of anyone who played there.

Barry Melton: Yeah, I've been twenty-six years in law. I'm the public defender of Northern California County. I spent almost twenty years on the road as a musician. I started playing music and becoming part of the civil rights and antiwar movements of the mid-'60s, I was—at least for a minute—a college student intending on becoming a lawyer. I dropped all that in a hurry when I found out that playing guitar for ten or twelve years was probably more important. So, in a way, years later I got to resume part of my life that I had dropped and became a lawyer at the age of thirty-five. I was late, but I got there. But there's not anyone who knows me who doesn't think that I'm doing anything inconsistent with my long-held views about freedom. Maybe I'm doing it in a bit more mature manifestation.

After whatever Barry's Caviar Dream was, the group launched into the one true song that defines their nonpolitical persona. It's the one called "Not So Sweet Martha Lorraine" that was a huge FM "turntable hit," a song that may not have been a hit in the quantifiable sense (copies sold, chart appearances) but still seeped into the public consciousness through widespread radio airplay and live performance. "Martha" was definitely one of those. The song they performed next, "Rock and Soul Music," also became one, thanks to its inclusion on the *Woodstock* soundtrack album.

The last three songs were "Thing Called Love," "Love Machine," and, saving the best for last, "The Fish Cheer / I-Feel-Like-I'm-Fixin'-to-Die Rag." Far from feeling it was anticlimactic, the crowd was ready for it, anticipated it, expected it, knew their part from Joe's "rehearsal" on Friday afternoon, and, for a second time, filled the skies with that once-and-future forbidden word! The audience screamed out those letters, yelling that word with abandon and wild-eyed enthusiasm. They gleefully sang along and mouthed every line in the song. Country Joe and the Fish left an indelible mark on the festival and on the culture during their weekend at Max's.

TEN YEARS AFTER

The name came from the fact that the group got going "ten years after" the beginning of rock 'n' roll. But the band's true roots went back much further than that to the classic blues of Willie Dixon, John Lee Hooker, Sonny Boy Williamson and similar artists. At a time when these masters were being ignored in their own country, they were being lionized by an extremely talented bunch of skinny English white kids with group names like the Bluesbreakers, Chicken Shack, Fleetwood Mac, the Rolling Stones, Savoy Brown, and the Yardbirds. Add to this mix the quartet known as Ten Years After and you've got a significant, formidable portion of the second wave of the British Invasion that swept the States in the late '60s.

Ten Years After evolved out of a pleasant, enthusiastic R&B covers group called the Jay Birds. Alvin Lee on guitar and vocals, Leo Lyons on bass, Ric Lee on drums, and Chick Churchill on keyboards had ambitions that went way beyond doing polite versions of old rhythm and blues classics. First of all, they had their own music to write, and, secondly, they just didn't do covers, they did total overhauls and reinventions of primary source material from a different era, a different culture, and a different country.

Among the words most often used to describe the group as a whole are *intensity, stamina,* and *indefatigability.* And when it came to lead guitarist Alvin Lee, the words were *fierce, fiery,* and "fastest fingers on the planet!" Getting such a raw sound and style down in the recording studio proved to be a great challenge on their debut album. The follow-up was more successful because it captured the group in their natural habitat performing live at the Klooks Kleek Club in London.

They released two albums in 1969 and just kept getting better and better. The first one in February was called *Stonedhenge,* and the follow-up just six months later neatly dovetailed with a tour of the US that summer that had them playing at the Newport Jazz Festival in July, and Woodstock in August. The album was called *Ssssh,* which always seemed incongruous to me because the group and their fans were anything but quiet. Explosive hysteria on and in front of the stage would be somewhat closer to the truth. The whole world was about to find that out for itself in the days following the festival, particularly after the movie was released in 1970. Ten Years After went from playing clubs to concert halls to five-thousand seaters to stadiums with blinding speed. Mostly thanks to that little soiree in Bethel.

Alvin Lee: It was just a name on a date sheet. We were in the middle of a tour. It meant nothing to us until we got there and they said, "You can't get there by vehicle, you have to go in by helicopter." And that was the first inkling that it was going to be a different sort of day. I saw kind of something, very cool.

They were supposed to play on Sunday afternoon, but Mother Nature made sure that wasn't going to happen.

Alvin Lee: When we got there, we were supposed to play about three o'clock, as far as I remember. And I got into the gig and I got out of the helicopter and tuned up and I was pretty much ready to go, and the rainstorm broke. Which kind of screwed things up for hours, and I just kind of went out into the audience and joined in, I suppose. And I came back about every hour to see if anything was happening, and it wasn't. And it was much better in the audience than it was backstage because there wasn't a lot of peace and love backstage. There were a lot of managers!

We told you in an earlier chapter how Country Joe and the Fish bravely took the stage to restart the music after the storm, and that's all true.

But it wasn't completely altruistic on their part. The old music business pecking order of who should follow whom, and which acts could easily upstage the other acts, was certainly in play as well.

Alvin Lee: Well, I'll tell you a secret that I've never told anyone else. On one of my ventures backstage the storm had eased up and I said, "Well, we can go on now," and the stage manager said, "No, because there's still sparks and things jumping around onstage and the technicians won't go on." And I said, "Well, I'll go on!" And it wasn't an argument, it was all talking, and I said, "Well, all those people out there, you know, we gotta do something." And so I said, "Well, I'm going to go on, and if I get struck by lightning, think how many records we'll sell!" And that went down well. And of course, then everybody said, "Yeah, yeah, let's go on, come on, it's the cool thing to do." And so we were set to go on again, I think Country Joe, who didn't like following Ten Years After, he nipped out in front of us. His crew went and just put all the amps onstage and they started the set as we were tuning up again. So we had to wait for them then. But that was cool. Backstage, it could've been anywhere. It could've been Madison Square Garden, because it's the same old story—all the managers, and who wants to go on when, and "My band's been here all afternoon." I chose not to get into that. That's the beauty when you're in the band, you don't have to get involved with that . . . I had a great time.

The group's set began with their delightfully lascivious version of Sonny Boy Williamson's "Good Morning, Little School Girl." It continued with Al Kooper's arrangement of Blind Willie Johnson's "I Can't Keep from Crying Sometimes" from the Blues Project's *Projections* album. Then it was on to their own, "I May Be Wrong, But I Won't Always Be Wrong" and "Hear Me Calling." But the pièce de résistance was the set closer: Alvin Lee's "I'm Going Home," which he introduced adding the ad lib, "by helicopter!" The song was exciting when it was captured live on the group's *Undead* album, but the Woodstock performance raised the level of excitement and enthusiasm and pure joy to completely unimaginable proportions.

Alvin Lee: Well now, you gotta remember that was probably the last song, we'd probably been playing for about an hour. I mean, it was a pretty high-energy set. We were just buzzing, you know? That's what Ten Years After is all about. To boogie down, have a good time, and play lots of riffs around, and that's basically it. And it's great. It's a good attitude. I actually did everything. I thought a lot of the things being said from the stage were embarrassing. They were all going on and going, "Oh wow, man, we've got a whole city here," and that kind of stuff. I think it's best to go on and say, "Let's have a good time, rock 'n' roll . . . bang the drums. Just boogie down." That's my message.

THE BAND

Though Bob Dylan outright turned down the invitation to perform at Woodstock, many thought that he might pull a Bob Dylan–ish move and just show up.

Jim Marion: When I first saw the ad for Woodstock, probably in the <u>New York Times</u>, my friends and I were thrilled because so many of our favorite performers were supposed to play—Hendrix, Creedence, the Dead, the Who, Jefferson Airplane, Jeff Beck Group, and the Band. We also came to the conclusion that, because the Band was on the bill, and Dylan lived nearby, it was a good bet he would show up, a bet we obviously would have lost.

Mike Jahn: You have to understand that those rumors happened all the time. Almost like the Paul Is Dead rumors were the Dylan Will Show Up Tonight rumors. It was like the map to the Lost Treasure of the Incas. They were everywhere. Later they were replaced by the Hendrix Will Show Up Tonight rumors. The difference being that Hendrix frequently showed up. I heard that rumor that Dylan would be there about Woodstock, but I didn't believe it. You just heard it all the time.

Greil Marcus: Willingly or not, Bob Dylan was the presence hovering over this three-day jamboree . . . he is the elder of this urban tribe . . . the tribally tom-tommed message of WOODSTOCK, Dylan's refuge, WOODSTOCK, Dylan's turf, WOODSTOCK, Dylan's bringing it all back home, was as much responsible for moving this massive surge of humanity onto a six-hundred-acre farm as any advertisements, promotion, publicity.

Arthur Levy: I counted myself among the people who already knew that it was silly to think that Dylan was going to show up for something he wasn't announced for. There were two kinds of people in the world. There were people who thought that Dylan was going to show up anywhere, to do anything at any time. And then there were people who understand: this is a business. If he was going to play, he would be advertised. I didn't expect him to be there. I knew that Dylan didn't work that way anymore. I think that rumor thing got started because in 1963, '64 he would show up unannounced at Joan Baez concerts because she took him under her wing. By '66, '67 he was not showing up magically at places.

John Morris: Dylan, the Stones, and the Beatles were the three major acts in the world. We had every other major act, except those three. And we tried all three of them. And we didn't make it. We had the bands that really counted. Dylan just plain decided that he didn't want to do it—upfront. Michael hammered Albert Grossman, Dylan's manager, and I guess Dylan himself—begged, pled, promised—he did everything in the world he could do to have Dylan there. And Dylan didn't want to do it. So he didn't. But what are you going to say? People would say, "Bob Dylan is coming to Woodstock," and you could tell them "No" but Bob Dylan was attached to it.

His legend, his history, his mystery, his mythology was already immense in 1969. Parts of it were self-created (or self-inflicted); parts of it were imposed by outside forces. His aura wafted and hovered over Woodstock like some rock 'n' roll Shroud of Turin. Hell! They called it the Woodstock Festival because *he* lived there. Even as the event moved further and further away from Dylan's actual residence—to Wallkill, to Bethel—the organizers clung to that name because of all the artsy, craftsy, bohemian trappings that Woodstock conjured up in your mind. But its main cachet was that *Dylan* lived there, and *Dylan* wrote great songs there, and that *Dylan*, when he put his mind to it, was going to save the world with his music!

Mike Wadleigh: Bob Dylan told me flat out that if he had known what it was going to be, surely he would've been there. John Lennon desperately wanted to play up there.

In typical Dylan contrarian fashion, he decided not to. He decided to stay home . . . and then go off to the Isle of Wight Festival in Europe the next month and play there instead.

When Dylan finally did play on the property, which is now the Bethel Woods Center for the Arts, in 2007, the only time he spoke to the crowd with tongue planted firmly in Woodstock-chic he said, "It's nice to be back here. Last time we played here we had to play at six in the morning, and it was a-rainin', and the field was full of mud."

So though the Messiah didn't make it to Woodstock, his disciples, or at least his backup band, which had gone on to carve a niche of their own, did play. The Band appeared on Sunday evening.

The psychedelic rock of 1967 and the blues rock and return to hard rock of 1968 ceded some turf in 1969 to a rootsier, simpler, countrified brand of music. It was exemplified by a new incarnation of the Byrds, the softer side of Poco and Crosby, Stills and Nash (out of the ashes of the Buffalo Springfield), and teen idol turned country rocker Rick Nelson and the Stone Canyon Band. Dylan himself had moved in that direction with his album *John Wesley Harding* in 1968 and even more so with *Nashville Skyline* in 1969. But the band that spearheaded the movement, that captured the imaginations of record buyers and concertgoers, that caught lightning in a moonshine jug was the Band!

Starting out in a rock ensemble called the Hawks, backing rockabilly legend Ronnie Hawkins, Garth Hudson, Richard Manuel, Rick Danko, and Robbie Robertson from Canada, and Levon Helm from Arkansas put together an irresistible gumbo of folk, rock, country, jazz, and blues that caught on like wildfire.

Settling down on Dylan's turf in Woodstock, the group rented a big pink house that became, for a while, one of the most famous structures in rock 'n' roll folklore. It was there that Dylan recorded the so-called Basement Tapes, which weren't officially released until a number of years later. It was also there that, now calling themselves the Band, the group put together the songs for their highly praised, warmly received 1968 debut album *Music from Big Pink*.

The group's producer was one of the most successful producers of rock 'n' roll projects at the time, John Simon, who had worked with giants such as Simon and Garfunkel; Janis Joplin; Blood, Sweat and Tears; Gordon Lightfoot; and Mama Cass Elliot; to name just a few. He's also a fine performing singer-songwriter in his own right. John's been a guest on my radio show a number of times, and I asked him recently if he was at Woodstock to see the Band.

John Simon: I was living then where I live now—about an hour's drive from Bethel. I knew about the festival, but having attended a lot of them because of the groups I was working with, I was ambivalent about going.

But the news of the festival was infectious so, on Sunday morning, my wife and I decided to take the drive over there. Fortified by a single glass of orange juice, we set out. We got as far as Liberty, where a road-block had been set up. We were told to go to the Holiday Inn, which was the off-site headquarters. There I happened to bump into John Fisher, who was a rock 'n' roll limo driver—I'd been in his limo quite a few times before. He offered to drive us to the heliport from which we could hop a chopper to Yasgur's farm.

The helicopter landing area was an ad hoc affair—a farmer's field that appeared as if it had just been bulldozed flat to accommodate the whirlybirds. As I recall, the helicopter had four seats for passengers. My wife and I were slated for the first two seats and another couple soon showed up to take the other two. We waited for the plane to arrive. As the chopper approached the field, I looked off to the west, and huge thunderheads were forming. Now, remember, I lived close by and I knew the weather came from the west. Nevertheless, we four passengers boarded the plane but, just before liftoff, some medics rushed up with many cartons of what they called "emergency medical supplies." Because of the amount of stuff, they said the other couple would have to take the next chopper, which disappointed them deeply. But, seeing this imminent tremendous storm on the way, I suddenly felt less inclined to be dropped in an area where emergency medical supplies were needed. So we gave up our seats to the others and decided to return home. A sheriff drove us back to the Holiday Inn, insisting that we duck down in the back in case his boss might be looking. When we got home, we lost our power for two days because of the storm. Now, forty years later, do I regret not having gone? You bet I do!

Keep in mind that Bob Dylan's hoped-for and constantly discussed possible appearance in Bethel was only inflamed and thought to be a sure thing when the Band was added to the bill. But obviously, it didn't work out that way. It was getting close to the originally announced time for the festival to pack up its tent and go home, but there were still several major acts to go. One often thinks in a concert environment that the more laid-back act should open for the more bombastic act. But Woodstock had turned those rules inside out so many times over the weekend that it made perfect sense for the Band to follow Alvin Lee and Ten Years After. They sauntered on at about 10:30 p.m. and captivated the crowd with their homespun brand of North Americana.

When the original Band decided to put the closing parenthesis to their own career, they did so with one of the best rock 'n' roll movies ever made, *The Last Waltz*. I asked guitarist Robbie Robertson about its legacy and, though he may disagree, I think his response applies as much to Woodstock as it does to *The Last Waltz*.

Robbie Robertson: I hope it says that this music was truly valid, and, you know, I think it will. It's not made up of tricks and gimmicks and fads, and it's based on its musical value and what poets could express. That everybody was trying to express and what these people were actually able to say and get across. I think it will be an extraordinary example of what these times really were, what this culture was made of—this whole generation of the '60s and '70s. And I think it will work as kind of a timeless capsule.

CROSBY, STILLS, NASH (AND YOUNG)

Crosby, Stills, Nash and Young didn't go to Woodstock for a concert, they went for a coronation—their own! When my friends and I heard about Woodstock, the list of bands had us very excited. The real clincher, however, was Crosby, Stills, Nash and Young, since we had been huge Buffalo Springfield fans, and an appearance by Crosby, Stills and Nash, scheduled for the Fillmore East in June, had not transpired for whatever reason. They were already names to be reckoned with individually. But collectively? Gangbusters! The term *supergroup* lost its meaning and luster very early on because of abuse, misuse, and underperformance, but there was a time in the late '60s when it really meant something. Crosby, Stills and Nash joining forces was definitely one of those times. Then along came Neil Young for what we call today "added value," and you really, really had something very special (and, as it turned out, very, very fragile).

The very existence of CSN was due, in part, to something akin to a Major League Baseball trade. Crosby was a free agent, thanks to his dismissal from the Byrds. Stills was under contract to Atlantic Records from his time as a member of Buffalo Springfield. And Nash was under contract to Epic Records from his days as a member of the British rock band the Hollies. The question on the table was "How do you spring Nash from Epic to join Crosby and Stills at Atlantic?" Simple. Fellow Springfield alumnus Richie Furay had already formed his own new band, Poco, and Epic was interested. Solution? Atlantic traded Furay for Nash, and two great new groups put out stunning debut albums in 1969.

There was a lot of shared history with these three guys. Crosby had played with the Springfield at Monterey Pop during one of Neil Young's absences from the group. And Nash was friends with the late Mama Cass Elliot, who knew intuitively how well he would blend with her California buddies David and Stephen.

Stephen Stills: Yeah, I was playing in basket houses, shuffling around, trying to get a life and figure out who I wanted to be. One week I'd sing these maudlin folk songs, the next week I'd sing blues, and then I'd do Latin the next week. "Please! Something work!! I'm dancing as fast as I can!"

David Crosby: Just slightly before that, I was doing the same exact thing—working the basket houses. I was running around here, singing folk songs to make a living. When I'd make enough to buy a sausage sandwich, that was a big night!

John Sebastian: At the demise of the Spoonful, I was actually in a very positive place because I had actually had all of this experience before the Spoonful of playing with lotsa great guys, playin' with Steve Stills, and I had by that time met Dallas Taylor and Kenny Altman, who had been part of the New York scene. Now I'm livin' half in Los Angeles and half in New York because it's the musical life and that's what's required. And so I start to hear Stephen and David singin' together and I also knew Graham by that time. And then the three of them start playing. And we still have fun arguing as to whether the first trio singing experience happened at Cass Elliot's swimming pool or my swimming pool or Paul Rothchild's living room. These various theories all abound. At some point I said, "Look, guys, why don't you come east? I got a garage behind my house and I've been playin' drums in it for a year and nobody complained."

At that point, things nearly took a dramatic turn.

John Sebastian: I'm an amateur drummer, and Stephen had said to me, "This band is gonna be a kind of an odd thing with these vocals as the focal thing. I don't feel like hiring a drummer, because he's gonna be insulted. Whereas you, Sebastian, aren't formed yet as a drummer. You could take this job on and kind of play into it. Then we'd have another

240

songwriter and another voice." And I thought pretty hard on this, but I'd been trying out these various things and learning to play alone, and had managed to carry a good part of my audience with me from the Lovin' Spoonful. I think if I'd got behind the idea, it could have happened. But I felt like my audience might have trouble making that many jumps from the Spoonful to John's solo to CSNS, or whatever it was gonna be. So I just said, "Guys, I think I gotta just tough it out here and be the one guy—one-guitar guy for a while and see how that works."

Imagine that for a moment: Crosby, Stills, Nash . . . and Sebastian. But with Sebastian refusing to perform aside the trio—they went onward on their own, eventually enlisting Dallas Taylor to play drums.

Ahmet Ertegun: From the first demos they made, I could hear that the harmony sound of this group was better than anything I had heard since the Everly Brothers. It was really very special. Stephen Stills had talked to me at length about how much he admired David and that Crosby was somebody who had a different understanding of life and a different approach to things and other people. He came from a motion picture family and had an understanding of art, was a jazz fan, and a great composer, a great singer. When I heard the music a few months later, after they'd holed up on Long Island rehearsing together, I said, "My God, this is really something very, very special."

The added value we referred to earlier came in midsummer, and it was something of a surprise. Tensions between Stephen Stills and Neil Young in Buffalo Springfield were legendary, but there was no denying the creative sparks that flew whenever they traded licks with their dueling guitars.

Ahmet Ertegun: One evening after we had our first big success with CSN, David came up with Elliot [Roberts] to my house for dinner, and after dinner I started to play these Neil Young records and I told them that as happy as I was to see Stephen Stills with Graham and with David, I was very sad that Neil Young was no longer with Stephen. There was a certain magic between them when they were with the Buffalo Springfield, and that evening they said, "You know, we ought to talk to Neil," and I think the whole idea of adding Neil Young to the group came about then.

Young joined Crosby, Stills and Nash so close to Woodstock that he barely considered himself part of the band, explains Larry Johnson, now-manager, then-filmmaker on the *Woodstock* film.

Larry Johnson: Neil didn't want to be in the movie. In fact, in the archives we have a version of "Mr. Soul." He didn't want to be filmed, so you can only see his arm. At that point and time he was a sort of add-on to CSN. It hadn't become "and Young" yet. It was only their second gig they had played live. He felt that he was a sideman and didn't want to be a part of it. He felt, "You can film those guys," and that's just how he is. I don't know if he regrets that now or not because we could've certainly have used the footage.

The fact that there was now a Crosby, Stills, Nash *and* Young was not common knowledge almost up until the moment they appeared together at Woodstock. (Neil wasn't mentioned in the print or radio ads.) The ramifications of this new union would not reveal themselves until months after the festival. The debut album was impressive, but their job on August 16–17, 1969, was to introduce themselves to their friends, their fans, their fellow musicians, and to the world as a dynamic, no-holds-barred live performing entity. There were some obstacles in their path, but the consensus was that they hit it out of the park.

Stephen Stills: Our equipment almost didn't get there, and we were going to use a potpourri of the Jefferson Airplane's and the Band's equipment to play, but it showed up just in the nick of time. It was pretty spacey, and I had a twenty-eight-inch waist and nothing hurt! That's what I remember mostly is like, "God! I was so skinny, and nothing hurt!" And right now, getting up and down the steps to the stage is really problematic [laughs].

Ellen Sander: That was kind of their first gig—it wasn't actually their first gig, but it was sort of their first major gig. I think they had played somewhere before but this was to be their major debut. And I remember them arriving and, you know, Crosby kind of bobbing up and down on his heels because he was so excited, and . . . just everybody looking like, "What?" They hadn't been there the day before, I didn't see them at the Holiday Inn, I don't know where they came from, where they went to, where they stayed. They just kind of arrived. And I had worked with them extensively before, I had been with them on their ramp-up, I had been to most of the sessions for their first album, so I knew them and they just arrived and they were just, like, quite impressed. And I don't think I should say intimidated, but it was . . . more than anybody expected, but if you had the major venture that you're unveiling at this point, it must have been rather daunting to look out and see what a huge production it was, and the monumental talent that had gone on before them and would go on after them. You know, it was clear that they were not going to be the . . . highlight of the evening. And although I don't know that that much mattered to them . . . I was looking toward the back of the stage, they arrived from the left, they came in, and it was like, [laugh] maybe they'd helicoptered in and they'd seen it from above or whatever, but they were, they were very impressed.

CSNY took the stage for their famously shaky nervous start.

Stephen Stills:	Hey man. I just gotta say that you people have gotta be the strongest bunch of people I ever saw! . . . Three days, man! Three days! We just love ya! We just love ya! . . . Tell them who we are."
David Crosby:	They'll know if you just sing. Hello . . . Test . . . forty-nine, sixty-five, hike!
Chip Monck:	Ladies and gentlemen, please welcome Crosby, Stills and Nash!
Stephen Stills:	Thank you. We needed that. This is our second gig. This is the second time we've ever played in front of people, man . . . We're scared shitless!

There was a reason for that famous remark at the event and in the film that David explained in his autobiography:

David Crosby: What wasn't said in the movie is why we were so nervous: everyone we respected in the whole goddamn music business was standing in a circle behind us when we went on. Everybody was curious about us. We were the new kid on the block, it was our second public gig, nobody had ever seen us, everybody had heard the record, everybody wondered, "What in the hell are they about?" So when it was rumored that we were about to go on, everybody came. Every band that played there, including all the ones that aren't in the movie, were all standing in an arc behind us, and that was intimidating, to say the least. I'm looking back at Hendrix and Robbie Robertson and Levon Helm and Janis and Sly and Grace and Paul, everybody that I knew and everybody I didn't know. We were so happy that it went down well that we could barely handle it.

Despite the newborn status of the group, they were heavily featured in the *Woodstock* film because of what they stood for.

Michael Wadleigh: I want to emphasize that one of the reasons we used so much of Crosby, Stills, Nash and Young was the idea that the movie was about community, a gathering, a sense of camaraderie, a Woodstock Generation thing. And there were three or four people singing in harmony. It was a real group. Their harmonies were so very good. How many groups can you say that about? Generally, there's a lead singer, like Fogerty, and that's it. But CSNY had such a group feeling because vocally you can hear all these parts, these brilliant harmonies. On the Monday after the festival, Crosby and Nash showed up for a taping of The Dick Cavett Show, still reeling with excitement over the events of the weekend. Stills proudly showed off the Woodstock mud on his boots to a studio full of fans and a national television audience. Crosby was effusive when Cavett asked him if he thought the festival was a success.

David Crosby: It was incredible. It's probably the strangest thing that has ever happened in the world. Can I describe what it looked like flying in on the helicopter, man? Like an encampment of the Macedonian army on the Greek hills! Crossed with the biggest batch of gypsies that you ever saw. It was amazing.

Johnny Carson was the king of late-night television, but in 1969 Dick Cavett offered from time to time a slightly hipper roster of guests, including such Woodstock luminaries as Jimi Hendrix, Janis Joplin, and Sly Stone. He and his producers had fortuitously booked an all-Woodstock show for taping the day after the festival. The guest list included Jimi Hendrix, Jefferson Airplane, and Joni Mitchell. Having just finished his set a few hours earlier, Jimi pleaded exhaustion and didn't show. The Airplane was there in full force. Crosby, Stills and Nash showed up as a consolation prize, but only David and Stephen made it on camera because Graham's green card covered only concert work, not TV appearances. Joni's managers David Geffen and Elliot Roberts thought the network television exposure for her was so vital that they forbade her to travel to Bethel that weekend for fear that she might not make it back in time for the taping. This resulted in a pretty amazing chain of events. Joni's friends David, Stephen and Graham came back raving about the spectacle. She reconciled her own disappointment about it with their unbridled enthusiasm, and created, almost by osmosis, the wistful, defining anthem about the festival called "Woodstock." Another irony? CSNY recorded the song as a full-tilt rocker and Geffen and Roberts used it as a bargaining chip with Warner Bros. for the rights to use CSN in the film (Neil wanted no part of it, not even allowing himself to be filmed).

There have been times in the last forty years that all three, but David in particular, were burned out talking about Woodstock and refused to address the subject. Recently however, he addressed the subject once again with fresh perspective in his book about music and activism called *Stand and Be Counted*.

I'm asked about Woodstock so often I usually feign only a dim recollection of it. But the truth is my memory of it is very good. I loved it. I thought it was a very heartfelt, wonderful, accidentally great thing where a lot of incredible music got played. There was a genuine feeling of brotherhood among the people who were there. Nobody killed anybody, nobody raped anybody, nobody shot anybody. In the history of humankind, I think it's probably the only group of people that size that didn't do any of that. Anytime you get half a million people together, even at a religious gathering, somebody beats somebody up. The most aggressive moment I can remember was when Pete Townshend kicked Abbie Hoffman off the stage for trying to use the Who's microphone to promote the Yippies . . . Woodstock was definitely not a political event in the traditional sense of that word, but because it was so <u>huge</u> it had a significant political impact just the same.

And so have Crosby, Stills, Nash and Young. Witness the controversy stirred by Neil Young in his recent documentary about the 2006 CSNY Freedom of Speech tour. While promoting the film, Neil made these comments.

Neil Young: I think that the time when music could change the world is past . . . I think it would be very naïve to think that in this day and age . . . I think the world today is a different place, and that it's time for science and physics and spirituality to make a difference in this world and to try to save the planet . . . If we didn't do that, it would just feel like a bunch of old hippies up there saying what they thought—and who cares? The goal was to stimulate debate among people, and I hope that to some degree the film succeeds in doing that.

I think Graham Nash's observation about Woodstock in this book's introduction trumps his erstwhile partner's current notions about the power of music. If you'll remember, Graham posited that as we continue into the future, "the legend, the myth of Woodstock becomes greater than the actual reality." And as we get into questions about the future, what about the future of Crosby, Stills and Nash? Will they keep on keeping on?

Graham Nash: It's working. Why not? Somebody asked me the other day, "When are you going to quit?" And I said, "Well, Chuck Berry is ten years older than I am, and he can rock my ass right off the stage."

Stephen Stills: Why on earth would I want to quit? Jesus, they still pay us!

David Crosby: I'm only just starting to get good at this.

BLOOD, SWEAT AND TEARS

As we have seen many times already, there are some nearly forgotten men and women of Woodstock. This is mostly because they were not chosen by director Michael Wadleigh to be in the movie, or by producer Eric Blackstead to be on the concert recordings. This affected lower-tier performers such as Bert Sommer and Sweetwater, as well as such high-profile acts as the Band; Creedence Clearwater Revival; the Grateful Dead; and Blood, Sweat and Tears.

It is easy to forget how big an act Blood, Sweat and Tears was in 1969. Their eponymous second album with a new lead singer (more on this later on) was one of the most successful and critically acclaimed recordings of that year. In fact, three of the singles from it rocketed up the Top 40 charts: "You've Made Me So Very Happy" in March, "Spinning Wheel" in June, and "And When I Die" in October. Each one ascended to the Number Two slot, stopping just short of becoming Number One singles—echoing the experience of those other humongous American hit makers in 1969—Creedence Clearwater Revival. But it didn't really matter. BS&T's successful run was etched into the consciousness of the record-buying public, and they received massive amounts of airplay on both AM and FM radio. Groups with that many hits were the eight-hundred-pound gorillas of the record business and could sit, play, and appear just about anywhere they wanted to, and that included Woodstock. The group's original drummer remembered.

Bobby Colomby: *Well, in the first place, I was playing with my band Blood, Sweat and Tears, and, at that time, we were one of the major acts that were going to perform there. When we okayed it, when we said we would do that festival, it sort of became an official gig. And then everyone sort of signed on.*

Robert Spitz: *Blood, Sweat and Tears was considered of superstar magnitude. Their signing was a conspicuous feather in Lang's frumpy leather cap. By mid-1969, their second album, <u>Blood, Sweat and Tears</u> (minus founder Al Kooper), was firmly stationed at the top of the charts, and their unique sound—a synthesis of electric blues and jazz—began to dominate commercial rock music. All of the up-and-coming recording artists were incorporating a horn section like BS&T's into their bands and were similarly experimenting with more spontaneous chord progressions . . . Lang went with the proven commodity.*

Truth be told, BS&T was so big that year that it even embarrassed themselves to a degree.

Bobby Colomby: *We won the Grammy for Album of the Year. And I remember when I got the Grammy—<u>Abbey Road</u> was out at the same time—and as soon as I was handed the Grammy, I kept looking, "There's got to be a Beatle somewhere I can give this to. I feel guilty. This is ridiculous!"*

Ellen Sander was a big fan and she recalled their set from Woodstock.

Ellen Sander: *They were always so well produced—a nice big robust band who were more technically musical than most of the other bands, so I appreciated them for that. They were really musicians: they had studied music, they made charts, they rehearsed a lot. They knew a lot about the Chicago blues sound that they were playing. They were outstanding.*

Through her writing, she came to know the band personally.

Ellen Sander: *Jimmy Fielder actually gave me a music lesson once, actually taught me what eight-bar blues really meant. And I sort of was sitting around, talking about stuff, and he said, "Oh, you don't know this* stuff!" And he just sat me down and gave me a music theory lesson. It was just incredible that he would care to do that. And it wasn't like he was being condescending, because he loved my work, he loved my writing, but he just wanted me to know more about music. It was one of the most special moments of my career.

Even in how they chose to spend their free time, Blood, Sweat and Tears were not like the other bands of the time.

Ellen Sander: Bobby Colomby was a very funny guy and I always enjoyed his company. I remember running into them on the road and they said, "What are you doing tomorrow night? Come hang out with us." So I went and hung out with them and with most rock bands, you'd imagine that hanging out with them would mean just sitting around and doing drugs all night, and someone would play the guitar, and they'd be rapping about politics and the future of the world. But Blood, Sweat and Tears were these New York guys, so we went bowling!

Alas, the group was not able to sustain their 1969 success. They got a couple of good years out of it all, including a US State Department–sponsored tour of Yugoslavia, Romania, and Poland, but some familiar bugaboos reared their ugly heads. Internal squabbling, personnel changes, the grueling nature of touring, and the ever-shifting tastes of the record-buying public gradually eroded the group's superstar status.

Blood, Sweat and Tears's road to Woodstock turned out to have an easier path than most in more ways than one. While just about every other act that appeared there has horror stories about mud, and traffic, and no access, BS&T—thanks to good timing and fortunate logistics—breezed in and breezed out. They were scheduled to play prime time Sunday, but ended up getting on sometime around midnight.

Bobby Colomby: We were playing in Massachusetts the night before, and everyone was saying, "Did you hear? Do you know what's going on?" "What?" "You can't get in; you can't get out! Millions of people! Wow! You have to helicopter." Well, we drove straight in. We played. And we drove straight out. I think I was home in an hour and a half, because everyone was frozen assuming you couldn't get anywhere.

The group's set included one of their biggest hits—"Spinning Wheel"—written by Kooper's replacement, the new lead singer from Canada, David Clayton-Thomas. Kooper's talents were represented by one of his contributions to the debut *Child Is Father to the Man*. It was called "I Love You More Than You'll Ever Know" and has become a blues standard. Paul Shaffer immortalized it by playing a piece of it every Friday night for a year as part of a James Brown homage on *Late Night with David Letterman*. In general, BS&T's repertoire consisted of a balanced mix of original compositions as well as equally "original" covers of some other great writers and musicians.

Bobby Colomby: In the first place, our singer had a soul, kind of rootsy approach to his singing. We had a four-piece horn section, and we were jazz influenced. So the songs [by other writers] had to harmonically have something in them that would allow us to go in that direction, and there were a million songs that we tried.

And what was it like standing on that stage?

Bobby Colomby: For me, personally? I mean, imagine this. I sit at the drum set. I'm getting ready to play. I pick up a stick. I hit a snare drum. It goes, "CRRRRSSSSHHHH" and I hear half a million people go [roars], and I'm thinking, Hey! I'm really good! Very good! I'm an excellent drummer! [laughs]

As for why the group is not in the movie or on the album, Bobby told interviewer Jeremiah Rickert:

Bobby Colomby: Our manager at that time was Bennett Glotzer. He felt that since we were one of the headliners [along with Janis Joplin and Jimi Hendrix], we should be paid accordingly. Seventy-five hundred dollars was not enough to "star" in a movie. He had not recognized that the event itself would supersede the status of the individual acts. The producers of the festival and documentary were not permitted to film the band's performance. However, they did succeed in shooting the opening song, "More and More," and then were told to get off the stage.

Missed opportunity for sure, but most of the artists who were lucky enough to be there have come to terms with however big or small a part they played. David Clayton-Thomas put it succinctly in his internet Q&A with interviewer Rickert.

David Clayton-Thomas: My three days of love and peace lasted about two hours. When you're onstage in front of six hundred and fifty thousand people, you just know that this is a momentous event and probably will never happen again, and it never did.

JOHNNY WINTER

Johnny Winter is and has been a distinctly unique performer and personality for very many reasons for a very long time. He and his equally successful younger brother Edgar, both albinos, were raised in Beaumont, Texas, in a musical family. Their mom played piano, and their dad, a builder by trade, played banjo and saxophone.

Johnny Winter: I wanted to play clarinet. It just seemed interesting to me. I played in the school band. My daddy played banjo, and he taught me a few things on ukulele, taught me a few chords. A four-string banjo is the same thing as a ukulele. Stuff like "Ain't She Sweet," "Bye, Little Blackbird," "Shine On, Harvest Moon," "Five-Foot-Two." My parents were both musical and it was just something that just naturally I got into.

What did they listen to?

Johnny Winter: Oh, country and western mostly. But I didn't like country that much. It just didn't move me. Just didn't have the feelin' that the blues did. Blues had more feeling to it, more emotion. But it's not really that sad. Blues is not just sad. Some of the music is sad, but some of it's very happy. It was just an emotional music. It was about life and about feelings. Willie Dixon said blues is the truth.

The brothers were veteran performers in a number of local rock and blues bands by their middle teens.

Johnny Winter: I learned guitar when I was about twelve. My great-grandfather bought me my first guitar. It was a Gibson ES-125. Oh, it was very exciting. I just loved playing guitar. It was natural to me, came natural. I mostly played old rock 'n' roll at first, stuff I was hearing on the radio—Buddy Holly, Little Richard, Fats Domino, Elvis Presley. I hadn't heard the blues yet. I didn't hear blues till—till I was twelve or fifteen . . . I copied the stuff that I was hearing on the radio.

Soon after discovering the blues, he formed his first band.

Johnny Winter: Edgar was on piano. We had a sax player named Willard Chamberlain. David Holiday was on drums. Dennis Drugan was on bass. We played pretty much around Texas. We played in Louisiana some, too. You could make more money in Louisiana because they could sell mixed drinks, and they couldn't in Texas at that point. I put a blues song in every once in a while, and, ah, the white people didn't really go for it that much. But I—I tried putting it in there anyway as much as I could. They didn't say anything. I could just tell they didn't really get off on it as much as they did the rock 'n' roll and R&B: Little Richard, Fats Domino, Chuck Berry. Chuck Berry was a big influence on me. I liked all his music.

One of the defining moments of Johnny's early career came courtesy of B.B. King, who will come up again later in this chapter.

Johnny Winter: I saw B.B. King at a black club called the Raven in Beaumont. That was excellent. I bothered him until he let me play. I asked him to let me play, right? He said no at first. He asked to see my union card, and I had one, and finally he just decided to go ahead and let me. He said he was afraid that I would have thought he didn't let me play because I was a white kid in the black club. So he decided to go ahead and let me. It was a big thrill and it went well. I played "Goin' Down Slow" if I'm not mistaken. He just let me use his guitar and I played, and I got a standing ovation. It was a couple of thousand people. It was a big club.

That night in Beaumont was just the beginning. In his early twenties, the lure of the blues drew Johnny to Chicago in the early '60s. There he soaked up the genre, apprenticed with great players and met future legends including Mike Bloomfield and Barry Goldberg. Indeed, Columbia Records came calling and, as often happens when a new star gets that kind of attention, an album of old demo tapes surfaced just as Johnny was releasing his self-titled debut album on the major label. Both sold well, were raved about from coast-to-coast, and Johnny was soon being heard everywhere on FM radio.

There were many different ways to become noticed in rock 'n' roll in the mid- to late '60s, but one of the newest was the rise of a serious rock press. Antithetical to the glut of fan rags and teen magazines, a slew of initially "underground" newspapers and magazines began to take the maturing rock 'n' roll of the time quite seriously. The most successful of these was *Rolling Stone* out of San Francisco. The first issue carried a publication date of November 9, 1967. By just one year later, both rock 'n' roll fans and the music industry were paying close attention to whatever the magazine had to say.

In a 1968 article about up-and-coming talent, *Rolling Stone* called Johnny Winter "a cross-eyed albino with long fleecy hair, playing some of the gutsiest fluid blues guitar you've ever heard." The result of all this was an invitation to two major events in 1969: the Newport Jazz Festival and Woodstock. We'll start with Newport.

In what has been described as one of that festival's highlights, Johnny once again shared a stage with B.B. King. What a warm-up that turned out to be for Johnny's next appearance on a big stage—the one in Bethel.

> **Johnny Winter:** We knew there was a huge crowd. We heard on TV before we even got there that it was huge. We didn't know exactly how many people. We came in, really tired. We had played Detroit and Chicago and we didn't get much sleep at all. We got Hendrix's spot at 12:30 at night. He didn't want to play then. That was a real good time to play. It was the biggest thing we'd ever played. And we had played a lot of big festivals, too. But Woodstock was the biggest. I played my regular songs that I had done on my first album, <u>Fluorescent Blues Experiment</u>. When we played, the rain had quit. So we went on at a real good time. I think we played a good set.

Personal demons and changing times prevented Johnny from keeping a sustained foothold in the rock hierarchy, but he is a road warrior, still plays clubs and concerts all over, and still gets the job done musically as well. He is a modest, self-effacing man who would rather play music than talk about playing music, but he describes the essence of performing very eloquently:

Johnny Winter: When you're out there onstage, you're playing your soul and your heart out. I love it. It's my whole life.

PAUL BUTTERFIELD AND SHA NA NA

Sam Phillips: *If I could find a white man who sings with the Negro feel, I'd make a million dollars.*

For Sam, the embodiment of that dream was Elvis Presley. But what it did was take the focus away from the originators of this wonderful music. Clearly, young Americans at large were more willing to accept black blues music from white interpreters than they were from the original artists, many of them still at the top of their game.

Most of the credit for the revival of interest in American blues music in the '60s is heaped upon British musicians. And rightfully so. The names Beck and Burdon and Clapton and Jagger and Mayall and Page and Plant and Richards all deserve praise for refocusing attention on the genuine greatness of the largely ignored American blues masters. Maybe not as noticed, maybe not as widespread as it was in England, there were young, white Americans equally devoted to the form as any of the artists mentioned above. Most notable among them was harmonica virtuoso Paul Butterfield, born December 17, 1942, in Chicago. His musical training included seven years of study with the first flautist of the Chicago Symphony, but he was inexorably drawn to the down-and-dirty blues music that emanated from the nightclubs on his birth city's legendary South Side.

Paul was one of the first white boys to venture into those clubs and soak up the intoxicating music that he found there. He apprenticed with historical figures such as Buddy Guy, Howlin' Wolf, Little Walter, and Otis Rush. The fruit of this influence was the formation of the Paul Butterfield Blues Band in 1963. It was an integrated ensemble featuring Mike Bloomfield on guitar, and the rhythm section from Howlin' Wolf's band, Sam Lay on drums and Jerome Arnold on bass. They released their self-titled debut album on Elektra Records in October of 1965. Founded as a folk label, Elektra was the home of Judy Collins, Phil Ochs, Tom Paxton, and Tom Rush. Butterfield delivered the first electric Elektra album, and the label subsequently moved into big time rock 'n' roll with the Doors, Love, and, later on, Queen.

The Butterfield Blues Band was not officially on the roster at Woodstock, but Paul was actually one of the musicians who lived in the town that the festival was named after. His ties to Albert Grossman, who delivered the Band and Janis Joplin, made it natural for Butterfield and Company to show up in Bethel just in case a jam broke out. On Sunday night, at John Morris's request, they ended up bridging the performances of Johnny Winter and Sha Na Na. They delivered a typically terrific set and ended up with a tune on the first Woodstock album ("Love March") and another one on *Woodstock Two* ("Everything's Gonna Be Allright"). Butterfield's post-Woodstock career was erratic at best. The Blues Band broke up in 1971, and his next vehicle never lived up to the optimistic promise of their name—Paul Butterfield's Better Days. Paul had one more great moment in the sun at the Band's *Last Waltz* in 1976. He soldiered into the '80s, but alcoholism and subsequent related health problems took their toll. He was found dead in his apartment in North Hollywood on May 4, 1987, at the age of forty-four. He may just be an asterisk at Woodstock, but no history of the American blues revival would be complete without mention of his name and his accomplishments.

Butterfield wasn't the only Sunday-Monday act to revive old music. While most notable bands at Woodstock were engaged in a musical revolution, another band on the bill was reframing the pop music of the '50s in a most unusual way by taking a step backward into the future. There are cartoons in the daily newspapers. There are cartoons on Saturday morning and even prime time TV. And there was a cartoon at Woodstock. Maybe not in the traditional sense—but a cartoon nonetheless. It was a rock 'n' roll group sending up an entire era, an entire decade, an entire subgenre of pre-hippie, primitive rock 'n' roll. The cartoon was named Sha Na Na, and far from the mean streets of New York City, the group's actual roots can be traced to the hallowed, ivied halls of Columbia University.

Michael Wadleigh: It's a view of the '50s before the '60s happened. And yet, they were bizarre. They were a satire of the '50s, of course. They were kind of like Mark Mothersbaugh, Devo, one of the all-time interesting bizarro groups. Anyway, there was something very bizarre about them. In their sort of automaton roteness that went beyond the '50s. Even though they were doing dance moves from the '50s, it seemed to me they were more out of Merce Cunningham or Twyla Tharp, a satiric choreographic group.

Columbia had a twelve-man choral group called the Kingsmen. One night at a concert early in 1969, they sang an old '50s hit by the Diamonds called "Little Darlin'" and the audience went wild. The brother of one of the group's members came up with the idea that the group should grease their hair back, wear gold lamé suits (à la Elvis on the cover of his second *Golden Hits* collection), and do a concert of all doo-wop and rock songs. One of the preppier Kingsmen quit the group in disgust and was replaced by a rock 'n' roll kid from Brooklyn College named Henry Gross. They did another show not as the Kingsmen, but as Sha Na Na, a name taken from a nonsense lyric in a 1958 hit by the Silhouettes called "Get a Job." They were a sensation. Henry Gross hinted that both Jimi Hendrix and Bill Graham might have had something to do with getting them noticed by the Woodstock promoters, but however it happened, they were booked to play at Bethel in August.

Contrary to the popular belief that twenty-year-old Santana drummer Michael Shrieve was the youngest musician to take the stage at Woodstock, Henry Gross was just eighteen years old at the time. Henry's offstage brushes with greatness at the festival were even more entertaining than the group's well-received performance.

Henry Gross: We got the booking . . . they wanted us for Sunday morning, so anticipating diabolical traffic, we left Saturday in the middle of the night. After talking our way through a billion roadblocks with police, we actually arrived at the Holiday Inn, Fernwood, at 9:00 a.m. Sunday morning. This is where the acts were staying and this is where you're going to stay until they want you to go on. But we were sort of the new kids on the block. Nobody knew who we were, so they wanted us there to get us on whenever they could.

So, I walk into the lobby of the Holiday Inn, and the first person I see is Jimi Hendrix. He's holding a quart bottle of Jack Daniel's and it's nine in the morning, this is true, and he offers me a drink. Now it's nine in the morning and I've been up all night. But you don't turn down possibly the greatest guitarist in the twentieth century when he offers you something to drink. So we passed the bottle back and forth and about an hour later, I'm pretty well gone when a guy taps me on the shoulder and says he wants to take me to the stage because they wanted us to be there to be available whenever they could.

So I say so long to Jimi and wobble out of the lobby . . . and we walk around the side of the building and I'm surprised to see this military-style helicopter sitting there. Now, flying is my second favorite thing. Everything else is tied for first! So I get into this helicopter with a couple of musicians going to the stage and a couple of strangers, and the pilot takes off straight up—that's how helicopters go, if you've never been in one—it was kind of a chopper. And he tilts the chopper so that we can see the half a million people down below, and it's the most incredible sight I'd ever seen, and I'd have been amazed <u>except</u> for the fact that the door is wide open and I almost fell out along with another guy. So I advised the pilot that unless he wanted to spend the rest of the day cleaning his machine, he should take us back where he found us. Believe it or not, he took my advice, and in a minute we were back where we started from.

So I retreat back to the lobby—it's true, all this is true—and Jimi is sitting there and he motions me to sit down and he sees that I'm mildly hysterical and he asks me what happened and when I tell him, he busts out laughing because he was a paratrooper in the army. So he couldn't stop laughing at me and says, "Have something to drink; it will calm you down." So we passed the bottle back and forth for a while and now I'm completely beyond comprehension, and a guy comes back, same guy, and says my car is there. I say so long to Jimi, fall out of the lobby, and there is a 1958 Cadillac with a driver . . . more my speed. So I'm flopped out in the back and we're just about to pull away when the door pops open and a guy slides in next to me. He's got round sunglasses and a beard and he's smiling like this. And I recognized him immediately. And I said, "I know you. You're Jerry Grateful of the Garcia Dead!" And he's grinning from ear to ear because he can see that I'm blotto from hair to toe. So he offers me something to smoke. Now I'm already high as Kilimanjaro, but you don't turn down arguably the greatest druggie of the twentieth century when he offers you something to smoke. So he reaches into the pocket of his denim jacket and produces a little bottle

PAUL BUTTERFIELD AND SHA NA NA

from which he rolls a very large joint. So he lights it up and we pass it back and forth, and now I'm . . . truckin'!

So between Jimi's hooch and Jerry's hemp, I'm hallucinating so intensely that the rest of the day is this magnificent washing machine of images . . . Joe Cocker's blue boots with the white stars on them, a lake full of naked ladies with breasts floating like life boats on a sea of love, Stephen Stills trying to get to the backstage area without a pass—the guard was not impressed—and backstage was an orgy of the most beautiful guitars surrounded by the Daily News headline "Hippies Mired in Sea of Mud." All this and Crosby, Stills, Nash and Young; Blood, Sweat and Tears; Johnny Winter; and my buddy Alvin Lee and Ten Years After!

Well, we were waiting to go on . . . let's just say I'm damaged permanently from that afternoon. A buddy of mine who was in my first band in high school was actually a security guard there and he said, "Man, we spent the whole day with Jimi and Jerry hanging out backstage," and I said, "Oh yeah, I remember that." I was gone. I thought we'd never get on. I was a big fan of all those bands—and people started showing up, like Paul Butterfield, unannounced, and they put him right on and I thought they'd never get to us. Finally at seven in the morning on Monday morning we went on.

Michael Wadleigh: They were such an extraordinary, far-out group. Of course, they occupied practically no film time. We couldn't help but put them in. They were just too hysterical for words. They're just out there.

As a novelty; as an appetizer for Jimi Hendrix; as additional comic relief in the movie and on the album, Sha Na Na was launched into the stratosphere by Woodstock and parlayed it into a successful syndicated television series in the '70s. Ironically, Henry Gross didn't stick around long enough to enjoy it, opting instead for a fairly successful solo career of his own.

Henry Gross: A lot of things went through my mind [onstage] that I do remember, but mostly I just remember being amazed and really feeling that something had gone right finally. But I also do remember, it was a real gut feeling, it was very strange, watching Jimi play when he went on may have been the moment when I knew I was leaving Sha Na Na. I'm pretty sure of that because I wanted to do that more than I wanted to . . . Sha Na Na was changing, even from the very beginning. You just got this feeling that you couldn't really grow with it because it was going to be locked into doing songs you didn't write. It was more like being in a Broadway show like <u>Grease</u>—you were an actor in a play. Didn't matter that I was in Sha Na Na. The fact that I played well and sang well didn't matter. Anyone could have done it that was a good singer and good guitar player.

But the twelve people who actually did do it have a memory to take with them for the rest of their lives. And Henry Gross in particular has one other postscript to add to his own personal story, and that is the fact that of all the acts who appeared there, he will *always* be the youngest musician that played Woodstock.

JIMI HENDRIX

Larry Johnson: A lot of people had left the night before. The crowd was very sparse for Hendrix's performance because most people had left because it was Monday. Most people had jobs. They weren't like hippies. They were like suburban kids. I mean, we were so exhausted by the end of that, that when Hendrix came out to play and did "The Star-Spangled Banner," I stood right at the bottom of the stage and stared up and thought, Man, is this over? There was Sha Na Na, which was weird enough, and then Jimi Hendrix. It was so surreal to have gone through those three days already.

Billy Altman: By the time Hendrix came on, most people were gone and I was no more than a hundred feet from the stage. I had started out a half a mile away on Friday night. It was fascinating to see him come onstage and start to play a very toned-down set. As over the top and in some respects clownlike and vaudeville-like as he had been in Monterey two years before, he wanted his performance at Woodstock to be the first day of the rest of his life as a musician. He really wanted to play a very serious show and the pyrotechnics would simply be coming out of his guitar, but he wasn't going to be rolling around onstage playing with his feet. He wanted to play a straightforward, "I'm a real musician" show. He was phenomenal.

Billy Cox: The people who were left merged toward the stage to really enjoy the music we were making.

I met Jimi once on Bleecker Street in Greenwich Village in the winter of 1970. He was trudging through the snow wearing a big fur coat that you've all seen on him in photos from that era. I introduced myself and he actually knew who I was! A reminder that even the musicians listened to WNEW-FM in New York in 1970. We chatted briefly, then went our separate ways. At that time, especially in the Village, it wasn't rare just to bump into people. All those artists keeping strange hours.

Ellen Sander: One night, really late, I was up writing. I was living in Chelsea at the time and I went down to Smiler's to get some Häagen-Dazs Rum Raisin ice cream. And I went to the vats of ice cream, and there was one Rum Raisin left. All of a sudden, this black hand in a paisley sleeve snaked past me and grabbed the Rum Raisin. I stood up, and there was Jimi Hendrix! I just looked at him, and he looked at me with this big grin, and we both just cracked up, and he handed me the last Rum Raisin. We just looked at each other. We both obviously had the two a.m. munchies. No words were exchanged. He took French Vanilla.

My other Hendrix memory is a sad one. Later in 1970, I was finishing up my morning show at the radio station, and a desk assistant from the newsroom rushed in with a bulletin: Jimi Hendrix had been found dead in a London apartment at the age of twenty-seven. He choked to death on his own vomit following an overdose of barbiturates. The coroner's decision could not make a definitive determination if it was deliberate or accidental.

One of the most difficult parts of the radio job is passing along tragic information like that to a mass audience. You remember what a punch in the gut it is to hear about the death of a legend you admire, particularly at a young age (think Buddy Holly in 1959), and you call upon that visceral sense memory to help you find a compassionate way to disseminate the tragic news. I've had to do it too many times—Brian Epstein in 1967, Brian Jones in 1969, Jimi and Janis in 1970, Jim Morrison in 1971, and on and on. There is also a tremendous difference between mourning a full life, well lived, such as Bo Diddley's, versus a life cut short by incomprehensible inside or outside forces that agonizingly leave you wondering about what might have been. Of course, you always wonder how much more he would have accomplished at that high artistic level.

The Monterey International Pop Festival in June of 1967 was a huge moment for Hendrix. Birth records indicate that he was born in Seattle on November 27, 1942, but some secretly think that he came from outer space to educate humans in the ways of the electric guitar that no one before him had even thought to pursue.

But, no. He was a naturally talented musician who really worked at his craft.

Michael Wadleigh: Hendrix was really competing with himself. He was really experimenting. Drawing from the outside but without an interest in commercialization. He was interested in the sounds. The other thing was that he practiced that guitar always. This was not a man who let it happen. He had discipline and played hours and hours every single day. I think people don't understand that. If you want to play like Hendrix, you have to work and work and work and work. It's well known that Clapton works like a dog. Springsteen rehearses all the time. The kids of the world don't seem to get that. They want to be famous, and want to do this that and the other thing.

John Morthland writes in *The Rolling Stone Illustrated History of Rock & Roll:*

As a guitarist, Hendrix quite simply redefined how that instrument could be played, in the same way that Cecil Taylor redefined the piano or John Coltrane the tenor sax. As a songwriter, Hendrix was capable of startling, mystical imagery as well as the down-to-earth sexual allusions of the bluesman. He sang in a wispy voice that at first seemed limited, but proved remarkably effective at conveying nuance and emphasis.

SUNDAY

Unheralded in his own country, Jimi had to go to England to reinvent himself and be discovered. It was Chas Chandler, an original member of the Animals, and his partner Michael Jeffery, who divined the Hendrix potential and mounted a reverse British Invasion by bringing back to these shores an American who would bewitch, bother, and bewilder audiences for the final thirty-nine months of his life.

Rock historians have gone so far as to call Jimi Hendrix the patron saint of revolutionary rock.

Christopher Farley: I don't think it goes far enough, because at the time we were writing "Clapton Is God!" across walls. So Jimi Hendrix has to be a lot more than just a patron saint. This is the man that reinvented rock 'n' roll guitar. And for years, the English had been taking blues-based music, selling it to Americans, saying, "Look at what we can do!" Here's Jimi finally taking command of the blues, of rock 'n' roll, R&B, mixing it all together and finally getting to present it as an American, as a [master] guitarist to other Americans again. So he was really reinventing the form, doing something new, reclaiming it for the US of A. It's an amazing thing he's doing here. This is the guy that other [guitarists]— Jeff Beck, Eric Clapton, the Beatles—they were going to see him and they were impressed! Stars were impressed by him, so that shows how bright his light was.

Unlike some of the other divas, Jimi was far from hesitant to book this concert in a cornfield.

John Morris: Jimi had rented a place upstate to rehearse and get ready for the event, but as the weekend arrived, he was reportedly terrified by the television accounts about Woodstock, fearful of the chaos and conditions he was hearing about, and threatening a last-minute cancelation. Calmer heads prevailed.

Originally, Michael Lang had imagined a very unique act to tie up the festival.

Michael Lang: My generation grew up with Roy Rogers on television. At the end of each show, Roy would sing "Happy Trails" and send us all to bed. So I thought, What a perfect way to end Woodstock. And I think Roy was the only artist who turned us down. He didn't get it at all.

According to John Morris, Johnny Winter was originally going to close the festival, but that's not the way it turned out:

John Morris: Well, we didn't end with Johnny Winter, but it's good we didn't. The way we ended was the way that I guess it was designed that we should—which was with Hendrix. I mean, Jimi drove around for two days around the outside of the festival not being able to get in and Mike Jeffery who was his manager, who a lot of people hated, but who I got along with, was the most cooperative manager you could ask for. He would say, "Well, what do you want to do, John?" "Well, can you stay out there for a few more hours? You know what, Mike, maybe you guys should get a motel room, and we should put this off until tomorrow?" And they were totally cooperative and did it. Jimi, he was the last act. And what we were trying to do was to get through the dark hours of Sunday night, because we didn't want to dump that number of people on the highway in the dark trying to get home, or trying to find their cars trying to get out of there. So we stretched it and stretched it and stretched it.

My old friend, and great singer and musician, Kenny Rankin, hung out with Jimi at the festival.

Kenny Rankin: I had just recorded Mind Dusters [his debut album], and my wife and I were invited, by two execs from Mercury Records, to join them at the Woodstock Festival in Bethel, New York . . . My good friend, Gerardo Velez was playing percussion with Hendrix for a while, and Gerardo had given me a backstage pass. I made my way to the rear of the stage, and with my pass, found myself standing behind the amplifiers. It was awesome!

At the end of the day, we all went back to a house that Jimi had rented. There was Paul Butterfield and a bunch of players that were jamming downstairs, on first floor. I was very intimidated. I played an unamplified classical guitar, and I felt so out of place, that I went to the third floor of the home with my guitar.

After a short while, Jimi climbed the stairs to where I was. He was wearing a burgundy velvet robe that went to the floor. He was carrying a flattop steel string guitar. I think it was a Martin guitar. He sat down, and we played for about an hour or so. There was a woman that came upstairs carrying a Bolex 35mm camera. She began to film us playing, or I thought she was. It turned out that there was no film in the camera. It was the '60s, you know. What I would have given to have just one frame of what I thought was a great moment in time. It is a memory that I will carry with me for the rest of my life.

Jimi was so much more of a guitar player, beyond the psychedelic, than most people knew. I recall an evening at my then manager and friend's home, Monte Kay. We were all sitting around, and Jimi began to explain his feelings about the sea. He said that he was fearful of the sea, because it was deep, dark, and mysterious. But after some time, he said that his feelings had changed, and that he now loved the sea, because it was deep, dark, and mysterious. He was one of a kind, and we all miss him.

Michael Wadleigh: By the time Hendrix was on, there were only three cameras working sometimes. Often mine was the only camera running. The motor was so hot that I had to wrap it in a towel in order to even hold it. We were down to the last few rolls of film. It was a bit like filming a war, I suppose.

Jimi—dressed in jeans, a white leather jacket with heavy-duty fringe, and a pinkish red scarf wrapped around his carefully coiffed Afro—stepped onto the stage with his experimental, informal ensemble called Electric Sky Church.

Billy Cox: He got in touch with me and told me he needed my help very desperately. I just dropped everything here in Nashville. I had a publishing company and a few other things going on. I heard the desperation in his voice, and I went to New York, and we got together. However, we did some other small jobs down in the Village and some other places. We constantly stayed in the recording studio coming up with ideas for songs. We found out that there was this festival that was fixing to happen in Woodstock. We just thought it was going to be an ordinary event. We didn't realize how astronomical it was going to be. We rehearsed in Chopin, New York, which is maybe fifteen minutes away. We got together with Larry Lee, a guitar player who was a friend from years gone by. Mitch Mitchell on drums. Juma Sultan on congas, and Jerry Velez on congas and Jimi and myself.

What was life like up there?

Billy Cox: I was kind of the entertainment director. I picked up this BB gun at a hardware store and we shot at cans and we rode the cows and motorcycles in between times because we knew there was going to be a time when we had to get down to some serious business. Jimi was going through some mental anguish about a group. Not necessarily that group, but trying to get his head together to project some new music to be able to perform a little better. We knew he was kind of reaching back to us, because a lot of times Jimi and I would get together and write these little riffs. We'd call them patterns and hook them all together, and he would say, "Man, if they heard us playing stuff like this, they'd lock us up."

That spirit of improvisation would pay huge dividends at Woodstock. How long did these sessions go on for?

Billy Cox: We rehearsed, I'd say, a good three or four weeks to get it all together. The Experience had come to the end of the road per se. Jimi had wanted to do something new, something different; he didn't quite know how to make his mind up to do that. So anyway, even as far away as we were when the Woodstock festival started, we could hear resounding in the ionosphere the excitement that was generated from this festival. We knew that was going to be something. Up in those mountains where we were, that sound carried for miles. We were under the impression that a helicopter was going to pick us up on the front lawn and take us over. It did not. I was disappointed. I was looking forward to my first helicopter ride.

What happened instead?

Billy Cox: We wound up staying the night prior to that at a place where some other entertainers were. Someone said it was Stephen Stills's old home. That morning the cars took us around the back of the festival itself. They made arrangements to get to the back of the stage, and the stage had a lift that took us up one floor, and when we got to the top we pulled the curtains back and it was the biggest crowd I'd ever seen or had to play in front of. We made it on with the help of some Blue Nun wine that Mitch brought along. It kind of bolstered our spirits.

Alan Douglas: Jimi's performance was a little bit different than normal because it was a transition band that he was with, you know. Mitch Mitchell was playing drums from the Experience. Billy Cox was playing bass from the Band of Gypsies. Juma Sultan was playing congas, who was kind of a hang-around buddy of Jimi's up in Woodstock. Larry Lee, who was just another buddy, you know, who he put onstage for rhythm guitar. So the band really didn't know his repertoire, as such. Mitch and

Billy had not played together very much before that—if not—that may have even been the very first time, or very close to the very first time. So there was an awful lot of improvisation in that show that really got done onstage. There are probably some of the best improvisations we've all heard Hendrix perform.

He does not appear tired or detached. To the contrary, he is engaged, in charge, at times playful, at other times intense. He seems to have grasped the extraordinary nature of the event itself, and his role in it as "the closer." He rips through a dozen songs that morning including "Message to Love," "Spanish Castle Magic," "Foxey Lady," and "Voodoo Chile/Slight Return." Whatever is left of the audience (one estimate puts it at about thirty thousand) is cheering each song, loving each lick, and enjoying every last musical grain as it free flows through the dwindling minutes of the Woodstock hourglass.

Billy Cox: It was a great performance. We missed a few notes, but we were proud of what we did, and Jimi was proud of us.

Ellen Sander: A lot of people had left. But he played everything. He gave everything. It was one of the best performances I'd ever seen him give. He was so totally there. He was like, "I'm closing this show, this is my place," and he did everything so incredibly. He was such an incredible musician. There were two people who changed rock music. One was Les Paul, who invented the electric guitar, and the other was Jimi Hendrix, who used feedback as part of his music. He incorporated the feedback into his music, and that influenced everybody after and everybody did it, but he did it. It was unbelievable, the sound. What a technician he is and what a soul, what a great light of our time that man was. It sounded beautiful, it sounded beautiful, it just echoed out and it just surrounded the whole place and it encapsulated the entire event. It was the perfect closing act, and he was not at all—or at least he didn't show—any disappointment in playing to a leaving house.

Billy Altman discusses another possible reason for the different approach Hendrix took at Woodstock.

Billy Altman: There had been a significant backlash against him, especially within the African-American community. Some people thought he was acting like a clown for white people in the way that he presented himself. Playing with his teeth and playing behind his back. Black power was coming in at the time, fairly heavy, and there were people who didn't like that about Hendrix. I never thought that way because his music was just unbelievable. But there were people who thought that he was deliberately being a clown. What was so striking at Woodstock was that he just stood there and played. He presented himself very different image-wise than he had done before.

Billy Cox: Jimi made this profound statement. He said, "You know, there are a lot of people out there and I'm ill at ease, but if we take the energy that they are giving us and give it back to them, this concert will be great." And with that in mind, we went out and stayed onstage almost two hours. With a lot of the songs, the originals that we were working on. And a lot of the old songs we were prepared to do.

As good as the first part of the set was, there was nothing in any of it to suggest what was about to come next. Without any warning, your ears tell your brain that you're hearing the opening notes of one of the most familiar, one of the most played, one of the most sung songs in the nation's history: "The Star-Spangled Banner."

Your ears are also telling your brain that—depending on your politics—you are hearing one of the most profane or one of the most profound versions of that song that you have *ever* heard. It is searing; it is soaring; it is stirring; it is majestic; it is mocking; it is shocking; it is appealing; it is appalling; it is calming; it is alarming. It is a brain-twisting, body-contorting, mind-fucking performance with no equal.

It is Jimi Hendrix "playing" the Vietnam War on the strings of his white solid-body electric guitar—with "Taps" thrown in for good measure. In a weekend of "Oh my God!" moments, at a festival of "Can you believe this?" performances, it was then, and it is now, one of the most talked-about moments in Woodstock history, in music history, even in American history.

Billy Cox: I remember specifically when he did "The Star-Spangled Banner." If you listen to the first five or six notes, I'm playing with him, and then I said, "Wait a minute, I better get out of this—we didn't rehearse this." And what a performance! What a solo! I've never heard another to compete with it. We did not have a set list. We just followed Jimi's lead. We never rehearsed that at all. I will never forget that, and that will always stay with me and be on my mind, and I'd just like to say I was glad to be a part of history.

Ellen Sander: I felt like patriotism was being redefined. The phrase had not emerged yet, but the "Woodstock Nation" notion was there already. It was such an incredible testament to his soul, soul itself, and the soul of this country. He was incredible.

Billy Altman: "The Star-Spangled Banner" just filled the air. It just sounded like the Vietnam War. It sounded like a firefight. It sounded like helicopters. It sounded like machine guns. He took that song and made it of the moment in a way that no one could've predicted you could do that to the national anthem. He made it sound like everything that was going on in that country, in our country, and around the world at the moment. I remember it filling the sky. I looked up and it filled the sky in a way that I hadn't thought about that and music for the entire weekend.

A discussion about it during an appearance by Jimi on *The Dick Cavett Show* in September led to this exchange:

Dick Cavett:	What was the controversy about the national anthem and the way—
Jimi Hendrix:	I don't know. All I did was play it. I'm American, so I played it. I used to have to sing it in school, they made me sing it in school, so it was a flashback, you know [*laughter*].
Dick Cavett:	This man was in the 101st Airborne, so when you write your nasty letters in—
Jimi Hendrix:	Nasty letters? Why?
Dick Cavett:	When you mention the national anthem and talk about playing it in any unorthodox way, you immediately get a guaranteed percentage of hate mail from people who say "How dare—"
Jimi Hendrix:	It's not unorthodox, it's not unorthodox.
Dick Cavett:	It isn't unorthodox?
Jimi Hendrix:	No, no. I thought it was beautiful. But there you go, you know [*applause*].

Earlier on, John Morris told us how the first words that came through the PA system at Woodstock were "holy shit." His observation upon first seeing the crowd:

John Morris: When I got them onstage and they started playing, that's when I went back to my trailer and collapsed. And woke up when he played "The Star-Spangled Banner" which nobody had ever heard. It was like, "holy shit!" So I guess we started with a "holy shit" and ended with a "holy shit!"

Michael Wadleigh: If you take a look at "The Star-Spangled Banner," every note, the way he bends it, the feedback, all of it. You watch him retuning in the middle of him doing all this stuff. And his concentration, what he's doing with his mouth, his whole body . . . as you know, that was not an improvisation. He told me that he worked on that really hard. He knew he would do it and that it would be the finishing touch. "Star-Spangled Banner" provided the perfect ending for the whole thing. Then he went off into this bizarre classical music, blues, if you listen to the totality of it he goes through every genre you could possibly cover. It's almost impossible to pin it down. Really a complete amalgam of classical, jazz, blues, rock 'n' roll, and electronics, it's all of those things altogether. I don't think we have an atmosphere now that's going to produce a musician like that ever again.

One of our collaborators, Bernie Corbett, witnessed an impressive display of the ongoing Hendrix legacy.

Bernie Corbett: I was out in Seattle about two years ago, and I went to the gravesite, and it was a Monday afternoon. A hot summer afternoon. When I got to the gravesite, there was a young kid . . . about sixteen . . . and he was sitting by the gravesite picking a guitar. I said, "Man, you couldn't have scripted anything like this in Hollywood."

Is there any Woodstock musician that casts a longer shadow than Jimi Hendrix? Probably not. In the end, there's the work, there's the memories, and there's the legacy. I asked Christopher Farley whom he would point to as carrying on that legacy.

Christopher Farley: If Prince were here, I'd point at him right now. Clearly, Prince has taken a lot from Jimi Hendrix, but not in a bad way, not in a way that is ripping the guy off. He's just paying tribute to him in his music and taking it in other directions. You see Wyclef Jean today, he's also taken a page out of Jimi Hendrix's book. He can't play like Jimi, but he learned the guitar and he's brought that to hip-hop—being able to play an instrument—so I think he's continued to influence people even today. In a way, the whole Seattle sound—that comes out of Jimi. I mean, Jimi was from Seattle. He had roots there and that Seattle sound would not have happened—Pearl Jam, Nirvana—if Jimi hadn't been there first.

And Woodstock wouldn't be what it was and is if Jimi hadn't been there last.

EPILOGUE:
THE WHOLE WORLD GOES TO WOODSTOCK

Martin Scorsese: There was the music. There was the idea of rejecting the rest of the world and living in a natural state. There was the drug culture. There was the political stance against the government, specifically its policy in Vietnam. And they all came together in this moment.

It's interesting that people called it the Woodstock Nation, because that's what people wanted—to be separate, to have their own community. And for three days, they had it.

When I look back at the second half of the sixties, I realize it is the only time I have ever heard people talk about love in serious terms, as a force to combat greed, hate, and violence. What it symbolizes is that things can happen, incredible events that are the product of many particular elements converging at a particular moment. And those events can't be repeated.

Life doesn't come with an owner's manual. At birth, children are not handed a survival guide. Existence does not have an instruction booklet.

But aspiring members of Woodstock Nation had all three by the spring of 1970: an owner's manual, a survival guide, and an instruction booklet. This all happened with the simultaneous release of *Woodstock* (the movie) and *Woodstock* (the album).

Everyone who was at the event could relive it on the big screen. But, even more important, everyone who was not at the event could claim legitimate citizenship in Woodstock Nation, all across the country and all around the world.

This final chapter will tell the story of yet another series of happy accidents that resulted in the definitive documentation of all things Woodstock '69. You didn't have to be at Woodstock to be at Woodstock. These are the recollections of some of the people who made that paradox possible.

Larry Johnson: We think of Woodstock as an event but I think it's really represented by the movie in people's minds as much as the people that were there.

Presenting both the music and sociological aspects of those three days of peace and music, the innovative three-and-a-half-hour film defined how Woodstock would be remembered. Director Michael Wadleigh wasn't just trying to make a film about music.

Michael Wadleigh: The idea that I had really was Pilgrim's Progress or The Canterbury Tales. This really came from talking to whacked-out people like Wavy Gravy and Allen Ginsberg, which I did. They were both up in Woodstock Village quite a lot. We talked ahead of time about the metaphors and what the festival might stand for. Ginsberg and Gravy were very clear this was about going back to nature, back to the garden. The great thing about it was that it would be a journey out of cities, which were complex and dirty and problematic, back to a pureness of nature. We talked about The Canterbury Tales, where the pilgrims journeyed from the cities to a cathedral, the idea that the stage at Woodstock would be a cathedral built in nature, that the pilgrims were walking and telling tales to one another. That became the structure of the film. You have the tavern keeper's tale, you have the police chief's tale, you have the television reporter's tale, the local farmer's tale, the nude bathers' tales, and so on. I deliberately wanted it to be as much out of time as possible. We were going for an epic. If you read the reviews from Ebert and others, they were on the bandwagon. They saw it that way, as a bigger metaphor than just a rock 'n' roll movie. Of course, that's why I ended up with a wasteland with Hendrix playing that moody music, and people walking around with casts and crutches and so forth. I personally felt that this wasn't going to work out. Even when we were finishing the film in 1970, there were indications that the future was not going to be good. Even though the war might end, historians would say, that by about 1972, America had taken a turn to the right that it would never recover from.

Despite the trials and tribulations, the storms, technical malfunctions, the shortage of food, Wadleigh and his crew managed to capture 172 hours of footage in the 72 hours of Woodstock. The filmmakers filmed without a contract, rightfully believing that the footage would be priceless to some company like Warner Brothers, who ultimately signed a contract for the film. Director Michael Wadleigh, sound designer Larry Johnson, editor Thelma Schoonmaker, assistant editor Martin Scorsese, producer Bob Maurice, and associate producer Dale Bell were among the many who hustled to complete the film.

Dale Bell: It would be Michael, Larry, Thelma, the editor, the assistant editor, and me . . . it was about a dozen people in there most of the time. And the editors were changing. When we were editing in New York, we were editing around the clock with three eight-hour shifts. At one point we might have fifteen people working between eight p.m. and one in the morning. We might have fifteen people working between five and midnight. We might have twenty-five people working between eight in the morning and five at night. There was rotating decisions with Thelma and Michael really being in the lead with most stuff. We might have really good images but crappy sound so we'd ask, "Can we improve the sound?" That's why we brought seventeen out of fifty people in New York to LA in December. We brought those seventeen people to California to help us get the rough cut, which was about eight or nine hours in length—probably ten or eleven hours—but it was also on multiple images. So it was ten hours of running time, but each hour might consist of four hours of film. They were on multiple projectors. We had six projectors set up in one room.

Larry Johnson: We relived it in the editing room. We relived it all the way through. We spent a whole year making the movie, and it was so exciting. Because we really did, every time we would see something, we would just go nuts. We'd say, "Come here! Look at this," and people would run over to the can, and we would all stand around and say, "Play that again!"

In general, Hollywood embraced the maverick filmmakers.

Larry Johnson: So we were on the Warner lot and Michael says to me, "John Wayne and [his son] Michael Wayne wanna see our system, so go meet them." I go down to the gate where they are coming in and bring them back to the thing, and there's John Wayne with a suit and a hat, and I have this long hair, and I'm wearing this jumpsuit, and I come up to him, and he goes, "I wanna see your hippie ass off this lot in five minutes," and I go like this [insert some sort of gesture] and he said, "Aw, I'm just kidding, Michael said to say that." He was real interested in moviemaking and we had these editing machines, and none of them had ever been in Hollywood, and we had three of them. It was about to break through and make editing a whole other thing. So people would come through because Michael was so technically advanced.

I remember Hugh Hefner threw a party for us on Sunset Boulevard. He had this top-floor penthouse party house. I think it was us and Country Joe and the Fish. And we were like, "What the hell is this all about?" It was a shock to us to be absorbed into Hollywood. And then the Academy Awards were a surprise to us. I got beat out of my sound award by Patton. It was like fake cannon explosions and stuff, but Hollywood was conservative. And we were a nonunion movie, and it was still a company town in those days.

Michael Wadleigh: It's a shame that Larry didn't get the Academy Award. He certainly deserved it for doing the sound for Woodstock. But Larry really did innovations. Panning the sound around—we knew it was technically feasible, but he really researched it and made effects. He was eighteen years old at the time. He would have been the youngest person to have won a technical Academy Award if he had won. Of course, it's a shame that Thelma didn't win it for editing. It was certainly a tour de force of editing. Certainly nothing that complex had ever been done. It was a union miscarriage of justice that those two people didn't get technical awards.

After months and months of editing down the footage, the filmmakers held a private screening for the Warner Brothers executives and local college students, hungry for the Woodstock experience.

Dale Bell: We refused to allow them to look at the film by themselves because they might not fully appreciate its value for the audience we were targeting. So we said, "Let's move this screening from this small room, where we had been looking at sections of the film, to a large one, a theater that held about five hundred people." We then called UCLA and USC and other groups that held younger people, and we invited these people to the screening on the Warner Brothers lot. The executives refused to allow them on the lot, so we finally came up with some accommodation. We went through a process. I think some time on a weekend afternoon, in filed five hundred young people in various forms of hippiedom. The clothes, the hair, the garb, whatever. And there were a dozen suits in the room.

We had some issues. We couldn't have it in one theater because the theater could not hold all the people we had invited. We had said we'd only invite as many people as there were seats. We exceeded that by a few, but not by a lot. So there were people who were also sitting and watching this in the aisles in the screening room. I think, if I'm not mistaken, that there were people who were puffing on weed. Which of course was probably against the rules. When the lights went off you couldn't tell who was and who wasn't.

The film then begins with a scratchy, grainy image of Sidney Westerfield standing in front of his inn. Then the film rolls. Four hours of uninterrupted projection. The projectionist didn't miss a beat. The sound was all around us. The images were just cascading on the screen. Single images ran for ten to twelve images before they became double images. Double images became triple images. Then returned to a single image of Richie Havens. The movie ran. People cheered. People wept. People shouted. People clapped. People moped. People were overwhelmed with the raw power that they were seeing.

Despite the obviously positive feedback, Warner Brothers was hesitant to release a four-hour cut of the film.

Dale Bell: Warner Brothers, in a private room, in a meeting we had with just a few executives, said that they could not possibly distribute a four-hour-long film. Their exhibitors would rebel. What would we cut it down to? Well, we were scared to death that they would cut it. We were fearful that it was already being cut behind our backs. There was all kind of paranoia. We had had to sue Warner Brothers three months earlier when we discovered that they were making duplicate copies of the opticals. The Technicolor laboratory that was processing the opticals that had been shot by the seven optical companies, Technicolor was sending copies of the opticals to New York where they were being screened for Warner Brothers executives. I discovered this. We all got together, Bob Maurice, Michael, and I, and decided we would stop editing the film until Warner Brothers stopped sending copies to New York City. It was outside the contract, against the contract. We did not want them to look at material totally out of context. Without sound, they would not understand what they were looking at. It would affect their opinion of the type of film we wanted to make. All throughout, we were really struggling for our artistic freedom. Bob Maurice was absolutely phenomenal at keeping the Warner Brothers at bay in that regard. Just before the release date, we had to reshoot optical, remix sound, and then we had to agree on the length of the negative and give it to Technicolor, who said that they could not possibly make prints fast enough to get them to the seven theaters here and one in Toronto.

Eventually, the film was pruned to three and a half hours. Filmmakers were satisfied, but despite the response to the screening, Warner Brothers was convinced it was going to bomb.

Michael Wadleigh: Warner Brothers thought it was going to be a disaster. They thought that three hours, three and a half hours would only be watched by dyed-in-the-wool hippies, no one would see it. We got reviews that were really, really awesome from the most famous reviewers of the day like Roger Ebert and Pauline Kael. They gave us a huge critical push. They weren't expecting anything but music, but so many of the journalists picked up on the metaphors. They saw it was very much about a social rebellion and social change in America. Richard Schickel from the <u>New York Times</u> especially liked it. Amazing reviews.

Dale Bell: Our film opened. There was a preview night. Of course, people were standing around the block. The theater opened the following day, on the twenty-first, there were people all over the place. In every city that we could monitor by phone, of course. There was no live television. You couldn't use a phone to convey an image. There was no computer, there was nothing besides verbal communication. You saw lines and lines and lines of people stacked up to want to go. The exhibitors were going nuts because they could only play it three or four times. Sometimes they started at midnight so they could run it all night long. It was extraordinary. You look at all the newspaper clippings and you'll see what the response was. Charlie Champlin, the critic out in Los Angeles, called it one of the most phenomenal films ever made. And then the rest of the world got to see it two months later. They were clamoring to see it, because they'd heard about the buildup. It would have to be translated into other languages and in some cases subtitled. Since no one had really seen the finished film before the ten days before opening night, all that translation into other languages took weeks.

Larry Johnson: Oh, in Hollywood it was great. It was rockin'. People were blown away. I mean, it was a four-hour, eight-minute movie. People were exhausted. It was like being at the event. It was rockin'. The audience was waiting for it. It was branded. It was already Woodstock the brand. It was a year later. It was already put in everybody's mind. They were waiting for it. It was huge. The nudity and people smoking pot, I mean, that was unheard of.

Michael Wadleigh: Immediately Warner Brothers made huge numbers of prints and we went right to the Cannes Festival, where we were by far the biggest hit. We were the film to see. It virtually went to every country. Warner Brothers made a huge amount of money on the soundtrack.

It also made quite a splash internationally. Michael Wadleigh himself made it to a number of openings of the film.

Michael Wadleigh: One of the significant things about the film was that it was a huge, huge hit around the world. And it did an awful lot to promote the counterculture in the world—culturally and politically. The film was banned in South Africa. The film was so popular—we're back in apartheid times—that people in South Africa demanded to see it. Of course, we had these black performers on the stage, which was completely forbidden. You could not have black and white people together at a performance. Or certainly performing on the same stage, even separately. So I went to South Africa and was greeted by tons of press. They interviewed me, asked me all these questions, took all these photographs, and the next day the press came out and there were no pictures of me at all except from my high school days when I had very short hair. There was an embargo on putting up shots of long-haired people. Then I found out that they nearly shaved my head at my airport. This happened to me any number of times.

I'm sure you heard that—they used to shave people at the airports. It's stupidly symbolic, but it's not a pleasant thing to go through. After giving this huge press conference, the thing that struck me was that I had never been in a country with such power of censorship. They simply had the ability with the newspapers to take out anything. And here all these reporters had asked me all these questions and taken all these pictures. There were completely innocuous comments in the articles. Nothing I had talked about: I had talked about American immigration, I had quoted Martin Luther King—talked about all this stuff. It was completely taken out. It was an amazing, amazing experience for me. The next thing that was amazing was that they opened the movie and they had cut out all the black performers. And they had cut any audience close-up where you could see a black person. They had ripped out Richie Havens, Sly, Santana because there was a black guy in that group, and once again I went to the journalists to say something and it did not work. To make a long story short, I made a couple of films secretly in South Africa about apartheid, and during one of my times there, I was in a Volkswagen with a very famous filmmaker and journalist, and we were struck by a truck. I was in a coma in a hospital and nearly died, as did he. It turned out it was the secret police who had rammed us. While we were in the hospital, of course, they took all the film equipment that was in the van, then they went to this guy's house and took everything. After I was released from the hospital, they put me in jail for a while and said, "You can either leave the country or continue in jail." That was it.

Woodstock was such a hit in Greece—it broke every single record. There was a military government in Greece. The Greek youth really saw Woodstock as a student free speech movement. When it came time for the film to be shown there, I flew to Greece and was met at the airport by thousands and thousands of people. They carried me through the streets. It was just amazing. It was all over the headlines that they were about to have the opening of the Woodstock film. These kids carried me down to the biggest theater in Greece—this big square—and the whole square was jammed. So they passed me over their bodies to the gates of the theater, which were pulled down. The police, squadrons of police came and forced the students out of the square and didn't show the movie. They thought that there would be riots for sure. So they put me under house arrest. They were going to throw me out of the country. I stayed in jail maybe one or two nights and then they put me in a hotel. And the students kept rioting. They decided to show the movie. When they did, the streets were filled again, and they made it a free film. They showed it around the clock, over and over and over. It immediately broke every single record Greece had had. That was an unforgettable experience.

In Tokyo, it was damn near the same thing. Tokyo went wild for the film. It broke every record there. No one really knew a lot about the festival, so the film became its own thing. It became the festival. Many, many times we'd go to a screening of this three-and-a-half-hour movie, and the kids would get up and stand through the whole three and a half hours of the film. It was truly amazing. And they would sing along with the songs and dance, and it was just . . . phenomenal. It was a hit at the Cannes Film Festival. It was a huge, huge, huge success. It was a super hit in England. When it came to England, it was in the most prestigious theater, the Empire Theatre. And literally every single musician showed up. It was like a Who's Who of all the Stones, Clapton, everybody you can think of. They all came to see the movie.

Why did it resonate so much?

Michael Wadleigh: It had been building up in the US and around the world. This sort of movement away from commercialization and toward essential values. Growing your hair long, expressing your own personality as you may in a nonconformist and exploratory fashion. To do something as interesting as have this gigantic music-peace festival out in nature. That sort of thing. You know that Woodstock, New York, got named after Woodstock, England, where Churchill was raised. The significance there, which was not really known at the time, was that Oxford, England, the king of the colleges from the Middle Ages onward, Oxford was a city and was highly polluted in the 1300s, 1400s, 1500s. There was a town called Woodstock, and students and professors used to go out there to the village of Woodstock, England, where nature could be found in an unspoiled fashion. We knew all these things ahead of time and we tried to capture that.

Why has nothing come close to Woodstock?

Michael Wadleigh: I deliberately tried to take the setting and the issues, Three Days of Peace and Music, and the issues of the day from ecology to civil rights to the war, and deal with them lyrically and cut away to the audience in a metaphoric fashion. I think that's why it's lasted. Why it still captures people's attention. You have a rare group of performers. A constant complaint I hear from kids is the coopting of music by commercialization. It's terrible. Woodstock may have been the last giant festival without any advertising, logos, or banners. Part of that was my doing. I fought like crazy to even get rid of a banner saying "Woodstock" in the back. Every fucking festival you see now has a fucking backdrop. You can't just look off on to a lake, or into the trees. There are no more simple, unpainted stages anymore. Everything is rehearsed, and painted, and decorated to the nth degree. We used Jimi Hendrix's system, the Electric Ladyland system, to record the sound for the film and for the album. A telling metaphor, I think, happened down at Ladyland before the festival when Jimi was looking for a costume. Today, you'd have eighteen different costumers submitting eighteen different costumes. I went with him. Walked down the street, went into one store after another, and finally found the white outfit that he wore, off the rack. No makeup artists, no choreographers, no handlers. It's a different world now. The college kids tell me when I appear at showings, we just live in an overproduced world, it's all money, money, money. Every rock 'n' roller has a line of clothing, lipsticks, lip gloss, you name it.

Back then, you'd slam the disc down and listen to it. You wanted originality. They wanted to hear what another band was coming out with. Originality was the name of the game. Imitation is now the name of the game. You hear a new sound and then you run it into the ground. A new sound to be imitated, commercialized, and make money off of.

In addition to its effects on the countercultural movements worldwide, Woodstock changed the face of marketing and the music industry forever.

Dale Bell: We directly impacted how music was marketed here and around the world. Woodstock gave a voice to young people for the first time—really, for the first time in this country. The cinematography that we used, virtually all of it handheld except for all of that that was done from the light towers, is still being imitated today. People try and shake the camera while it's sitting on the tripod to get that sense of urgency. The use of multiple screens that you see in half a dozen commercials today in different ways, you see one image come up and then you see two images come up, it's the same thing we did. The use of the full soundtrack and wraparound so that you've got a totally different moviegoing experience was directly enhanced and affected by how we designed that soundtrack. THX1138, which was George Lucas's sound system—you hear that first buzz before the feature's played and that tests the surround sound. The use of Dolby sound–suppressing device, music tracks—whether they be albums or live—was first inaugurated by us. There was a whole lot of technical innovation. There are many techniques we invented on the spot that are still being employed. We take great pride that we were the first.

Michael Wadleigh: That's why they call me the father of MTV. When they were starting MTV, which I was invited to join, they kept running Woodstock over and over again. Santana was one of their favorites. I'm not a big fan of MTV at all—but it's been pointed out that MTV was a direct result of Woodstock because it showed you could make razzle-dazzle rock 'n' roll videos. If you look at other films that were made like the one of Monterey before Woodstock, there wasn't much technique at all. Even in the Beatles films, for which they had endless sums of money, they were just walking through fields and jumping from this, that, and the other thing. But our film showed that the technological experiments you could do were just endless. Woodstock broke every financial record. And in a way, I'm sad that It wrecked the innocence of rock 'n' roll and turned it into a gigantic business.

There have been many attempts to re-create Woodstock. None of them nearly as successful as the original. The Altamont Speedway Free Festival, just months after Woodstock, was marred by violence.

Chris Langhart: I have a general theory that I codified in my mind as Woodstock came together. There's something about people on the East Coast, this became more apparent after Altamont. There's something about East Coasters—they're used to be shoved into subway cars and that kind of thing. The space you have around you is whatever space you have around you. It's not very big, it reaches up to the edge of you, and that's pretty much it. So it's not like it's next to you . . . On the West Coast there's a lot more space, my space includes me and my motorcycle and if you spit on my motorcycle, that's like spitting on me. But that's not the way it is in New York. In New York, a motorcycle is a motorcycle and a human is a human, and those are different things. So all the Woodstockers were imbued with this "Let's all get along together and make it as peaceful as possible," whereas at the Altamont there was a territorial area aspect to it. Even though they were all crowded together there was kind of a West Coast territorial aspect. I don't know if any study has been done on this. But I just find it to be the case that there's a difference there. That difference helped make the Woodstock thing fit together very sweetly . . . Also the farm environment is certainly different from a city. The Yasgurs' was a beautiful place.

Dale Bell: There were two anniversary concerts. There was an attempt at an anniversary concert in '94 and another one in '99 that Mike Lang did. It was incredibly messy.

Maybe we should just appreciate Woodstock as a phenomenon that could have only happened at that unique moment in time in Bethel.

Larry Johnson: The crowd was so beautiful. For no organization, it went well. It could've been chaos; it could've been like Altamont. But it wasn't like that at all. It was truly peace and love; it lived up to its reputation. The crowd was peaceful and into it. Everybody was helping each other. It was a community.

The movie's role in contributing to Woodstock's legacy is undeniable, even for the people who were there.

Jim Marion: Despite my grumbling at the festival, it didn't take long for me to realize that Woodstock was a milestone event. We had no idea of the magnitude of it until afterward, and five hundred thousand people attending a show together under pretty difficult conditions and doing it without incident is really pretty amazing, then and now. Truth be told, I didn't appreciate a lot of what went on there until I saw the movie a year or two later. I guess for me at the time, it was just another concert to attend and, musically, not a particularly impressive one, despite the incredible lineup. In the years since, I guess I've come to see it a lot more for all the other aspects I didn't appreciate while I was actually there.

We'll give the last word to the legendary film critic Roger Ebert. In his review of the film, he wrote:

> Michael Wadleigh's <u>Woodstock</u> is an archaeological study of that [Woodstock] nation, which existed for three days a year ago. Because of this movie, the Woodstock state of mind now has its own history, folklore, myth. In terms of evoking the style and feel of a mass historical event, <u>Woodstock</u> may be the best documentary ever made in America. But don't see it for that reason; see it because it is that good to see.
>
> <u>Woodstock</u> does what all good documentaries do. It is the bringer of news. It reports, it shows, it records, and it interprets. It gives us maybe 60 percent music and 40 percent on the people who were there, and that is a good ratio, I think. The music is very much a part of the event, especially since Wadleigh and his editors [including cinema <u>wunderkind</u> Martin Scorsese] have allowed each performer's set to grow and build and double back on itself without interference.

And perhaps his most prescient observation:

> <u>Woodstock</u> is a beautiful, complete, moving, ultimately great film, and years from now when our generation is attacked for being just as uptight as all the rest of the generations, it will be good to have this movie around to show that, just for a weekend anyway, that wasn't altogether the case.

EPILOGUE

ACKNOWLEDGMENTS

It was a daunting task from the start. There are at least four hundred thousand people to thank and I was originally going to list them all here alphabetically. Cooler heads prevailed, however, which is why it is so important to work with great editors. On that front, I thank Zach Schisgal and my son Peter Thomas Fornatale. Zach has been a pleasure to work with. Not only has he been an immense help gaining support for the book throughout Simon & Schuster, but his cuts really helped this to read more like a narrative. Peter Thomas was my rock. His knowledge, enthusiasm, advice, and talents propelled this project. He must have gotten those qualities from his mother because I certainly don't possess them.

This book wouldn't have happened without the talents of Anna Kerrigan, a terrific researcher, interviewer, and writer. I am particularly grateful for her efforts in spearheading the chapter about the *Woodstock* film. Anna is a talent to follow.

Frank Scatoni was the biggest supporter of the book from the day I first mentioned it to him in the Blind Tiger Ale House. Thanks so much for your belief in this, your fine agenting, and your keen editorial eye.

Shawna Lietzke helped the book along in countless behind-the-scenes ways and deserves credit as well.

Mark Gompertz is my mentor in anything publishing related and has been for more than thirty years. Thanks, Mark.

Bernie Corbett was invaluable, traveling across the country to get several key interviews including the one with Country Joe.

All my interview subjects were cooperative and helpful and deserve great thanks, but two in particular, John Morris and Joshua White, merit extra praise. Joshua went above and beyond in terms of support and contacts, and John's interview really provided the narrative spine of the book.

Thanks to Phil Gordon for his efforts in putting together the proposal for this book.

Richie Bienstock of *Guitar World,* a fine musician in his own right, was a big help with a few technical questions about guitars.

Thanks to Phoebe Lithgow and Jona Tuck for help in research and transcribing the interviews.

Special thanks to my intern extraordinaire, Patty Bernstein, a great music fan and an even greater person.

For their audio archive contributions, I am indebted to two terrific radio personalities: Darren DeVivo of WFUV and Fred Migliore of FM Odyssey. WFUV news director George Bodarky's Woodstock documentary was a valuable resource, as were my old friend Mike Eisgrau's tapes and transcriptions from August 1969.

From the print world, Jeff Tamarkin and Robbie Wolliver could not have been more generous or cooperative. Same holds true for all the good people at the Long Island Music Hall of Fame, especially Tony Traguardo and Tom Bensen.

Then there are the usual suspects: Joan Auperlee, Marty Brooks, Henry Gross, Tom Malone, Chip Rachlin, and Kenny Rankin, who dug deep for their great Woodstock stories and recollections.

One hundred years from now, if there still is a planet, people will talk about and want to know about the Woodstock Music and Art Fair of August 1969. We hope that this book remains through time a valuable resource in figuring out what it was and what it meant.

And if anyone along the way needs to know the correct spelling of the author's last name, the answer is very easy. Just start off by screaming:

"Gimme an F!"

ACKNOWLEDGMENTS

290

NOTES

Unless otherwise noted, all quotes in *Back to the Garden* either were conducted by the author or are part of his personal audio archives. Page numbers refer to the page on which the quotation begins.

Introduction
page
xvi   *Time* magazine, August 29, 1969.
xvii   This quote appears at http://www.law.umkc.edu/faculty/projects/ftrials/Chicago7/Hoffman.html; accessed June 2008.
xviii   Walter Cronkite, *I Can Hear It Now/The Sixties,* 1970, Columbia/Legacy.
xix   Margaret Mead, "Woodstock in Retrospect," *Redbook,* January 1970.
xix–xx Ayn Rand, *The New Left: The Anti-Industrial Revolution* (New York: Signet, 1971).
xxi–xxii Citations from *The New York Times:* http://www.woodstockpreservation.org/PastPresent/NYTcomPilation.htm; accessed June 2008.
xxii–xxiii The Bernard Collier quote and the *Rolling Stone* quote: Andy Bennett, ed., *Remembering Woodstock* (London: Ashgate, 2004).
xxiii   Rollo May, "Departments: An Opinion on Bethel and After," *Mademoiselle,* November 1969.
xxiv   Joseph Campbell (with Bill Moyers), *The Power of Myth* (New York: Doubleday, 1988).

Richie Havens
5   John Sebastian quote: courtesy of the Archives of The Museum at Bethel Woods.
10–11   All quotes (with the exception of Joshua White's, which came from an original interview): reprinted with permission from Joel Makower, *Woodstock: The Oral History* (Albany, NY: SUNY Press, 2009). Copyright © Joel Makower.

| 14 | The quote from the stage: the motion picture *Woodstock (The Director's Cut)*, directed by Michael Wadleigh (DVD release, Warner Home Video, 1997); hereinafter *Woodstock (The Director's Cut)*. |

The Swami

18	This quote is from the motion picture *Woodstock (The Director's Cut)*.
19	Swami Satchindananda quotes: Douglas Martin, "Swami Satchidananda, Woodstock's Guru, Dies at 87," *New York Times*, August 21, 2003.
20	Peter Max, Swami Satchidananda, and Felix Cavaliere quotes: *Living Yoga: The Life and Teachings of Swami Satchidananda*, DVD (Integral Yoga Multimedia, 2008).
21	Swami's speech from the stage: the motion picture *Woodstock (The Director's Cut)*; it is copyrighted, and I graciously thank the Integral Yoga Institute for permission to use it here.

Free Concert

| 23 | John Morris quote: from the motion picture *Woodstock (The Director's Cut)*. |

John Sebastian

49	John Sebastian quote: courtesy of the Archives of The Museum at Bethel Woods.
50	John Sebastian quotes: courtesy of the Archives of The Museum at Bethel Woods.
50–51	Quotes from the stage: from the motion picture *Woodstock (The Director's Cut)*.
52	First John Sebastian quote: courtesy of the Archives of The Museum at Bethel Woods.
52–53	John Sebastian quote that spans the two pages: courtesy of the Archives of The Museum at Bethel Woods.

Sweetwater

| 58 | James Poniewozik, "Sweetwater: A True Rock Story," *Time*, August 16, 1999. |

Bert Sommer

| 60 | This quote appears at http://www.bertsommer.com/introduction.htm; accessed June 2008. |

Tim Hardin

63	Chip Monck quote: from the motion picture *Woodstock (The Director's Cut)*.
64–65	John Sebastian quotes: Robbie Woliver, *Bringing It All Back Home* (New York: Pantheon, 1986).
68	"Woodstock," *Life*, August 1969.

Ravi Shankar

| 73 | Ravi Shankar quote: Ravi Shankar, *Raga Mala* (New York: Welcome Rain Publishers, 1999). |

74	Ibid.
74	George Harrison quote: George Harrison, *I, Me, Mine* (New York: Simon & Schuster, 1980).

Joan Baez

90	Joan Baez, *And a Voice to Sing With* (New York: Summit, 1987).
91	Conversation: from the motion picture *Woodstock (The Director's Cut)*.
93–94	Joan Baez, speech from the stage: from the motion picture *Woodstock (The Director's Cut)*.
95–96	Jeffrey Shurtleff comments: from the motion picture *Woodstock (The Director's Cut)*.

Founders, Quill, the Keef Hartley Band, the Incredible String Band

101	John Roberts quote: reprinted with permission from Joel Makower, *Woodstock: The Oral History* (Albany, NY: SUNY Press, 2009). Copyright © Joel Makower.
103–104	All the quotes on these pages except the John Roberts quote on 104 (which is from my personal archive): reprinted with permission from Joel Makower, *Woodstock: The Oral History* (Albany, NY: SUNY Press, 2009). Copyright © Joel Makower.
105	Artie Kornfeld quote: from the motion picture *Woodstock (The Director's Cut)*.
107	Mel Lawrence quotes: from Robert Spitz, *Barefoot in Babylon* (New York: Viking, 1979).
111	Miller Anderson quote: Dmitry M. Epstein's website, http://www.dmme.net/interviews/mander.html; accessed June 2008.
112	Joe Boyd and Rose Simpson quotes: the Incredible String Band online magazine, *Be Glad,* at http://www.makingtime.co.uk/beglad/index1.htm.

Santana

118–25	Michael Shrieve quotes: courtesy of the Archives of The Museum at Bethel Woods.
120	Bill Graham quotes: Bill Graham and Robert Greenfield, *Bill Graham Presents* (New York, Da Capo, 2004).

Canned Heat

129–30	*Downbeat* magazine, date unavailable; from Canned Heat's website, http://www.cannedheatmusic.com/biography.html; accessed June 2008.
131	Bob Hite quotes: *Sounds,* March 4, 1974.

Mountain

133–36	Felix Pappalardi quotes: "Talking to Felix Pappalardi & Leslie West of Mountain," *ZigZag,* May 20, 1971.
134–36	Leslie West quotes: courtesy of the Long Island Music Hall of Fame.
137	Leslie West quotes: *Modern Guitars* magazine website, http://www.modernguitars.com/archives/004075.html; accessed June 2008.

Janis Joplin

139   Janis Joplin quotes: from the motion picture *Woodstock (The Director's Cut)*.

143   The Nick Gravenites quote: Michael Lydon, *Rock Folk* (New York: Dial Press, 1971).

144   Janis Joplin quote: Richard Goldstein, *Goldstein's Greatest Hits* (New York: Prentice-Hall, 1970).

145   Clive Davis quote: Clive Davis, *Clive: Inside the Record Business* (New York: Morrow, 1975).

145   "Janis," lyrics by Country Joe McDonald, used with McDonald's permission.

149   Michael Lydon quote: Lydon, *Rock Folk*.

149   Ellen Willis quote: "Janis Joplin," in Jim Miller, ed., *The Rolling Stone Illustrated History of Rock & Roll*.

Grateful Dead

150–52   Jerry Garcia quotes: Peter Joseph, *Good Times* (New York: Charterhouse, 1973).

150   Leslie West quote: courtesy of the Long Island Music Hall of Fame.

151–52   Phil Lesh quotes: Phil Lesh, *Searching for the Sound* (New York: Little, Brown, 2005).

156   Jerry Garcia quote: Peter Joseph, *Good Times*.

157   Jerry Garcia quote: Michael Lydon, *Rock Folk*.

Creedence Clearwater Revival

158   Leslie West quote: courtesy of the Long Island Music Hall of Fame.

158   John Sebastian quote: courtesy of the Archives of The Museum at Bethel Woods.

160–61   Michael Lang quote: panel discussion, "Oscar's Docs, Part Two: Academy Award–Winning Documentaries 1961–1976," Beverly Hills, CA, October 24, 2006. Hereinafter cited as "Oscar's Docs" panel discussion, 2006.

Sly Stone

166   Sly Stone quotes: "The Sly Stone Interview," http://www.youtube.com/watch?v=A2BXgpIqiDw; accessed June 2008.

167   Dave Marsh quote: "Sly Stone," in Jim Miller, ed., *The Rolling Stone Illustrated History of Rock & Roll*.

169–71   The Family Stone band member quotes: Joel Selvin, *Sly & the Family Stone: An Oral History* (New York: Avon Books, 1998), courtesy of Joel Selvin.

173–74   Sly Stone quotes from the stage: from the motion picture *Woodstock (The Director's Cut)*.

The Who

179–80   Pete Townshend quotes: Bill Graham and Robert Greenfield, *Bill Graham Presents*.

179–82   Abbie Hoffman and Henry Diltz quotes: reprinted with permission from Joel Makower, *Woodstock: The Oral History* (Albany, NY: SUNY Press, 2009). Copyright © Joel Makower.

190   Peter Townshend quotes: the first, Bill Graham and Robert Greenfield, *Bill Graham Presents;* the second is from my personal audio archive.

Jefferson Airplane
199   Jann Wenner quote: Jeff Tamarkin, *Got a Revolution! The Turbulent Flight of Jefferson Airplane* (New York: Atria, 2003).
203–204 Grace Slick quotes: Grace Slick and Andrea Cagan, *Somebody to Love* (New York: Warner Books, 1998).

Joe Cocker
213   Joe Cocker, Michael Lang, John Morris quotes: "Oscar's Docs" panel discussion, 2006.

Max Yasgur
217–24 Sam Yasgur quotes: courtesy of the Archives of The Museum at Bethel Woods.
217–20 All quotes (except Sam Yasgur's; see above): "Oscar's Docs" panel discussion, 2006.

Country Joe and the Fish
225   Phil Lesh quote: Phil Lesh, *Searching for the Sound.*
227   John Roberts quote: Robert Spitz, *Barefoot in Babylon.*

The Band
234–35 Greil Marcus quote: "The Woodstock Festival," *Rolling Stone,* September 20, 1969.

Crosby, Stills, Nash and Young
240–41 John Sebastian quotes: courtesy of the Archives of The Museum at Bethel Woods.
241   Ahmet Ertegun quotes: David Crosby and Carl Gottlieb, *Long Time Gone* (New York: Doubleday, 1988).
243   Quotes from the stage: from the motion picture *Woodstock (The Director's Cut).*
243–44 David Crosby quote: Crosby and Gottlieb, *Long Time Gone.*
244   David Crosby to Dick Cavett, *The Dick Cavett Show,* August 18, 1969.
245   David Crosby quote: David Crosby and David Bender, *Stand and Be Counted* (San Francisco: HarperOne, 2000).
245   Neil Young quote: various sources, including Associated Press, "Neil Young Presents 'CSNY Déjà Vu' at Berlin Film Festival; Says Music Can't Change the World," *Houston Chronicle,* February 8, 2008.

Blood, Sweat and Tears
248   Robert Spitz quote: Robert Spitz, *Barefoot in Babylon.*
250   Bobby Colomby quotes: from Jeremiah Rickert, "Interview with Bobby Colomby," conducted April 2, 1998; available at http://www.rdrop.com/users/rickert/bobby.html; accessed June 2008.

NOTES

251   David Clayton Thomas quote: Jeremiah Rickert, "David Clayton Thomas Interview," conducted August 25, 1999; available at http://www.rdrop .com/users/rickert/dct-int.html; accessed June 2008.

Johnny Winter

252–55   Johnny Winter quotes: courtesy of the Archives of The Museum at Bethel Woods.

Jimi Hendrix

264   John Morthland quote: "Jimi Hendrix," in Jim Miller, ed., *The Rolling Stone Illustrated History of Rock & Roll*.

265   Michael Lang quote: *Jimi Hendrix: Live at Woodstock* DVD (Experience Hendrix, 2005), "Special Features."

271–72   Jimi Hendrix and Dick Cavett: *The Dick Cavett Show*, September 9, 1969; available as a DVD, *Jimi Hendrix: The Dick Cavett Show* (Experience Hendrix, 2002).

INDEX

INDEX

Max, Peter, xxvii, 20
May, Rollo, xxiii–xxiv
McCartney, Paul, 214, 215, 222
McDonald, Joe, 32–45, 83, 90, 175,
        180–82
    "Bring Back the Sixties, Man," ix–x
    Country Joe and the Fish, xxvii, 32,
        33, 36, 228
    and "F" cheer, 36–39, 43–45, 225,
        229
    "Janis," 36, 145–46
McGhee, Brownie, 85
McGuinn, Roger, 47, 85, 95
McKernan, Ron "Pigpen," 154–55
Mead, Margaret, xix
Melanie (Safka), xxvii, 4, 77–81, 112,
        136, 141
Melcher, Terry, 70
Melton, Barry, xxvii, 228–29
Merry Pranksters, 128
Miami Pop Festival, 71
Miles, Buddy, 122
Mitchell, Joni, 13, 65, 81, 136,
        244–45
Mitchell, Mitch, 267, 268
Monck, Chip, 10, 27–31, 50, 51, 243
    announcements by, xxviii, 11, 28,
        63
    lighting by, xxviii, 92–93, 120
Monterey International Pop Festival,
        4, 70–71, 73, 130, 143–45, 200,
        203, 262, 264
Moon, Keith, 67, 183, 186, 188, 189
Morris, John, 102, 107–8, 221
    on the crowd, 3, 4
    and free concert, 23–28, 31, 105
    and Graham, 114, 115–16
    on the performers, 22, 43, 65–66,
        75, 83, 91–93, 94, 98, 121, 122,
        130, 134, 146–47, 152, 153,
        172, 213
    as production manager, xxviii, 115,
        120, 169, 186–87, 226–27
    and program changes, 20, 32–34,
        38, 49–50, 53, 112, 235, 257,
        265–66, 272
    and the *Times,* xxi–xxii
Morrison, Jim, 131, 148, 263
Morthland, John, xxviii, 264

Mountain, xxviii, xxix, 81, 133–37
Muir, John, 127
Murray the K, 69, 114

Nash, Graham, xvi, xxviii, 239–46
Nelson, Gaylord, 127
Nelson, Tracy, 149
Nevins, Nancy, xxviii, 55–57
Newport Festival, 69, 72, 84, 86–87
New York Times, xxi–xxiii, 8
Nietzsche, Friedrich, xix
North, Roger, 106
Nyro, Laura, 65

Objectivism, xix
Ochs, Phil, 40, 42, 257
Oxendine, Eric, 11

Pappalardi, Felix, xxviii, 133–37
Parker, Dorothy, 37
Parsons, Gram, 95
Paul, Les, 269
Paxton, Tom, 40, 47, 95, 257
Penn, Arthur, 222
Peter, Paul and Mary, 11, 12
Phillips, John, 47
Phillips, Sam, 256
Pomeroy, Wes, 128, 192, 195
Presley, Elvis, 32, 143, 159, 200,
        212, 256
Prince, 273

Quill, 106–7, 108–9

Rachlin, Chip, xxviii, 216
Rakha, Alla, 73
Rand, Ayn, xix–xx
Rankin, Kenny, xxviii, 266–67
Redding, Otis, 70, 140, 141, 143
Reeves, Martha, 149
Reston, James, xxii
Rivers, Johnny, 70
Roberts, Elliot, 241, 245
Roberts, John, xxviii, 25, 101–2,
        104–5, 107, 218, 220, 226, 227
Robertson, Robbie, xxviii, 236, 238
Robinson, Cynthia, 165, 166
Rockefeller, Nelson A., 25, 107, 226
Rolie, Gregg, 117